D0916436

RACE AND
JUVENILE JUSTICE

Race and Juvenile Justice

Edited by

Everette B. Penn

Helen Taylor Greene

Shaun L. Gabbidon

CAROLINA ACADEMIC PRESS
Durham, North Carolina

Copyright © 2006
Everette B. Penn
Helen Taylor Greene
Shaun L. Gabbidon
All Rights Reserved

Library of Congress Cataloging-in-Publication Data

Race and juvenile justice / edited by Everette B. Penn, Helen Taylor
  Greene, Shaun Gabbidon.
     p. cm.
   Includes bibliographical references and index.
   ISBN 0-89089-572-4
   1. Juvenile justice, Administration of--United States. 2.
Discrimination in juvenile justice administration--United States. 3.
Juvenile delinquency--United States. 4. Minority youth--United States.
   I. Penn, Everette B. (Everette Burdette) II. Greene, Helen Taylor,
   1949-   . III. Gabbidon, Shaun L., 1967-   .
   HV9104.R23 2004
   364.36'089'00973--dc22

     2004024034

Carolina Academic Press
700 Kent Street
Durham, NC 27701
Telephone (919) 489-7486
Fax (919) 493-5668
www.cap-press.com

Printed in the United States of America

In memory of Mrs. Mary Plummer Penn
Beloved Mom
of
Everette

To my niece and nephew, Karen and Joseph Powell
Helen Taylor Greene

CONTENTS

PART I

PERSPECTIVES ON RACE AND JUVENILE JUSTICE

PART II

ISSUES ON RACE AND JUVENILE JUSTICE

ACKNOWLEDGMENTS

A number of organizations were instrumental in the completion of this volume. We first extend our appreciation to Carolina Academic Press for its continuing encouragement (and patience) as our manuscript has undergone revisions. We also thank Penn State University-Capital College, School of Public Affairs; Prairie View A&M University, College of Juvenile Justice and Psychology; Old Dominion University, Department of Sociology and Criminal Justice for their support. Finally, we thank the Academy of Criminal Justice Sciences (ACJS) and Sage Publishing for granting us permission to reprint articles in this volume.

A number of people were also instrumental in the completion of this book. We thank our contributors for lending their academic talents to the manuscript. Two persons warrant specific acknowledgment and thanks: first, Dr. Patti Mills, Interim Assistant Dean for Graduate Studies, who provided book subvention funds which paid for some copyright expenses; second, Ms. Patricia Patrick, Dr. Gabbidon's graduate assistant, for doing some of the more mundane but important tasks required for preparing the manuscript.

Finally, we would be remiss if we did not thank our beloved families for their inspiration and patience during the time our book was in progress.

ABOUT THE AUTHORS

Dr. Myrna Cintrón is Associate Professor of Juvenile Justice and Department Head of Justice Studies at Prairie View A&M University. She earned her B.A. degree in Sociology from the University of Puerto Rico; her M.A. in Criminal Justice from the Inter-American University of Puerto Rico; and her Ph.D. in Criminology from Florida State University. Her research and publications concern the treatment of minorities, in particular Latino(a)s in the criminal justice system; drug control; and teaching issues. She has published several articles, book chapters, and other works in the fields of criminal justice and Latino issues in the United States. Dr. Cintrón has been elected to several positions in the Academy of Criminal Justice Sciences (ACJS).

Dr. Barry Feld is Centennial Professor of Law at the University of Minnesota Law School. He received his B.A. in Psychology from the University of Pennsylvania, his J.D. degree, magna cum laude, from the University of Minnesota Law School, and his Ph.D. in Sociology from Harvard University. He has written eight books and more than sixty law review and criminology articles and book chapters on juvenile justice administration, with special emphasis on serious young offenders, procedural justice in juvenile court, youth sentencing policy, and the role of race in juvenile justice administration. Among his most recent books is *Bad Kids: Race and the Transformation of the Juvenile Court* (Oxford, England: Oxford University Press, 1999), which received the "Outstanding Book Award" from the Academy of Criminal Justice Sciences (ACJS), 2001, and the Michael J. Hindelang "Outstanding Book Award" from the American Society of Criminology (ASC), 2002. His additional works include *Cases and Materials on Juvenile Justice Administration* (Egan, MN: West, 2000; 2nd ed., 2005); and *Juvenile Justice Administration in a Nutshell* (Egan, MN: West, 2002).

Dr. Laurence Armand French is Senior Research Associate for the Justice Work Institute at the University of New Hampshire. He is also Professor Emeritus of Psychology at Western New Mexico University. He received his B.A., M.A., and Ph.D. in Sociology at the University of New Hampshire, as well as an M.A. in Educational Psychology at Western New Mexico University and a

Ph.D. in Cultural Psychology at the University of Nebraska. A student of Native Americans for over thirty years, he has worked with Cherokee, Sioux, Navajo, and Pueblo tribes, as well as with Mexicans, Mestizos, and Mexican Americans. His interests include social, human, criminal justice, and clinical issues in neuropsychology and forensic psychology. He has published over two hundred academic works, including eleven books—ten of which are on the subject of Native Americans.

Dr. Shaun L. Gabbidon is Associate Professor in the School of Public Affairs at Pennsylvania State University, Capital College. He received his Ph.D. in Criminology from Indiana University of Pennsylvania. He has served as a summer fellow at Harvard University's W. E. B. DuBois Institute for Afro-American Research and has published numerous works on race and justice issues. He is coauthor of both *African American Criminological Thought* (2000), published by the State University of New York Press (Albany, NY), and *African American Classics in Criminology and Criminal Justice* (2002), published by Sage Publications (Thousand Oaks, CA). In the fall of 2001, he became the inaugural editor of the Southern Illinois University Press's Series, *Contemporary Studies in Crime and Justice.*

Dr. Daniel E. Georges-Abeyie is Professor and Associate Dean for the College of Juvenile Justice and Psychology at Prairie View A&M University. He has served in various positions at several universities across the country, including Associate Dean at Florida State University. His research concerns race, ethnicity, and social distance; the geography of crime and justice; political terror and terrorism; the heterogeneity of African-Americans and the diaspora of other African peoples; and "petit apartheid" in the United States Criminal Justice System. He is the author or editor of numerous publications, including *The Criminal Justice System and Blacks* (1984), published by Clark Boardman (New York). He has won awards for his pro bono work for Amnesty International USA and was named Professor of the Year at Florida State University, California State University-Bakersfield, and Arizona State University-West.

Dr. Helen Taylor Greene is a Professor of Administration of Justice in the Barbara Jordan-Mickey Leland School of Public Affairs at Texas Southern University. She completed her Ph.D. in Criminology at the University of Maryland, College Park. Her research interests include Black issues in the justice system such as policing and juvenile delinquency. She has published numerous articles on integrating Black perspectives into the criminology and criminal justice body of knowledge. She is coauthor of *African American Criminological Thought* (2000), published by the State University of New York Press

(Albany, NY), and is coeditor of *African American Classics in Criminology and Criminal Justice*, published by Sage Publications (Thousand Oaks, CA).

Dr. Michael Leiber is a Professor in the Department of Sociology/Anthropology and Criminology and the Director of the Sociology Graduate Program at the University of Northern Iowa. Dr. Leiber has published numerous articles and reports on juvenile delinquency, juvenile justice, and race/ethnicity. He also conducted a study on race and juvenile justice decision making in Iowa, the results of which were compiled in his book, *The Context of Juvenile Justice Decision Making: When Race Matters*, published by the State University of New York Press (Albany, NY). He serves on the Governor's Juvenile Justice Advisory Group in the state of Iowa (SAG) and is Chair of the Disproportionate Minority Confinement (DMC) subcommittee. He also acts as a consultant for the Office of Juvenile Justice and Delinquency Prevention (OJJDP). Dr. Leiber received a B.A. in Liberal Arts from Marquette University and a M.A. and Ph.D. in Criminal Justice from the State University of New York at Albany.

Dr. Marilyn D. McShane is a Professor in the Department of Criminal Justice at the University of Houston-Downtown. She also serves as the Director of the Community Justice Institute. She has taught at the graduate and undergraduate levels since 1985 and has received awards and tenure from several universities. She was a founding faculty member of the Ph.D. program in Juvenile Justice at Prairie View A&M University. She has served on the boards of a number of national criminal justice professional organizations and reviews research proposals for the National Institute of Justice. Dr. McShane has published a substantial number of works and received numerous grants. She coedited the award-winning *Encyclopedia of American Prisons*, published by Garland Publishing (New York), and the *Encyclopedia of Juvenile Justice*, published by Sage Publications. In addition, she coauthored the 4th Edition of *Criminology Theory*, published by Prentice Hall (Upper Saddle River, NJ).

Dr. Everette B. Penn is Assistant Professor of Criminology at the University of Houston-Clear Lake. He received his Ph.D. in criminology from Indiana University of Pennsylvania. Previously he served as Master's Coordinator at Prairie View A&M University and was a founding faculty member of the University's Ph.D. program in Juvenile Justice. He has also served as a Corporation for National Service Fellow and as an elected/appointed director of several national and local organizations. Dr. Penn was recently recognized as Fulbright Scholar to Egypt, where he taught criminology and juvenile justice. He is the author of several publications on juvenile justice, criminal justice pedagogy, and race issues in criminal justice.

Dr. Pam Preston is Assistant Professor of Criminal Justice in the School of Public Affairs at Pennsylvania State University-Schuylkill. Her research interests include special-needs populations in the criminal justice system, race/ethnicity issues, prostitution, drug use, and immigration issues related to crime.

Dr. Lee Ross is Associate Professor of Criminal Justice at the University of Central Florida, where he serves as coordinator of the Honors Program in Criminal Justice. A graduate of Rutgers University, his research interests span a variety of areas—from his seminal work on religion and social control theory to more recent African-American interests in law enforcement. The study of crime and delinquency among African-Americans is a centerpiece for many of his numerous publications. His recent work with the Task Force on Family Violence in Milwaukee, Wisconsin, has spawned his latest interest—race and domestic violence.

Dr. Franklin P. Williams III is a Professor in the Department of Criminal Justice at the University of Houston-Downtown. He also serves as the Director of the Security Management Program. A Professor Emeritus at California State University-San Bernardino, he has over twenty-five years of experience in criminal justice, serving in positions of chair, coordinator, and director in six universities. He was a founding faculty member of the Ph.D. program in Juvenile Justice at Prairie View A&M University and directed the program for several years. He has served on boards of national scholarly organizations and chaired several national and regional criminal justice committees. He has published more than a hundred books, articles, research monographs, and government reports. He has served as editor or deputy/associate editor of several journals and publisher's book and monograph series. His most recent books are *Imagining Criminology,* published by Garland Publishing; *The Encyclopedia of Juvenile Justice,* published by Sage Publications (Thousand Oaks, CA); and *Criminology Theory,* (4th Ed.), published by Prentice Hall (Upper Saddle River, NJ).

Dr. N. Prabha Unnithan is Professor of Sociology at Colorado State University in Fort Collins, Colorado. He has been on the faculty since 1987. His research interests are the study of violence (specifically, homicide) and a variety of criminal justice organizational issues. Dr. Unnithan teaches criminology and corrections (at the undergraduate level) and policy analysis and program evaluation (at the graduate level). He has published numerous works, and from 1999 to 2002 he served as Editor of the *Journal of Criminal Justice Education,* a publication of the Academy of Criminal Justice Sciences (ACJS).

List of Acronyms

ACJS	Academy of Criminal Justice Sciences
ASC	American Society of Criminology
BIA	Bureau of Indian Affairs
CHINS	Children in need of supervision
CIS	Cities in Schools
CSPV	Center for the Study and Prevention of Violence
DARE	Drug Abuse Resistance Education
DMC	Disproportionate Minority Confinement
DRO	Office of Detention and Removal
EOP	Michigan Early Offender Program
FAE	Fetal Alcohol Effect
FAS	Fetal Alcohol Syndrome
FBI	Federal Bureau of Investigation
GREAT	Gang Resistance Education and Training
HRW	Human Rights Watch
ICE	U.S. Immigration and Customs Enforcement
IIM	Individual Indian Money fund
INS	Immigration and Naturalization Service
JJDP	Juvenile Justice and Delinquency Prevention
LAPD	Los Angeles Police Department
LULAC	League of United Latin American Citizens
MALDAFE	Mexican American Legal Defense and Education Fund
MALE	Making attitude Adjustments in order to Lead more Effective lives
MST	Multisystemic Therapy
NAACP-LDF	National Association for the Advancement of Colored People-Legal Defense Fund
NCADP	National Coalition to Abolish the Death Penalty
NCCD	National Council on Crime and Delinquency
NCLR	National Council of La Raza
NCPTP	National Campaign to Prevent Teen Pregnancy

NIDA	National Institute on Drug Abuse
OJJDP	Office of Juvenile Justice and Delinquency Prevention
OMB	Office of Management and Budget
POSIT	Problem-Oriented Screening Instrument
SAG	State Advisory Group (Governor's Juvenile Justice Advisory Group in Iowa)
UCR	Uniform Crime Report

PERMISSIONS

Permission has been given to Carolina Academic Press to reprint the following:

As **Chapter 10**:

Feld, Barry C. (2003). The politics of race and juvenile justice: The "due process revolution" and the conservative reaction. *Justice Quarterly, 20* (4), pp. 765–800.

Copyright 2003 © by Barry C. Feld

Reprinted with Permission of the Academy of Criminal Justice Sciences.

As **Chapter 9**:

Lieber, Michael. (2002). Disproportionate minority confinement (DMC) of youth: An analysis of state and federal efforts to address the issue. *Crime and Delinquency, 48* (1), pp. 3–45.

Copyright 2002 © by Michael Lieber

Reprinted by Permission of Sage Publications, Thousand Oaks, CA.

RACE AND
JUVENILE JUSTICE

INTRODUCTION

Race and ethnicity have been and continue to be subjects of contention in the justice literature. Yet it is germane to this text to understand the difference between race and ethnicity. A race is often defined as a human population from the same locality, having distinguishable genetic physical features (Morris, 1973). In addition, Reasons, Conley, and Debro (2002) note that "race has come to mean largely skin pigmentation" (p. 3). In contrast, ethnicity is the grouping of persons according to their commonalities of cultural customs, language, religion, food, and family patterns (Walker, Spohn, & DeLone, 2004). Hispanics/Latinos are more closely aligned with the ethnic definition because of their many geographical origins and common culture (United States Census, 2001).

According to the census taken on April 1, 2000, there were 281,421,906 persons residing in the United States. The count includes five race categories as defined by the Office of Management and Budget (OMB). The five racial categories and their percentage of the U. S. population are as follows: "White"—people having origins in any of the original peoples of Europe, the Middle East, or North Africa, and representing 75.1 percent of the population; "Black or African-American"—people having origins in any of the Black racial groups of Africa (including people who identify themselves as Negro or Afro-American), and representing 12.3 percent of the population; "American Indian and Alaska Native"—people having origins in any of the original peoples of North, Central, and South America, and representing 0.9 percent of the population; "Asian"—people having origins in any of the original peoples of the Far East, Southeast Asia, or the Indian subcontinent, and representing 3.6 percent of the population; "Native Hawaiian and Other Pacific Islanders"—people having origins in any of the original peoples of Hawaii, Guam, Samoa, or other Pacific Islands, and representing 0.1 percent of the population. For respondents unable to identify with any of the above categories, a sixth choice, "some other race," was available. Most people who responded with this category identified themselves as "Hispanic" or "Latino." Considered the largest minority group, they represent 12.5 percent of the United States population. The Hispanic/ Latino category is complex because it indicates an ethnic rather than a racial group (United States Census, 2001).

A caution must be made regarding the use of OMB/U. S. Census racial and ethnic categories. Definitions change and have little direct relation to geographic region. For example, people from the North African countries of Egypt, Algeria, and Morocco are defined as White. Therefore, race (together with ethnicity) is a socially constructed concept. Thus this text, just as those before it, will begrudgingly use the racial/ethnic terms "White," "Latino," "Black," "Asian," and "Native American."

During the past few decades, more publications than ever before have devoted considerable attention to the widening racial disparities in the juvenile justice system. Numerous articles have appeared in the leading criminology and criminal justice journals. In addition, during the 1980s and 1990s, more book-length works appeared (Georges-Abeyie, 1984; Mann, 1993; McNeely & Pope, 1981; Tonry, 1995; Wilbanks, 1987). Missing from these publications, however, was a volume devoted entirely to race and juvenile justice. Except in a few cases, interest in racial disparities in the juvenile justice system took a backseat to interest in racial disparities in the *adult* justice system. During the 1990s, however, the tide began to turn with the publication of the pioneering work on race and juvenile justice, *Minorities in Juvenile Justice,* edited by Leonard, Pope, and Feyerherm (1995). Since then, several additional books on race and juvenile justice have been published (see, for example, Joseph, 1995; Feld, 1999; Tatum, 2000; Leiber, 2003). Moreover, scholars are now arguing that juvenile justice is an independent discipline (Williams, McShane, & Rodney, 2001), which has its own journal, *Youth Violence and Juvenile Justice,* and a doctorate program at Prairie View A & M University. Furthermore, because funds are being made available at the federal and state levels to study and ameliorate racial disparities, more scholars are researching the topic.

Our purpose in writing this book is to fill the gap that currently exists in the coverage of minority youth both in textbooks on juvenile justice and juvenile delinquency, and among interested readers. We envision a volume of essays that will be a resource of information on juvenile justice issues among Asian-American, Black, Latino, Native American, as well as White youths in the United States. Through these essays we hope that juvenile justice professionals, community activists, scholars, and students will become more aware not only of the magnitude of the problems of minorities in the juvenile justice system but also of the promising theoretical formulations and policy initiatives that address these problems. We particularly hope that the essays will inspire our students to seek careers which will help reduce disparities concerning race and youth in the justice system.

The book is divided into two parts. Part I, "Perspectives on Race and Juvenile Justice," includes chapters on each racial group: Whites, Latino(a)s,

Blacks, Asians, and Native Americans. These chapters explore causes of delinquency, juvenile justice, and social issues related to minority involvement in the juvenile justice system. Part II, "Issues of Race and Juvenile Justice," presents chapters on relevant topics such as domestic violence, gang activity, the death penalty, an historical analysis of race in juvenile justice, disproportionate minority confinement, and lessons learned about the prevention of juvenile delinquency.

Part I begins with the chapter "White Delinquency" by Pam Preston. Though Whites make up the largest racial group in the United States, White juvenile delinquency has not received the amount and quality of scholarly attention given to delinquency among most other racial groups. This chapter presents trends of delinquency, as well as drug and alcohol usage among White youths through an analysis of national and self-reported data. It concludes with theoretical explanations of White delinquency. Chapter two, by Myrna Cintrón, explores several impediments related to Latinos and Latinas in the juvenile justice system (e.g., language barriers and immigration status). In addition, Cintrón explores the most useful theoretical linkages for explaining Latino delinquency. In chapter three Everette Penn focuses on delinquency among Black youths. Penn reviews the several stages of operation in the juvenile justice system and notes the disproportion in the system's treatment of Black youths in comparison to its treatment of youths of other races and ethnic groups. By reviewing theoretical explanations for the over representation of Black youths in the juvenile justice system, the chapter concludes that "being Black" is a significant variable that should be used to explain Black youths' disproportionate involvement in the juvenile justice system.

Chapter four, by N. Prabha Unnithan, examines Asian-Americans and juvenile justice. Unnithan first notes the reasons for the scarce research on Asian-American delinquency. Even though Asian-American youths are underrepresented in delinquency statistics, he shows the trends in their current offenses. In addition, he reviews the emergence of Asian-American street gangs. Part I ends with chapter five, "Native American Youth and Delinquency," by Laurence French. Because, like their counterparts among Asian-Americans, delinquent Native American youths are small in number in the U. S. population, they receive considerably less scholarly attention than other groups. Even so, they are the beneficiaries of a rich history, which is profiled in detail by French. Unfortunately, some of this history includes the various means by which Native Americans have been mistreated. The chapter further shows that, despite this mistreatment, they have, for the most part, maintained their indigenous cultural traditions. Besides providing figures on crime and delinquency among

Native American youths, French presents a case study showing how the Navajo juvenile justice system operates.

Part II includes six chapters. Five of them focus on contemporary topics related to race and juvenile justice; the final chapter provides an overview of delinquency intervention strategies for youths. Chapter six, by Lee Ross, explores the connection between domestic violence and delinquency among African-American youths. Ross surveys the juvenile justice literature and shows how violence within the family increases the likelihood that African-American youths will be involved in violence outside the family. As a means of addressing this issue, he points to both traditional and nontraditional avenues through the use of a hypothetical case study.

Youth gangs have been a concern of police agencies and communities across the country. In chapter seven, Marilyn McShane and Frank Williams III define the issues concerning youth gangs and present the various approaches which have been used to reduce the involvement of minorities in gang activity. Chapter eight, by Daniel Georges-Abeyie, provides a look at the neglected issue of minority youths and the death penalty. His unique approach applies international law to the use of the death penalty for juveniles in the United States. The chapter presents evidence that, by continuing to execute those who committed offenses as juveniles, the United States continues to violate international law.

Chapters nine and ten are reprints of two essential articles on the subject of race and juvenile justice. The first reprint, by Michael Leiber, provides one of the most recent and comprehensive analyses of the disproportionate minority confinement (DMC) initiative. The chapter notes the progress made by states in identifying and remedying the excessive representation of minorities in the states' juvenile justice systems. Additionally, it reveals some of the political issues involved in administering the DMC initiative. The second reprint, by noted juvenile justice scholar Barry Feld, provides a significant historical analysis of the social context surrounding the current disproportionately high representation of minorities in the juvenile justice system (especially that of African-Americans). A key theme of his analysis is the role of the Supreme Court led by Earl Warren and the wave of conservatism (i.e., support for more punitive policies) that followed. As he convincingly argues through social and legal documentation, the movement toward due process in the juvenile justice system radically changed its nature and practice. Moreover, decades of conservatism have led to policies which have only increased and aggravated racial disparities in the system.

In the final chapter, Helen Taylor Greene and Everette Penn provide promising strategies for reducing juvenile delinquency, especially among minority youths. Following a brief historical overview of juvenile justice programs and policies, the authors review prevention and intervention strategies that are successful and also identify those that have not been effective. The chapter concludes by noting important issues and challenges regarding the future of minority youths in the juvenile justice system.

REFERENCES

Feld, B. (1999). *Bad kids: Race and the transformation of the juvenile court.* New York: Oxford University Press.

Georges-Abeyie, D. (Ed.) (1984). *The criminal justice system and blacks.* New York: Clark Boardman.

Joseph, J. (1995). *Black youths, delinquency, and juvenile justice.* Westport, CT: Praeger.

Leiber, M. J. (2003). *The contexts of juvenile justice decision making: When race matters.* Albany, NY: State University of New York Press.

Leonard, K. K., Pope, C. E., & Feyerherm, W. H. (1995). *Minorities in juvenile justice.* Thousand Oaks, CA: Sage Publications.

Mann, C. R. (1993). *Unequal justice: A question of color.* Bloomington, IN: Indiana University Press.

McNeely, R. L. & Pope, C. (Eds.) (1981). *Race, crime, and criminal justice.* Beverly Hills, CA: Sage Publications.

Morris, B. S. (1973). *Imperialism and revolution; An essay for radicals.* Bloomington, Indiana University Press.

Reasons, C., Conley, D., & Debro, J. (2002). *Race, class, gender, and justice in the United States.* Boston: Allyn and Bacon.

Tatum, B. L. (2000). *Crime, violence and minority youth.* Brookfield, VT: Ashgate.

Tonry, M. (1995). *Malign neglect.* New York: Oxford University Press.

United States Census (2001). *Overview of race and Hispanic origin: Census 2000 brief.* Washington, D. C.: United States Census Bureau.

Walker, S., Spohn, C., & DeLone, M. (2004). *The color of justice* (3rd Ed.) Belmont, CA: Wadsworth.

Wilbanks, W. (1987). *The myth of a racist criminal justice system.* Monterey, CA: Brooks/Cole.

Williams, F. P., McShane, M. D., & Rodney, H. (2001). Juvenile justice: A rationale for a new discipline. *Perspectives, 4,* 1–10. Retrieved March 21, 2003: http://www.aabss.org/ journal2001/.

Part I

Perspectives on Race and Juvenile Justice

CHAPTER ONE

WHITE DELINQUENCY

Pamela Preston

INTRODUCTION

Juvenile delinquency is often linked to social class, but it is more strongly related to race. There is no denying that White youths have, since Revolutionary America, been involved in delinquency and crime (Grennan, Britz, Rush, & Barker, 2000). At least until recent years, most research on delinquency among White youths focused on what used to be called "other races"— the Irish, Jewish, or Italian immigrant youths, who were the minority youths of their day. The study of delinquency among White, or dominant-group, youths (especially middle-class or affluent White youths) seemed of minor importance when compared to street crime, gang warfare, and the drug wars of the1980s. White America's insular perception that delinquency and violence were problems limited to the poor and to the minority community came to an abrupt end in the 1990s with a spate of shootings in White, middle-class schools, culminating in the Columbine High School shootings in Littleton, Colorado, an affluent White suburb of Denver. Delinquency and violence were no longer "their" problems, but became "our problems" as well. This chapter explores trends in delinquency among White youths throughout the1990s; patterns of offending in rural, suburban, and urban areas; substance use and offending by White youths; and theoretical explanations for White delinquency.

TRENDS IN WHITE DELINQUENCY

By the late 1990s White America was scared of its own children. After Columbine, many White American parents took a good look at their children and didn't like what they saw. Hip suburban White youths dressing "gangsta" style and alienated high school outsiders in rural and suburban areas dressed in "Goth'" or "punk" gear brought home to White American parents that their children's generation was indeed far more dangerous, and far more deadly, than earlier ones. The spate of school shootings in the late 1990s raised the specter of a generation of young White males out of control. On September 25, 2003, the son of a rural Minnesota sheriff's deputy opened fire on fellow students, killing one ("Cold Spring School Shooting," 2003, September 25). In March 2001, a senior at Santee High School in San Diego County, California, shot and killed two classmates ("Two Killed in San Diego School Shooting," 2001, March 6). A recent list of White male youths who appear to have randomly shot and/or killed their classmates follows:

1) a thirteen-year-old who opened fire in Fort Gibson, Oklahoma, 6 December 1999;
2) a fifteen-year-old in Conyers, Georgia, 20 May 1999;
3) two seniors at Columbine High School in Littleton, Colorado, 20 April 1999;
4) a seventeen-year-old in Springfield, Oregon, 21 May 1998;
5) a fifteen-year-old in Edinboro, Pennsylvania, 24 April 1998;   ·
6) two boys. eleven and thirteen, in Jonesboro, Arkansas, 24 March 1998;
7) a fourteen-year-old in West Paducah, Kentucky, 1 December 1997;
8) a seventeen-year-old in Pearl, Mississippi, 1 October 1997; and
9) a sixteen-year-old in Bethel, Alaska, 19 February 1997. ("Other Recent School Shootings," 2001, March 6)

In spite of the hysteria surrounding the school shootings of the 1990s, delinquency among White youths has, for the most part, declined over the past decade. Data on self-reported delinquency among high school seniors compiled by the Sourcebook of Criminal Justice Statistics (Pastore & Maguire, 2003) are obtained from a national survey of approximately 2,500 youths. Increases and decreases in offending were calculated for each year for selected offenses, and are presented in Charts 1 through 3.

As indicated in Chart 1, the percentage of White seniors who reported getting into a serious fight, taking part in a group fight, or hitting someone hard enough for that person to need bandages or a doctor declined between 1990 and 2002. The percent of White seniors who reported hitting a supervisor/instructor increased by 21 percent. It appears that White youths have become less likely to assault their peers, while the increase in assaults on instructors or supervisors may reflect a decreased respect for authority figures, or it may simply reflect that a greater number of White youths have jobs and hence have supervisors.

**Chart 1.   Percentage of White High School Seniors
Reporting Involvement in Personal Crimes**

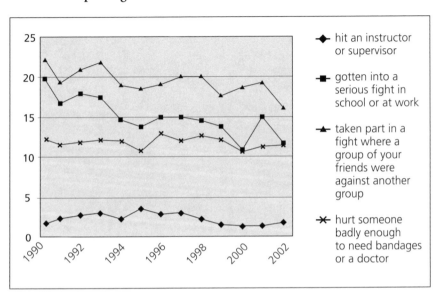

Source: Pastore, A. L. & Maguire, K. (Eds.). *Sourcebook of Criminal Justice Statistics.*

Self-reported involvement in property crimes also decreased. "Taking something worth less than $50" decreased by 47 percent; "taking something worth more than $50" decreased by 12.9 percent; "taking something from a store without paying for it" decreased by 16 percent; and "taking a part of a car without permission" decreased by 39 percent. Only joyriding (taking a car not belonging to one's family) increased, although only by 2 percent. White youths also appear to have been less involved in property crime than they were in 1990.

However, more serious offending by White youths increased during the 1990s and into 2002. The number involved in robbery (using a knife or gun to take something from someone else) increased by nearly 24 percent; the number involved in arson increased by 70 percent; and the number having been arrested or taken to a police station in the past twelve months increased by nearly 20 percent. While the increase in the percentage of youths arrested or taken to a police station may be a reflection of the demonization of White youths that occurred because of the school shootings of the 1990s, there has also been some increase in self-reported crime.

**Chart 2.   Percentage of White High School Seniors
Reporting Involvement in Property Crimes**

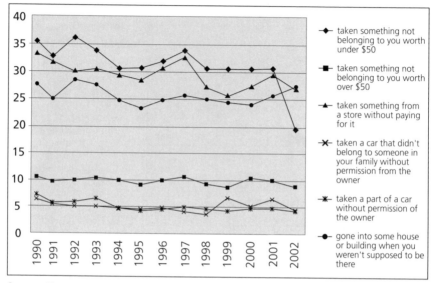

Source: Pastore, A. L., & Maguire, K. (Eds.). *Sourcebook of Criminal Justice Statistics.*

A COMPARISON OF RURAL, SUBURBAN, AND URBAN WHITE YOUTH ARRESTS

Uniform Crime Report (UCR) data from the *Sourcebook of Criminal Justice Statistics* (Pastore & Maguire, 2003) show arrests of White juveniles as a percentage of all White arrests and as a percentage of all juvenile arrests in rural, urban, and suburban areas. UCR defines suburban areas as cities with populations of less than 50,000, as well as unincorporated areas within a metropolitan statistical area. Rural counties are those outside of metropolitan statistical areas and are not under the jurisdiction of city police departments. Data on arrests of juveniles according to race and age group for the year 2001 are presented in tables 1 and 2. These data suggest that White youths in different types of areas are prone to different types of offending. Table 1 shows the arrests of White juveniles as a percentage of all White arrests for selected offenses. Urban White juveniles account for a great share of White arrests (as compared to those in rural and suburban areas) for murder, robbery, larceny/theft, violent and property crime, forgery/counterfeiting, fraud, embezzlement, stolen property offenses, and offenses against family and children.

**Chart 3.   Percentage of White High School Seniors
Reporting Involvement in More Serious Offenses**

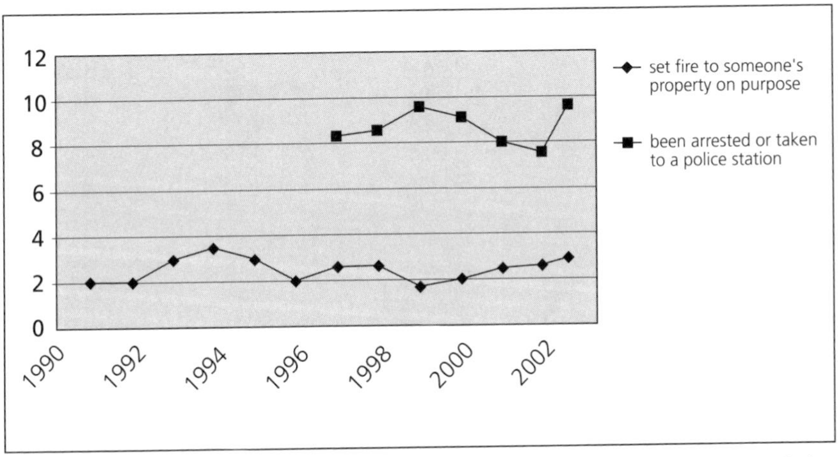

Source: Pastore, A. L. & Maguire, K. (Eds.). *Sourcebook of Criminal Justice Statistics.*

Rural White youths account for a greater share (as compared to suburban and urban White youths) of arrests for weapons offenses, prostitution/commercialized vice, and vagrancy. Suburban White youths account for a greater share of White arrests for suspicion, disorderly conduct, drunkenness, liquor law violations, drug abuse violations, sex offenses (excluding forcible rape), vandalism, assault (not aggravated), arson, burglary, and forcible rape. These data suggest that violent White juvenile offenders are more likely to be found in urban areas rather than the suburbs. Suburban White youths are more likely to be involved in less serious crimes, such as substance use offenses and what is sometimes considered "kid stuff"—vandalism and disorderly conduct. Rural White youths, reflective of the gun culture of rural areas, are most likely to engage in weapons-related offenses.

Table 2 shows the percentages of arrests for selected offenses of White juveniles in comparison to that of all juveniles. While these percentages indicate, to a certain extent, the racial composition of the specific areas, they also suggest what types of offending White juveniles are most likely to engage in, in comparison to non-White juveniles. Caution should be used regarding the percentages because arrests do correspond to offending. White youths in rural

Table 1.   A Comparison of Rural, Suburban, and Urban White Juvenile Delinquency as Percentage of All White Arrests

	Rural	Suburban	Urban
Murder and nonnegligent manslaughter	5.53%	7.45%	10.95%
Forcible rape	14.68%	17.17%	16.89%
Robbery	10.88%	20.26%	22.14%
Aggravated assault	9.80%	13.70%	13.71%
Burglary	30.08%	33.28%	32.93%
Larceny theft	24.20%	30.57%	31.94%
Motor vehicle theft	32.91%	31.17%	32.81%
Arson	36.18%	56.12%	55.78%
Violent crime	10.93%	14.47%	15.05%
Property crime	27.36%	31.54%	32.45%
Other assaults	11.89%	19.27%	18.48%
Forgery and counterfeiting	4.83%	5.82%	5.83%
Fraud	1.19%	2.34%	3.89%
Embezzlement	2.77%	9.74%	11.07%
Stole property—buying, receiving, possessing	16.47%	21.07%	23.29%
Vandalism	36.99%	44.47%	42.77%
Weapons—carrying, possessing, etc.	59.37%	25.61%	26.66%
Prostitution and commercialized vice	2.17%	1.79%	1.46%
Sex offenses	19.37%	20.99%	18.21%
Drug abuse violations	9.29%	15.73%	15.43%
Gambling	6.67%	6.66%	6.47%
Offenses against family and children	5.14%	6.04%	11.19%
Driving under the influence	1.44%	1.42%	1.65%
Liquor laws	26.17%	27.00%	23.33%
Drunkenness	2.99%	4.35%	3.62%
Disorderly conduct	21.47%	30.71%	26.89%
Vagrancy	18.65%	14.56%	9.42%
All other offenses	7.67%	12.97%	13.93%
Suspicion	12.99%	35.27%	30.88%

Source: Pastore, A. L. & Maguire, K. (Eds.). *Sourcebook of Criminal Justice Statistics.*

areas make up the greatest share of arrests of all juveniles for prostitution/commercialized vice, violation of liquor laws, driving under the influence, drunkenness, and offenses against family and children. White youths in suburban areas make up the greatest share of arrests of all juveniles for driving under the influence, violation of liquor laws, drunkenness, vandalism, and curfew/loitering. White urban youths make up the greatest share of all juvenile arrests for vandalism, driving under the influence, violation of liquor laws, drunkenness, and arson. The data suggest that, regardless of location, White youths are most likely to be arrested for alcohol-related offenses, while suburban White youths are most likely to be arrested for a "status offense": curfew violation.

SUBSTANCE USE BY WHITE JUVENILES

Self-reported data from the 2001 National Household Survey of Drug and Alcohol Use for 11,626 White juveniles (ages twelve through seventeen) are presented in table 3. Nearly one-half of White juveniles have, at some time, drunk alcohol, with about one in five reporting that they have used it within the past thirty days. One in five juveniles report having at some time used marijuana, while nearly 9 percent appear to be regular users (i.e., within the past month). Other drugs most often used by White youths include pain relievers (used by 10 percent), inhalants (used by 9.9 percent), and hallucinogens (used by 6.9). The most regularly used drugs among White juveniles are 1) alcohol, 2) marijuana, 3) pain relievers, 4) hallucinogens, 5) stimulants, 6) ecstasy. Table 3 indicates the average number of days each drug is used per year. On the average, White youths drink alcohol fourteen days per year and smoke marijuana thirteen days per year. More White youths report having driven under the influence of alcohol in the past year (4.3 percent) than under the influence of illegal drugs (3.9 percent); a percentage of 5.6 report having driven under the influence of one or the other.

CAUSES OF WHITE DELINQUENCY

The fact that White juveniles engage in criminal and delinquent behavior cannot be denied. The usual explanations for incidents like the shootings at Columbine (which seem to defy conventional wisdom about youth and delinquency) focus on the perpetrator's peers, the media, or the absence of parental control. Social learning and social control theories formalize these explanations.

The earliest social learning model, Differential Association (Sutherland, 1947; Sutherland & Cressey, 1978), theorizes that persons engage in illegal or delinquency acts as a result of associating with persons who hold norms and values favorable to deviance and to attitudes not opposed to rule violation. According to this perspective, the act of associating with delinquents, criminals, or deviants may lead one to become delinquent, criminal, or deviant. Social learning theories are most effective in explaining delinquency and crim-

Table 2.   A Comparison of Rural, Suburban, and Urban White Juvenile Delinquency as Percentage of All Juvenile Arrests

	Rural	Suburban	Urban
Murder and nonnegligent manslaughter	60.42%	69.88%	40.79%
Forcible rape	81.34%	71.10%	55.70%
Robbery	48.18%	47.02%	39.22%
Aggravated assault	70.00%	71.40%	58.48%
Burglary	84.43%	79.19%	69.01%
Larceny theft	84.60%	72.22%	68.24%
Motor vehicle theft	83.87%	74.05%	51.78%
Arson	88.11%	87.60%	79.88%
Violent crime	75.38%	66.21%	52.47%
Property crime	85.11%	74.07%	66.97%
Other assaults	77.48%	72.57%	60.95%
Forgery and counterfeiting	89.06%	79.08%	75.18%
Fraud	83.63%	72.12%	64.86%
Embezzlement	84.62%	71.81%	68.81%
Stole property—buying, receiving, possessing	84.92%	67.12%	54.83%
Vandalism	90.51%	86.22%	95.57%
Weapons—carrying, possessing, etc.	78.64%	76.25%	64.18%
Prostitution and commercialized vice	100.00%	67.01%	47.59%
Sex offenses	88.82%	77.78%	64.94%
Drug abuse violations	87.07%	85.56%	68.38%
Gambling	86.67%	47.31%	9.81%
Offenses against family and children	91.57%	80.65%	76.13%
Driving under the influence	92.10%	95.02%	92.41%
Liquor laws	94.64%	94.24%	91.00%
Drunkenness	92.08%	93.24%	89.70%
Disorderly conduct	74.74%	71.69%	61.05%
Vagrancy	66.67%	79.81%	75.15%
All other offenses	82.54%	80.63%	73.50%
Suspicion	67.35%	62.21%	73.76%
Curfew and loitering	85.09%	84.08%	69.68%
Runaways	88.23%	8.24%	72.71%

Source: Pastore, A. L. & Maguire, K. (Eds.) *Sourcebook of Criminal Justice Statistics.*

inality within a group context and self-reported delinquency (Shoemaker, 1996). Tests of all or part of social learning/differential association theory have consistently shown significant effects on crime and delinquency (Elliot, Huizinga, & Ageton, 1985; Dembo, Grandon, La Loie, Schmeidler, & Burgess,

Table 3.   Percentage of Drug and Alcohol Use for White Juveniles Age 12–17 (Relative Recency) (n=17,429)

	Within past 30 days	More than 30 days ago but within the past 12 months	More than 12 months ago	Never used
Alcohol	19.6	17.6	8.3	54.5
Marijuana	8.7	7.4	4.4	79.6
Cocaine	.6	1.3	.7	97.5
Crack	.2	.3	.3	99.3
Hallucinogen	1.6	3.5	1.8	93.1
LSD	.6	2.0	1.4	96.0
PCP	.1	.5	.6	98.8
Ecstasy	.8	2.1	.9	96.2
Inhalant	1.0	2.9	5.9	90.1
Pain reliever	2.8	4.1	3.1	90.0
Tranquilizer	.7	1.4	1.1	96.8
Stimulant	.9	1.8	2.1	95.2
Methamphetamine	.3	.6	.8	98.3
Sedative	.2	.3	.4	99.1

	Mean	Standard Deviation*
Alcohol	14.03	40.27
Marijuana	13.15	52.23
Cocaine	.57	8.354
Crack	.18	5.259
Hallucinogen	1.22	12.22
Ecstasy		
Inhalant	1.04	11.47
Pain reliever	2.63	19.14
Tranquilizer	.66	8.88
Stimulant	1.21	13.69
Methamphetamine	.36	7.54
Sedative	.20	4.97

	Yes	No
Drove under the influence of alcohol and illegal drugs	4.3	95.7
Drove under the influence of alcohol	4.3	95.7
Drove under the influence of illegal drugs	3.9	96.1
Drove under the influence of either alcohol or illegal drugs	5.6	94.4

Source: *National Household Survey on Drug Abuse* (2001).

* Standard deviations reflect data not normally distributed

**Table 4.   Theoretical Foundations for White Delinquency:
Social Learning and Social Control**

Cause of White Delinquency	Theoretical Perspective Social Learning	Independent Variable (Measurement)	Indicators
Deviant peers	Social Learning	SOCLEARN	Friends' involvement in drug use
Media			
Lack of parental control	Social Control	PARINVOL	Amount of time parents spend helping and monitoring behavior
Lack of interest in school		POSATT	Feels that school is worthwhile
Lack of involvement in conventional activities		CONVINVO	Number of school-, community-, faith-based and other similar activities

1986; White, Johnson, & Horowitz, 1986; Sellers & Winfree, 1990; Winfree, Sellers, & Clason, 1993; Winfree, Vigil-Backstrom, & Mays, 1994a; 1994b; Mihalic & Elliott, 1997; Skinner & Fream, 1997; Esbenswen & Deschenes, 1998).

Control theories suggest that deviant impulses are omnipresent, and control (either internal or external) must be exercised to prevent deviant behavior (Hirschi, 1969). Personal controls are internalized controls, rather like the superego. External controls include the effects of religion, family, school, and involvement in conventional activities. Empirical support for social bonding as a control is not strong; for the most part it is related only to minor delinquency (Krohn & Massey, 1980; McIntosh, Fitch, Wilson, Wilson, & Nybert, 1981; Agnew 1991) and marijuana use (Akers & Cochran, 1985).

Data on White juveniles (n=11,626) from the 2001 National Household Survey of Drug Use were used to compare the effects of peers (social learning) and social control variables (attachment to school, involvement in conventional activities, and parental supervision). The theoretical perspectives and indices used to measure their relative effects are presented in table 4.

There are four independent variables in each analysis. The independent variables include the following:

   1) Social learning: Subjects were asked how many students they knew in their grade who smoked cigarettes, used marijuana or hashish, drank alcohol, and got drunk weekly. Scores range from 4 to 16, with 4 indicating the respondent knew no one using any of these sub-

stances to 16 indicating the respondent knew everyone used all of these substances.

2) Positive attitudes toward school: how the youth felt about going to school during the past year, whether he/she felt schoolwork was important in the past year, how important he/she thought the things were he/she learned in the past year, and if he/she felt classes were interesting in the past year. Scores ranged from 4 to 8, with 4 indicating the most positive attitude toward school and 8 indicating the least positive attitude toward school.

3) Involvement in conventional activities: the number of school-based, community-based, faith-based, and other activities in which a youth was involved during the past year. Scores ranged from 0 (indicating no involvement in conventional activities) to 12 (indicating the highest level of involvement in conventional activities).

4) Parental involvement: A parent verifies that a child has done homework, helps with homework, makes a child do chores, limits TV time, limits time out with friends, lets the child know he or she was doing a good job, tells the child the parent is proud of him or her. Scores ranged from 7 to 28, with 7 indicating the highest level of parental involvement and 28 indicating no parental involvement.

Ten dependent variables were analyzed separately. The first six dependent variables are numeric, reflecting the frequency with which each event occurred: (1) A youth has gotten into a serious fight at school; (2) a youth has taken part in a group fight at school; (3) a youth has carried a handgun; (4) a youth has sold illegal drugs; (5) a youth has stolen or tried to steal something; or (6) a youth has attacked someone with the intent to seriously hurt the person. The final four dependent variables are dichotomous and include the response categories "yes" or "no": (7) Has a youth ever been arrested and booked? (8) Has a youth ever run away and slept on the street? (9) Has a youth ever hacked into a government system? Or (10) Has a youth ever intentionally set a fire?

The first six models were analyzed using OLS regression to allow analysis of the numeric dependent variables, while the last four models were analyzed using binary logistic regression to allow analysis of the dichotomous dependent variables. The results of the analysis are presented in table 5.

Social Learning (the number of friends involved in illegal activities) is positively associated with some types of delinquency/criminality among White youth, and negatively associated with others. Youths with peers who drink, smoke, and use marijuana are more likely to sell illegal drugs, steal, take part

Table 5. **Relative Effects of Social Learning and Social Control on White Delinquency**

	Standardized Coefficients and Significance			
	SOCLEARN	POSATT	CONVINVO	PARINVOL
Gotten into a serious fight at school [R=.225]	.08*	.138*	.004*	.090*
Taken part in a group fight at school [R=.195]	.085*	.113*	.028*	.077*
Carried a handgun [R=.103]	.040*	.055*	-.007	.043*
Sold illegal drugs [R=.212]	.126*	.073*	-.028*	.080*
Stolen or tried to steal something [R=.175]	.092*	.066*	.015	.086*
Attacked with the intent to seriously hurt [R.179]	.062*	.094*	-.016	.083*
Ever arrested and booked [-2 LL=4195]	-.256*	-.162*	.125*	-.054*
Ever run away and slept on the street [-2 LL=2773]	-.129*	-.100*	-.026	-.033*
Hacked into a government system [-2 LL=1797]	-.061*	-.137*	-.052*	-.030
Intentionally set a fire [-2LL=1788]	-.065*	-.190*	-.028	-.019

* sig. at p<.05
SOCLEARN: social learning
POSATT: positive attitudes towards school
CONVINVO: involvement in conventional activities
PARENINV: parental involvement

in a group fight, get into a serious fight, attack someone with the intent to seriously hurt the person, and carry a handgun. However, the number of peers who drink, smoke tobacco, and smoke marijuana is negatively associated with having ever been arrested and booked, run away and slept on the street, hacked into a government system, or intentionally set a fire. It may be that youths who get arrested, or run away, or hack into computer systems, or set fires are the loners and outsiders of their grade: They are not aware of or included in what their peers are doing.

However, the relationship between **positive attitudes toward school** and involvement in delinquent/criminal activity is the exact inverse of the relationship between **social learning** and involvement in delinquent/criminal activity.

Negative attitudes toward school are positively associated with getting into fights, taking part in gang fights, attacking someone with the intent to hurt the person, selling illegal drugs, stealing, and carrying a handgun. Those White youths who have intentionally set a fire, ever been arrested and booked, hacked into a computer system, or run away are more likely to report positive attitudes toward schools.

Students involved in **conventional activities** are more likely to have never been arrested and booked, taken part in a group fight, or gotten into a serious fight at school. Student less involved in conventional activities are more likely to have hacked into a government system or sold illegal drugs. Participation in conventional activities has no significant effect on carrying a handgun, stealing, attacking with the intent to hurt, or running away.

Students with less **involved parents** are more likely to get into serious fights, steal, attack with the intent to hurt, sell illegal drugs, take part in group fights, and carry a handgun. Students with more involved parents are more likely to have never been arrested and booked and to have run away and slept on the street. Parental involvement has no significant effect on hacking.

White youths who get into fights have more peers who engage in deviant behavior, have negative attitudes toward school, are more involved in conventional activities, and have less involved parents. White youths who carry handguns, steal, or have attacked someone with the intential to seriously hurt the person have more deviant peers, negative attitudes toward school, and less involved parents. Those who sell illegal drugs have more deviant peers, more negative attitudes toward school, less involved parents, and are involved in fewer conventional activities. Those who have been arrested have (or are aware of) fewer deviant peers, have more positive attitudes toward school, are involved in more conventional activities and have greater parental involvement. Runaways have fewer deviant peers, positive attitudes toward school and greater parental involvement. Hackers have fewer deviant peers, like school, and are less likely to be involved in conventional activities. Arsonists have fewer deviant peers and positive attitudes toward school.

These data reveal some interesting patterns. First, the number of (known) deviant peers is negatively associated with having been arrested and booked. One aspect of social learning/differential association is that one's deviant peers teach one not only *how* to commit a crime but *how not to get caught.* Youths outside a circle of deviant peers may be no more deviant but are, simply, easy targets for the criminal justice system. Youths who like school (again, outside the circle of deviant peers) are more likely to have been arrested and booked, are more often involved in conventional activities, and are more attached to their parents. It would seem that, at least regarding

White youths, social learning/social disorganization can explain, if not deviant behavior, the forces behind being arrested. The youths with more deviant peers are more likely to engage in group-oriented crime and delinquency, since fighting, selling drugs, and stealing are all, to a certain extent, social activities.

A second surprise is the relationship between involvement in conventional activities and crime/delinquency. While hackers (computer criminals) and drug dealers are less likely to be involved in school, church, and community activities, violent behavior is more common among White youths involved in them.

CONCLUSION

Contrary to common perception, self-reported crime and delinquency among White youths has been, for the most part, declining over the past decade. However, arrests have increased. This trend may be the result of increased public fear of what is (wrongly) perceived as an increasingly violent juvenile population. Furthermore, the image of the suburban, White, gun-toting male delinquent does not appear to be supported. Rural White youth account for more weapons arrests than suburban White youth, who are most likely to be arrested for drug- and alcohol-related offenses, as well as status offenses.

The role of movies, video games, deviant peer groups, and disinterested parents in White delinquency is also unclear. While association with deviant peers is positively associated with some types of White delinquency, it is negatively associated with others. Nor is there any clear association between the social bond and all types of delinquency. Blazak and Wooden (2000) make note that the Japanese produce and play more violent video games and that most of the school shooters in that country did have friends. Traditional, media-friendly perspectives on why kids engage in crime and delinquency are inadequate to describe why White youths engage in crime. Many White suburban youths do, in fact, feel disenfranchised and powerless (Blazak & Wooden, 2000). Only four years ago teens demonstrated in Orange, California, carrying signs that read "Youth is not a Crime."

Further research needs to be done not only into the possibility that today's White youths constitute an awakening group, aware of its relatively disadvantaged position in society, but also into the possibility that, rather than approaching White youth crime from interactional or structural positions, we may best approach it from a conflict or critical perspective and begin to look at White youth crime and delinquency as a adaptation to what is an increasingly unequal playing field as younger Whites increasingly have to compete with their baby boomer parents for a place in society.

REFERENCES

Agnew, R. (1991). The interactive effect of peer variables on delinquency. *Criminology, 29*, 47–72.

Akers, R. L., & Cochran, J. K. (1985). Adolescent marijuana use: A test of three theories of deviant behavior. *Deviant Behavior, 6*, 323–346.

Blazak, R., & Wooden, W. S. (2000). *Renegade kids, suburban outlaws*. New York: Wadsworth Publishing.

Cold Spring School shooting; A fatal day at school; 1 student dies, 2nd is critically wounded at Cold Spring Rocori; 15-year-old freshman is in custody; Motive remains unclear. (2003, September 25). *Minneapolis Star Tribune*, p. A1.

Dembo, R., Grandon, G., La Loie, L., Schmeidler, J., & Burgess, W. (1986). Parents and drugs revisited: Some further evidence in support of social learning theory. *Criminology 24*, 85–104.

Elliott, D. S., Huizinga, D., & Ageton, S. S. (1985). *Explaining delinquency and drug use*. Beverly Hills: Sage Publications.

Esbenswen, F., & Deschenes, E. P. (1998). A multi-site examination of youth gang membership: Does gender matter? *Criminology, 36*, 799–827.

Grennan, S., Britz, M. T., Rush, J., & Barker, T. (2000). *Gangs: An international approach*. Upper Saddle River, New Jersey: Prentice Hall, Inc.

Hirschi, T. (1969). *Causes of delinquency*. Berkeley, CA: University of California Press.

Krohn, M. D., & Massey, J. L. (1980). Social control and delinquent behavior: An examination of the elements of the social bond. *Sociological Quarterly, 21*, 529–543.

McIntosh, W. A., Fitch, S. D., Wilson, J. B., & Nybert, K. L. (1981). The effect of mainstream religious social controls on adolescent drug use in rural areas. *Review of Religious Research, 23*, 54–75.

Mihalic, S. W., & Elliott, D. S. (1997). A social learning theory model of marital violence. *Journal of Family Violence, 12*, 21–36.

Other recent school shootings. (2001, March 6). *St. Louis Post-Dispatch*, p. A10.

Pastore, A. L., & Maguire, K. (Eds.). *Sourcebook of Criminal Justice Statistics*. Retrieved September 15, 2003: http://www.albany.edu/sourcebook/.

Sellers, C. S., & Winfree, T. L. (1990). Differential associations and definitions: A panel study of youthful drinking behavior. *International Journal of the Addictions, 25*, 755–771.

Shoemaker, D. J. (1996). *Theories of delinquency: An examination of explanations of delinquent behavior*. New York: Oxford University Press.

Skinner, W. F., & Fream, A. M. (1997). A social learning theory analysis of computer crime among college students. *Journal of Research in Crime and Delinquency, 34*, 495–518.

Sutherland, E. H. (1947). *Principles of criminology* (4th ed.). Philadelphia: J. B. Lippincott.

Sutherland, E. H., & Cressey, D. R. (1978). *Criminology* (10th ed.). Philadelphia: J. B. Lippincott.

Two killed in San Diego school shooting. (2001, March 6). *The Independent.*

United States Department of Health and Human Services Substance Abuse and Mental Health Services Administration, Office of Applied Studies. (2001). *National household survey on drug abuse.* [Computer file]. ICPSR version. Research Triangle Park, NC: Research Triangle Institute [producer, 2002]. Ann Arbor, MI: Inter-university Consortium for Political and Social Research [distributor, 2003].

White, H. R., Johnson, V., & Horowitz, A. (1986). An application of three deviance theories for adolescent substance use. *International Journal of the Addictions, 21,* 347–366.

Winfree, L. T., Jr., Sellers, C., & Clason, D. L. (1993). Social learning and adolescent deviance abstention: Toward understanding reasons for initiating, quitting, and avoiding drugs. *Journal of Quantitative Criminology, 9,* 101–125

Winfree, L. T., Jr., Vigil-Backstrom, T., & Mays, G. L. (1994a). Social learning theory, self-reported delinquency, and youth gangs: A new twist on a general theory of crime and delinquency. *Youth and Society, 26,* 147–177.

Winfree, L. T., Jr., Vigil-Backstrom, T., & Mays, G. L. (1994b). Youth gangs and incarcerated delinquents: Exploring the ties between gang membership, delinquency, and social learning theory. *Justice Quarterly, 11,* 229–256.

CHAPTER TWO

LATINO DELINQUENCY: DEFINING AND COUNTING THE PROBLEM

Myrna Cintrón

INTRODUCTION

With the arrival of the twenty-first century, the Latino[1] population has emerged as the largest minority group in the United States. Latinos and Latinas are also becoming a large component of both the adult and juvenile justice systems. While there are serious inadequacies in the official national crime statistics, research findings indicate that Latino males, young and adult, are overrepresented in the nation's justice systems. This chapter discusses current research on as well as the social, historical, and environmental causes of Latino youths' involvement in delinquency. The chapter begins with an overview of the Latino population: who they are and where they stand in several national indices; the overview is followed by an exploration of criminal justice research findings relevant to the group. Next the discussion focuses on several group characteristics and experiences that influence delinquency rates. These characteristics and experiences underscore the complexity and challenges that Latinos face in the nation's justice system.

---

1. Latino refers collectively to Mexicans, Puerto Ricans, Cubans, Central and South Americans, Dominicans, and others of Spanish and Latin American descent. In addition, "Latino" can refer to males; "Latina" refers to females. Latinos can be of any race.

General Demographic Characteristics
of the Latino Population

Census Population Profile

According to the United States Census Bureau, the Latino population is composed of people "of Cuban, Mexican, Puerto Rican, South or Central American, or other Spanish culture or origin regardless of race" (Grieco & Cassidy, 2000, p. 2). There are 35.3 million Latinos in the United States (Guzmán, 2001). According to the latest census, the Latino population makes up the largest minority group in the United States: About one in eight people in the nation is of Latino origin. While the overwhelming majority of the Latino population in the United States is of Mexican, Puerto Rican, or Cuban descent, the 2000 census reports that the proportional distribution of these three subpopulations actually decreased (Guzmán, 2001), while the distribution of the "new-Latino immigrants" increased: a large wave of Latino immigrants coming from Central and South America and the Caribbean. While the Latino groups are concentrated in several states (e.g., California, Texas, New York, Florida), Latinos are also present in some counties within states with low Latino populations (e.g., Iowa, Kansas, North Carolina) (Guzmán, 2001). In nineteen locations throughout the nation, Latino people are in the majority (Guzmán, 2001).

Despite the diversity that exists within the Latino subpopulations (Myers, Cintrón, & Scarborough, 1994) and despite the overall achievements of the groups, when the groups are compared with the non-Latino White population, brief census reports are not encouraging. According to the reports, a disproportionate number of Latino "families, youth, and children in both urban and rural areas are significantly disadvantaged. These disadvantages are multiple, and each tends to compound the others in a progressively deleterious cycle" (Pabón, 1998, p. 943). For example, Latinos are more likely than non-Latino Whites to live in the inner city or within a metropolitan area (Guzmán, 2001; Therrien & Ramírez, 2000). The median age for the group is 25.9 years, compared to 35.3 years for the entire United States population. (Close to 36 percent of the Latinos are less than eighteen years of age.) (Guzmán, 2001; Therrien & Ramírez, 2000). Nearly 31 percent of Latino households consist of five or more members, compared to nearly 12 percent of non-Latino White family households (Therrien & Ramírez, 2000). While educational attainment varies among the Latino subpopulations, more than 2 in 5 have not graduated from high school (Therrien & Ramírez, 2000). Latinos are more likely than non-Latino Whites to work in service occupations or as laborers and are more likely to be unemployed (6.8 percent versus 3.4 percent) (Therrien & Ramírez, 2000). Among full-time year-round workers, Latinos earn less than non-Latino Whites. (Only 23.3 percent of Latinos versus 49.3 percent of non-Latino Whites earned $35,000 or more according to the 2000 U.S. census.) Also, Latinos are more likely to live in poverty than non-Latino Whites. (Latinos represent 13 percent of the United States population but make up more than 23 percent of those living in poverty.) While Latino children represent about 16 percent of all children in the United States, they make up more than 29 percent of all children living in poverty (Therrien & Ramírez, 2000).

The above census statistics concerning the Latino population have several implications for the juvenile justice system. First, this population is expected to continue to grow at a faster rate than any other population group in the United States. This group is younger, has higher fertility rates, and has higher levels of immigration than other groups. Second, it has been estimated that the proportion of Latino youth in the United States will increase by 59 percent between 1995 and 2015 (Snyder & Sickmund, 1999). Finally, as indicated above, low income, low levels of educational attainment, lack of training to compete in a constantly changing marketplace, as well as language and cultural barriers, all combine to predict social problems in general and delinquency in particular (Arthur, Mildon, & Briggs, 1990; Fagan, Piper, & Moore, 1986; Pabón, 1998; Pope & Feyerherm, 1990a; Pope & Feyerherm, 1990b; Tonry 1995). Pabón (1998, p. 943) argues: "[T]hese indicators are strongly associated throughout the scientific literature and by providers of human services with heightened danger of involvement in delinquent and criminal behavior."

LATINO REPRESENTATION IN THE JUVENILE JUSTICE SYSTEM

Inadequate Data

Among the first lessons learned in introductory criminal justice courses is that official data sources are plagued with weaknesses. However, most textbooks fail to mention that among these weaknesses is the absence of a systematic collection process that routinely distinguishes Latinos from Whites, Blacks, or other groups. As a result, the data available for research and policy are limited. Such is the case with the Office of Juvenile Justice and Delinquency Prevention (OJJDP) bulletins. Most of the tables in this agency's reports rely on aggregate data, which put Latino youths and White youths in the same category. Finley and Schindler (1999, p. 12) write:

> [T]he Office of Juvenile Justice and Delinquency prevention's 1996 national report on juvenile offenders and victims, reflecting data colleted by the states, includes Latinos youth as "white when counting violent crime and transfers to adult court, then lists them as "minority" in its confinement statistics. As a result, data on the extent to which Latino youth are overrepresented in the juvenile system are incomplete.

This method of classifying creates some practical, theoretical, and research issues that must be addressed by the criminal justice student. First, Latinos and Whites are not homogenous groups. For example, any U.S. Census Bureau index (income, employment, educational attainment) shows that the gap between the groups is abysmal. Second, by definition the groups White and Latino represent racial and ethnic categories, respectively. Simply stated, race refers to skin color and the physical characteristics commonly associated with a group. Ethnicity refers to the cultural practices and traditions commonly associated with a group. Because group categories are established by the U.S. Census Bureau, their definitions have been bureaucratically redefined for agency efficiency in identifying national population trends every ten years. By definition, these categories — "White" and "Latino" — assume there are marked and significant differences between the groups. Why, therefore, are Latinos lumped together with Whites in national crime statistics? Aggregating the groups results in an overestimation of the delinquency rates for Whites but an underestimation of the rates for Latinos. As a result, current practices mask disproportionate minority confinement rates for the Latino group.

Another issue is that Latinos are often considered a homogeneous group in official government reports based on research that fails to distinguish among the different Latino subgroupings and the demographic variations within the groups. For example, the above census data, while offering a broad generalization concerning the Latino group, fail to capture the diversity within the group. Closer inspection of the Census 2000 data shows not only the high levels of intragroup diversity (Mexican, Puerto Rican, Cuban, Central and South American) within this group, but also indicates that in some indices (such as education and income) subpopulation groups (Cubans in particular) are more similar to Whites than to other Latino groups. Relying on broad generalizations about Latinos can lead researchers to inaccurate and misleading statements (Lee, Martínez, & Rodríguez, 2000; Martínez, 2000; McNulty & Bellair, 2003). Juvenile justice professionals in particular should be aware of the differences that exist within the Latino group. For example, while Latinos share a common language, in Spanish, pronunciation and dialect vary among speakers, just as in English (Urbina, 2004). Also, the same word can have different meanings and implications, depending on national origin. For example, "la migra," Spanish slang referring to the Immigration and Naturalization Service (INS), has a different connotation to a Mexican immigrant than to a Cuban or Puerto Rican immigrant. In addition to their variations in the Spanish language, Latinos vary greatly in terms of their history in the United States. Latinos can be found in a variety of legal statuses; some examples include "new immigrant," "undocumented person," "fifth generation American," and "recently naturalized American." Some might have difficulties in school because they lack English language skills but not intellectual abilities. In addition to immigration experiences, juvenile justice professionals must be aware of the trauma Latino youths might have suffered in their countries of origin. For example, many have personally experienced the consequences of civil war; others are members of minority groups in their country of origin and have experienced oppression; for those that are undocumented, the fear of deportation is a constant burden. These experiences are likely to influence their perceptions, expectations, support, and trust in the American justice system (Urbina, 2004).

Overrepresentation in the Juvenile Justice System

While racial and ethnic bias in the American justice system is well documented (Pope & Feyerherm, 1990a; Pope & Feyerherm, 1990b; Bishop & Frazier, 1996), most of the research evidence relies on comparisons between Blacks and Whites. Empirical studies devoted to the exclusive examination and comparison of Latinos in the juvenile justice system are limited. Sampson and Lauritsen (1997, p. 364) state:

> Despite the volume of previous research on race and ethnic comparisons, we know very little about criminal justice processing other than for blacks and whites. Quite simply, there is little empirical basis from which to draw firm conclusions for Hispanics.

The research problem continues to be that it is difficult not only to calculate crime rate differences between Latinos and non-Latinos but also to collect data systematically on the nature and extent of Latino overrepresentation in the juvenile justice system (Steffensmeier & Demuth, 2001). Despite the problems with official data, researchers have documented not only the overrepresentation of Latinos in the American justice system but also the cumulative disadvantages faced by the group as they are processed through the system (Albonetti, 1997; Hebert, 1997; Hamparian & Leiber, 1996; Holmes,

Hosch, Daudistel, Perez, & Graves, 1996; Klein, Petersilia, & Turner, 1990; Petersilia, 1985; Spohn & Holleran, 2000; Steffensmeier & Demuth, 2000, 2001; Unnever & Hembroff, 1988; Zatz, 1984).

Researchers have documented that Latinos are overrepresented in the juvenile justice system and receive harsher treatment than White youths, even when charged with the same offense. Poe-Yamagata and Jones (2000) reported that Latino youth were three times more likely to be incarcerated than White youth. Juskiewicz (2000) also reported that Latinos made up 24 percent of the youths charged with felonies who were tried as adults. Juskiewicz also found that Latino youths released on bail before trial received, on the average, higher bail amounts ($13,556) than those of Whites ($10,174) and Blacks ($8,761) and were more likely than Whites to receive incarceration instead of split sentence or probation. Villarruel and Walker (2002) found that between 1983 and 1991 the percentage of Latino youths in state-run detention facilities increased by 84 percent, compared to an 8 percent increase for White youths. Other researchers (Hamparian & Leiber, 1997; Snyder & Sickmund, 1999) have also found evidence of Latino overrepresentation at the state level. For example, admission rates to state-run public facilities are higher for Latinos with no prior admission to them and for those with one or two prior admissions than for whites with the same number of previous institutional admissions for all offense categories (Villarruel & Walker, 2002). Similarly, the National Council on Crime and Delinquency (NCCD) (1993) found that the average length of incarceration for Latino youth is longer than for any other racial or ethnic group in every offense category. This inequitable incarceration is happening at a time when national crime rates are declining among both juveniles and adults—for most offense categories—and at a time when confinement rates have declined for White and Black youth (Villarruel & Walker, 2002). Other researchers have argued that the Latino youths' commitment rates will continue to increase over the next several years (Hayes-Bautista & Nichols, 2000; Males & Macallair, 2000; Poe-Yamagata & Jones, 2000). Males and Macallair (2000) found that of all ethnic and racial groups, Latino youths were more likely than any other youths to be tried for felonies as adults in Los Angles County.

Human Rights Watch (2002) found that Latino youths' incarceration rates are higher than those of White youths in 39 states; they are incarcerated, in jails and prisons, more than 3 times the rates of White youths in eight states (Connecticut, Michigan, North Dakota, Pennsylvania, South Dakota, Vermont, West Virginia, Wisconsin) and at 7 to 17 times the rates of White youths in four other states (Connecticut, Hawaii, Massachusetts, New Hampshire). Finally, Strom (2000) found that the percentage of Latino youths in adult state prisons was larger than the percentage of Latino youths in the general U.S. population.

Service Issues in Justice Agencies

As the above discussion has demonstrated, it is likely that the number of Latinos processed by the juvenile justice system will continue to grow. As a result, juvenile justice systems across the nation will have to address two other issues: first, the provision of bilingual and culturally sensitive services to this population and second, the immigration status of the Latino youths being served.

As the Spanish-speaking population of the United States continues to increase, an issue for juvenile justice agencies is the provision of services for non-English speakers (Cintrón & Lee, 2002). While it is possible that the population being processed by these agencies is able to speak English, several issues must be addressed by them. The first is the level of English proficiency: the ability to communicate (write, read, and speak) in English. A characteristic of the criminal justice system is that legal proceedings in general are difficult to understand, even for native-English speakers (Mann, 1993; Urbina, 2004). For example, juvenile justice agencies and their representatives use legal and professional jargon (e.g., "*parens patriae*" and "intake") that is not clearly understood by their serviced population. In addition, court proceedings are, at best, difficult to follow (e.g., advocacy versus prosecutorial roles, private versus public proceedings). There are even instances when the wheels of justice might move too quickly (e.g., through selective incapacitation and waivers). Most of all, legal proceedings have uncertain and unpredictable results (e.g., diversion, institutionalization, probation, intensive supervised probation). As a result, it is possible for an individual and/or families without proficiency in English to become lost in these proceedings.

Bilingual services are needed to prevent parents from being unable to communicate with system officials and thus avoiding misunderstandings. While English might be spoken by the juvenile who is being processed or by a sibling, parents or guardians might not speak the language at all. Several issues concerning miscommunication and misunderstanding must be addressed by juvenile justice agencies. For example, should a sibling (most likely a minor) translate for the adults? Will a child (as the defendant or as the translator for the family) be able to understand the proceedings, given their seriousness and their use of legal jargon? In cases where a translator is used, does the translator have the necessary language and cultural-competency skills? If a parent or guardian cannot communicate with the authorities but the juvenile in question is fluent in English, will the juvenile be trusted to translate? If parents cannot communicate in English, will they be perceived as lacking in parenting skills? Will they, for example, be perceived as unable to control and supervise their own children? Is it possible that risk assessment decisions, treatment plans, and aftercare plans are affected by language proficiency? Are constitutional due-process rights compromised because bilingual services are lacking?[2] This line of inquiry continues to be ignored by researchers in criminology and criminal justice, although it has been carried out by national Latino organizations such as the National Council of la Raza (NCLR), the Mexican American Legal Defense and Education Fund (MALDAFE), and the League of United Latin American Citizens (LULAC). Since the 1970s the U.S. courts have indicated that the appointment of an interpreter was entirely within the trial court's discretion. In *United States ex rel. Negron v. New York,* for example, the state and federal courts recognized that both the Sixth Amendment and "simple humaneness" require that the state provide interpreters to non-English-speaking defendants during criminal proceedings. However, only twenty-four states are members of the National State Courts Consortium for State Court Interpreter Certification (Urbina, 2004), an organization whose goals are to develop and share information to address the above issues.

The second issue is the immigration status of Latino youths in the juvenile justice systems throughout the United States. Data on the circumstances and the incidents used by local justice agencies to contact the Office of Detention and Removal (DRO), a division of the U.S. Immigration and Customs Enforcement (ICE),[3] are sketchy and at times conflicting (Villarruel & Walker, 2002). Cintrón (1997) found that among Texas law enforcement departments, agencies closer to the Mexican border were likely to contact the INS[4] to verify the residency status of suspects. It was also found that among departments closer to the border, the INS visited jails on a daily basis. Generally, undocu-

---

2. Defendants have a constitutional right to an interpreter; however, it has been reported that about 91 percent of the people who take the test to become certified court interpreters fail it. Therefore, if a court cannot find a certified interpreter, a mistrial could be declared (Poverty, welfare, labor, 2003).

3. The Office of Detention and Removal (DRO) is a division of the United States Immigration and Customs Enforcement (ICE) (the old Immigration and Naturalization Services), Bureau of U.S. Citizenship and Immigration Services, Department of Homeland Security.

4. Because of reorganization plans, the INS (Immigration and Naturalization Services) is now the ICE (Immigration and Customs Enforcement) in the U.S. Department of Homeland Security.

mented persons who are apprehended and not released from custody are placed in detention facilities until deportation.[5] The Department of Homeland Security's Detention and Removal Office also handle alien juveniles who have entered the United States illegally, who violate their legal status, or who commit deportable crimes.[6] In 2001 the INS Office of Juvenile Affairs reported it had 4,896 juveniles in custody, 3,540 males and 1,356 young females, their ages unknown (U.S. Immigration and Naturalization Service, 2002).

Many of these youths are detained for months at a time, and for some their only violation is a lack of proper documentation concerning their immigration status. In addition, even if their status is legal, some youths are not afforded rights guaranteed under the U.S. Constitution (Human Rights Watch, 1997; Human Rights Watch, 1998; U.S. Office of the Inspector General, 2001). For example, previous INS policies prohibited keeping juveniles in secure juvenile detention facilities longer than seventy-two hours, unless the juvenile was considered likely to escape, was at risk of being harmed (by smugglers, gangs, etc.), was considered by the courts to be a delinquent or was facing a delinquency hearing, was charged with a crime, or was convicted of a crime (U.S. Immigration and Naturalization Service, 2002).

It has been reported that a high percentage of federal immigration violation prosecutions results in convictions. In 2001 about 87 percent of such prosecutions resulted in convictions (Security: hearings, detention, visas, 2002). Moreover, because tougher U.S.-Mexico-border controls make it harder for parents to go back and forth across the border, undocumented parents who have settled in the U.S. are using "coyotes" (smugglers of illegal immigrants)) to get their children into the country (DHS: Border, visas, 2004). This kind of smuggling is happening at a time when other kinds of smuggling along the U.S.-Mexico border are becoming more dangerous because of increased security measures implemented after September 11, 2001. It has been reported that the increased security has led some groups to cease smuggling drugs and start smuggling immigrants (DHS: Border, visas, 2004). As a result, unaccompanied youths are at a higher risk of being victimized by coyotes. In addition, such youths run a greater risk of being apprehended by immigration authorities. Since the Federal Bureau of Prisons does not have its own facilities for juveniles, ICE contracts with state and local juvenile detention facili-

---

5. http://www.ice.gov/graphics/enforce/imm/index.htm.

6. http://www.ice.gov/graphics/enforce/imm/imm_dro.htm. The Department of Homeland Security has three bureaus responsible for immigration: the Customs and Border Protection (www.cbp.gov), the U.S. Citizenship and Immigration Services (www.uscis), and the Immigration and Customs Enforcement (www.ice.gov).

ties (U.S. Immigration and Customs Enforcement, 2004).[7] However, in some states these facilities are far from border towns, making it difficult for families to find these youths.

Research and Theoretical Issues

Research into the causes of delinquency among Latino youths has led to the examination of several theoretical factors: demographic characteristics (such as age, socioeconomic status, education, residency, and working status) and sociocultural influences (such as family relations and acculturation).

In the criminological literature, several of the demographic characteristics used earlier in this chapter to describe Latino youths have been associated with higher risks for delinquency and crime. Age, socioeconomic status, education, residency, and working status put many Latino youths at risk for delinquency. For example, about 80 percent of Latinos are twenty-four years of age and younger (Marotta & Garcia, 2003), the age range of persons considered at risk for delinquency and prosecution (Coyle, 2003; Arboleda, 2002).

In the criminological literature, socioeconomic status is commonly associated with delinquency. Such status is generally considered a variable reflecting education, occupation, and income. Poverty levels, which are also measured by the U.S. Census Bureau, are indicated in the literature as potential barriers to improving socioeconomic status (Marotta & Garcia, 2003). National poverty rates are a function of family size. The median household income for the United States is $67,721; for Latinos it is $45,338. When income is measured according to the number of family members, the average for the nation is $26,641; for Latinos it is $15,415 (Marotta & Garcia, 2003). Without taking family size into account, the average income is $82,000 for the nation and $53,251 for Latinos. According to the 2000 census 27 percent of Latinos were below the poverty level compared to 19 percent of the U.S. population (Marotta & Garcia, 2003).

Educational status affects the income-producing potential of individuals and families. Additionally, it affects the crime rate among a group of persons. For example, official criminal justice statistics show that convicted adult criminals were school dropouts and underachieving juveniles. According to several sources of data for educational indices, among Latinos educational statuses vary according to national origin (whether a Latino was born in the United States or outside of it) and family generational status (whether one or both parents were born outside the United States) (Marotta & Garcia, 2003). Martínez-Ebers, Fraga, López, and Vega (2000) report that at the national level Latinos—

---

7. http://www.ice.gov/graphics/about/contact/con_dro.htm.

particularly Latina teens—have the lowest high school graduation and college enrollment rates and the highest drop out rates. They also report that 75 percent of the students classified as "limited English proficient" are Latinos. Rodríguez (1996) found that youths who are not working are less likely to become delinquent than those who hold jobs. Rodríguez also found that being in school is associated with nondelinquency and argues in favor of policy programs that focus on learning skills and on convincing adolescents to stay in school. Arboleda (2002), in a National Council of La Raza report, wrote:

> The lack of adequate education, high poverty, and the need for healthy recreational activities contribute to disproportionate numbers of Latinos in all stages of the criminal justice system. The latest data show that 27.8% of Latinos between the ages of 16 and 24 are not currently in school and have not graduated from high school and only 57% of Latinos 25 years and older have a high school diploma. In part because of limited education and, subsequently, poor earnings ability, the Latino population has had a persistently high poverty rate over the past two decades, even during time of economic prosperity. In 2000, 21% of Latinos and 28% of Latino children were poor. Both low educational attainment and high poverty are associated with a greater likelihood of contact with the criminal justice system. Another issue especially relevant for Latino and African American youth is that they tend to live in urban areas with few resources, and often lack sufficient opportunities for sports, recreation, or other activities that would deter them from becoming involved with the criminal justice system. (pp. 1–2)

One of the most consistent and strongest findings in delinquency research is that having delinquent-prone peers increases the likelihood of delinquent behavior (Agnew, 2001). Peer pressure, poor achievement in school, peer involvement in drug use, deviance, and gang activity have all been associated with the onset and later persistence of delinquency (Elliot, Huizinga, & Ageton, 1985) and of participation in gang activity. A report on Latinos in the Texas criminal justice system summarizes the status of the group nationally:

> The entire juvenile offender population shared various social factors, which speaks clearly to the need to provide these children with services rather than adult-like criminal treatment. Three-quarters (74%) identified as having school problems such as failing a grade or dropping out of school. Half (49%) had a family member with a history of criminal activity or incarcerations, or were suspected of being in a gang, or were involved with a gang. Almost a third (32%) was en-

gaged in frequent alcohol or drug use. More than one in five (22%) was identified as having mental health or mental retardation problems. One-fifth (20%) had no contact with either parent, two or more changes of residence in the prior year, and/or prior contact with a child protection agency (Coyle, 2003).

Two common themes in the interdisciplinary study of the sociocultural influences on the Latino population are the role of the family and acculturation. The family variable (encompassing family solidarity and familism) has been broadly defined. In some studies, the term "family influences" refers to bonding with significant figures, such as parents involved in the adolescents' activities (Brook, Whiteman, Balka, Win, & Gursen, 1998; De la Rosa & White, 2001; Pabón, 1998; Dinh, Roosa, Tein, & López, 2002). In other studies the family variable has some psychological components, such as the adolescents' perceptions of the activities and behaviors the family will likely sanction (Brook, Whiteman, Balka, Win, & Gursen, 1998; De la Rosa & White, 2001; Pabón, 1998; Dinh, Roosa, Tein, & López, 2002). Criminology theory and research suggests an association between family life and involvement in delinquent behavior. (See, for example, Farrington, 1987; Elliot, Huizinga & Ageton, 1985; Hirschi, 1969.) Studies that have examined family influences among different groups of Latino youths have found that the Latino family has a significant, direct effect on delinquency in contrast to weaker effects found among mainstream White youths (Sommers, Fagan, & Baskin, 1992; Rodríguez & Weisburd, 1991). That is, high levels of family solidarity and familism have been identified as the dominant difference between Latino and mainstream youths. A high level of family solidarity among Latinos means that the family unit, which might include the extended family in the United States and abroad, exerts influence and control that effectively inhibits delinquency among adolescents whose other background characteristics might predict delinquency (Pabón, 1998). "Familism" means that Latinos hold a strong belief in the sanctity of the family and a high respect for family members (who are not always blood related, such as godparents and close family friends, who are called *tio y tia,* "uncle and aunt"). (Buriel, Calzada, & Vázquez, 1982; Coohey, 2001; De la Rosa & White, 2001; Fernández-Marina, Maldonado-Sierra & Trent, 1958; Pabón, 1998; Peñalosa & McDonagh, 1966; Rodríguez & Weisburd, 1991; Sommers, Fagan, & Baskin, 1992; Sabogal, Marín, Otero Sabogal, VannOss Marín, & Pérez-Stable, 1987; Vega, Gil, Warheit, Zimmerman, & Apospori, 1993).

Acculturation refers to the adaptation processes and the changes groups and individuals from different cultures go through as they come in contact with a different culture. Research assessing different levels of acculturation have used, as relevant constructs, length of time in the new country (Burman, Hough, Kamo, Escobar, & Telles, 1987; Griffith, 1983; Lang, Muñoz, Bernal, & Sorenson, 1982; Valentine & Mosely, 2000), preference of language (Cuellar, Harris, & Jasso, 1980; Marín, Sabogal, Marín, Otero-Sebogal, & Pérez-Stable, 1987; Norris, Ford, & Bova, 1996), and expression of cultural values and identity (Cuellar et al., 1980; Marín et al., 1987). Acculturation scales have also been developed by several researchers. What impact, if any, does acculturation have on delinquency? The empirical evidence is mixed. Some studies have found acculturation to be positively associated with delinquency (Buriel, Calzada, & Vázquez, 1982; Cuadrado & Lieberman, 1998; Fridrich & Flannery 1995; Scheier, Botvinet, Díaz, & Ifill-Williams, 1997). Other studies have found a negative association between acculturation and delinquency (Markides, Krause, & Méndes de León, 1988; Zapata & Katims, 1994). Still others have found no significant relationship between acculturation and delinquency (Carvajal, Photiades, Evans, & Nash, 1997; Wall, Power, & Arbona, 1993). While the evidence is inconclusive, it seems that Latino youths will be particularly at risk for delinquency since this variable may play an important role in their lives. The intergenerational conflict that naturally occurs between parents and children might be exacerbated in Latino families for several reasons. Latino youths assimilate more quickly to the American lifestyle than their parents. These youths may become isolated from their parents who wish to maintain traditional cultural values and language. The families of these youths might have had different expectations of and experiences with the justice system in their country of origin; thus, the trauma youths and parents might have suffered may influence their trust in the American justice system.

Conclusion

The preceding discussion not only explores the impact of the juvenile justice system on the youthful Latino population; it also stresses the need for researchers, policy makers, practitioners, and academicians to refocus their agendas if juvenile justice is to have an impact on the future of the largest minority group in the nation. However, the discipline lacks a basic knowledge and understanding of this population to meet the growing needs of the group and researchers. The discipline is also ill prepared to meet these needs—for several reasons. First, the criminal justice system lacks a uniform definition for the Latino group. "Latino" and "Hispanic" are used interchangeably. and in many jurisdictions terms of national origin (such as "Puerto Rican" and "Cuban") are used to identify persons. Second, the system does not separate ethnicity from race. (Persons of Latino origin can be of any race.) As a result, counting Latinos as White inflates the proportion of Whites in the criminal justice system while ignoring (i.e., underreporting) the proportion of Latinos in the system.

Fourth, there is evidence that Latino youths are disproportionately arrested, detained, and tried in adult criminal courts. Their sentences are harsher and their commitments are longer than those for White youths who have committed the same offenses. Latinos are significantly overrepresented in federal and state facilities, but arrest data about the group is lacking or inconsistently collected across jurisdictions.

Finally, the juvenile justice system must recognize and address the challenge that the Latino population represents. The growth of the population, coupled with the impact and effects of age, low educational attainment, immigration, adaptation process (acculturation), poverty, language, and discrimination, place Latino youths and their families at a higher risk for juvenile justice intervention.

Criminal justice professionals and academicians must broaden the scope of their knowledge so that the discipline can develop policies that will ameliorate the impact of the system on the generation that will lead this nation in the years to come. The author hopes that the characteristics, concepts, and issues discussed in this chapter—all of which underscore the complexity and challenges of the Latino experience in the nation's juvenile justice systems—will be the foundation for further inquiry and study.

REFERENCES

Agnew, R. (2001). *Juvenile delinquency: Causes and control.* Los Angeles: Roxbury Publishing Co.

Albonetti, C. A. (1997). Sentencing under the federal sentencing guidelines: Effects of defendant characteristics, guilty pleas, and departures on sentence outcomes for drug offenses, 1991–1992. *Law and Society Review, 31,* 789–822.

Arboleda, A. (2002). Latinos and the federal criminal justice system. *National Council of La Raza,* Statistical Brief No. 1 (July).

Arthur, L. G., Mildon, M. R., & Briggs, C. (Eds.). (1990). *Minority youth in the juvenile justice system: A judicial response.* Washington, DC: National Council of Juvenile and Family Court Judges.

Bishop, D. M., & Frazier, C. (1996). Race effects in juvenile justice decision-making: Findings from a statewide analysis. *Journal of Criminal Law and Criminology, 86,* 392–414.

Brook, J. S., Whiteman, M., Balka, E. B., Win, P. T., and Gursen, M. D. (1998). Similar and different precursors to drug use and delinquency among African Americans and Puerto Ricans. *The Journal of Genetic Psychology, 159,* 13–30.

Buriel, R., Calzada, S., & Vázquez, R. (1982). The relationship of traditional Mexican-American culture to adjustment and delinquency among three generations of Mexican-American male adolescents. *Hispanic Journal of Behavioral Sciences, 4,* 41–55.

Burman, M. A., Hough, R. L., Kamo, M., Escobar, J. I., & Telles, C. A. (1987). Acculturation and lifetime prevalence of psychiatric disorders among Mexican Americans in Los Angeles. *Journal of Health and Social Behavior, 28,* 89–102.

Carvajal, S. C., Photiades, J. R., Evans, R. I., and Nash, S. G. (1997). Relating a social influence model to the role of acculturation in substance use among Latino adolescents. *Journal of Applied Social Psychology, 27,* 1617–1628.

Cintrón, M. (1997). Undocumented citizens and language skills. *Texas Law Enforcement Management and Administrative Statistics Program (TELEMASP Bulletin), 4,* 4, 1–8.

Cintrón, M., & Lee, W. J. (2002). Bilingual workforce needs in Texas community supervision and corrections departments: Survey results. *Texas Probation, 17,* 4–7.

Coohey, C. (2001). The relationship between familism and child maltreatment in Latino and Anglo families. *Child Maltreatment, 6,* 2, 130–142.

Coyle, M. J. (2003). Latinos and the Texas criminal justice system. *National Council of La Raza,* Statistical Brief No. 2.

Cuadrado, M., & Lieberman, L. (1998). Traditionalism in the prevention of substance misuse among Puerto Ricans. *Substance Use and Misuse, 33,* 2737–2755.

Cuellar, I., Harris, L. C., & Jasso, R. (1980). An acculturation scale for Mexican American normal and clinical populations. *Hispanic Journal of Behavioral Sciences, 2,* 199–217.

De la Rosa, M. R., & White, M. S. (2001). A review of the role of social support systems in the drug abuse behavior of Hispanics. *Journal of Psychoactive Drugs, 33,* 3, 233–241.

DHS: Border, visas. (2004) *Migration News,* 1–2. Retrieved January 11, 2004: www. http/migration.ucdavis.edu/mn.

Dinh, K. T., Roosa, M. W., Tein, J. Y., & López, V. (2002). The relationship between acculturation and problem behavior proneness in a Hispanic youth sample: A longitudinal mediation model. *Journal of Abnormal Child Psychology, 30,* 3, 295–309.

Elliot, D., Huizinga, D., & Ageton, S. (1985). *Explaining delinquency and drug use.* Newbury Park, CA.: Sage Publications.

Fagan, J., Piper, E. S., & Moore, M. (1986). Violent delinquents and urban youth. *Criminology, 24,* 439–471.

Farrington, D. (1987). Implications of biological findings for criminological research. In S. Mednick, T. Moffitt, & S. Stack (Eds.), *Causes of crime.* Cambridge, MA.: Cambridge University Press.

Fernández-Marina, R., Maldonado-Sierra, E., & Trent, R. (1958). Three basic themes in Mexican and Puerto-Rican family values. *Journal of Social Psychology, 48,* 167–181.

Finley, M., & Schindler, M. (1999). Punitive juvenile justice policies and the impact on minority youth. *Federal Probation, 58,* 2, 11.

Fridrich A. H., & Flannery, D. J. (1995). The effects of ethnicity and acculturation on early adolescent delinquency. *Journal of Child and Family Studies, 4,* 69–87.

Grieco, E. M., & Cassidy, R. C. (2000). *Overview of race and Hispanic origin: Census 2000 brief.* Issued March 2001, C2KBR/01-1, U.S. Census Bureau, Washington, D.C.

Griffith, J. (1983). Relationship between acculturation and psychological impairment in adult Mexican Americans. *Hispanic Journal of Behavioral Studies, 5,* 431–459.

Guzmán, B. (2001). *The Hispanic population: Census 2000 brief.* C2KBR/01-3 U. S. Census Bureau, Washington, D.C.

Hamparian D., & Leiber, J. M. (1997). *Disproportionate confinement of minority juveniles in secure facilities: 1996 national report.* Washington, D.C.: Office of Juvenile Justice and Delinquency prevention.

Hebert, C. G. (1997). Sentencing outcomes of black, Hispanic, and white males convicted under federal sentencing guidelines. *Criminal Justice Review, 22,* 133–156.

Hirschi, T. (1969). *Causes of delinquency.* Berkeley, CA.: University of California Press.

Holmes, M., Hosch, H., Daudistel, H., Perez, D., & Graves, J. (1996). Ethnicity, legal resources, and felony dispositions in two southwestern jurisdictions. *Justice Quarterly, 13,* 11–30.

Hayes-Bautista, D. E., & Nichols, M. (2000). *American dream makers: Latino profiles study report.* Los Angeles, CA: Latino Profiles Committee.

Human Rights Watch (2002). *Race and incarceration in the United States.* Washington, D.C. Available at http://www.hrw.org/press/2002/02/race027.htm.

Human Rights Watch (1998). *Detained and deprived of rights: Children in the custody of the U.S. Immigration and Naturalization Service.* Washington, D.C.

Human Rights Watch (1997). *Slipping through the cracks: Unaccompanied children detained by the U.S. Immigration and Naturalization Service.* Washington, D.C.

Juskiewicz, J. (2000). *Youth crime, adult time: Is justice served?* Building Blocks for Youth. Washington, D.C.

Klein, S., Petersilia, J., & Turner, S. (1990). Race and imprisonment decisions in California. *Science, 247,* 812–816.

Lang, J. G., Muñoz, R. F., Bernal, G., & Sorenson, J. L. (1982). Quality of life and psychological well-being in a bi-cultural Latino community. *Hispanic Journal of Behavioral Sciences, 4,* 443–450.

Lee, M. T, Martínez, Jr., R., & Rodríguez, S. F. (2000). Contrasting Latinos in homicide research: The victim and offender relationship in El Paso and Miami. *Social Science Quarterly, 81,* 375–388.

Males, M., & Macallair, D. (2000). *The color of justice: An analysis of juvenile adult court transfers in California.* Building Blocks for Youth, Washington, D.C.

Mann, C. R. (1993). *Unequal Justice: A question of color.* Bloomington, IN: Indiana University Press.

Marín, G., Sabogal, F., Marín, B. V., Otero-Sebogal, R., & Pérez-Stable, E. J. (1987). Development of a short acculturation scale for Hispanics. *Hispanic Journal of Behavioral Sciences, 9,* 183–205.

Markides, K. S., Krause, N., & Méndes de León, C. F. (1988). Acculturation and alcohol consumption among Mexican Americans. *American Journal of Public Health, 78,* 1178–1181.

Marotta, S. A., & Garcia, J. G. (2003). Latinos in the United States in 2000. *Hispanic Journal of Behavioral Sciences, 25,* 13–34.

Martínez, R. (2000). Immigration and urban violence: The link between immigrant Latinos and types of homicide. *Social Science Quarterly, 81,* 363–374.

Martínez-Ebers, V., Fraga, L., López, L., & Vega, A. (2000). Latino interests in education, health, and criminal justice policy. *Political Science & Politics, 33,* 3, 547–554.

McNulty, T. L., & Bellair, P. E. (2003). Explaining racial and ethnic differences in adolescent violence: Structural disadvantage, family well-being, and social capital. *Justice Quarterly, 20*, 1–31.

Myers, L. B., Cintrón, M., & Scarborough, K. E. (1994). Latinos: The conceptualization of race. In J. E. Hendricks & B. Byers (Eds.), *Multicultural perspectives in criminal justice and criminology.* Springfield, IL: Charles C. Thomas.

National Council on Crime and Delinquency (1993). *The juveniles taken into custody research program: Estimating the prevalence of juvenile custody rates by race and gender.* Washington, D.C.

Norris, A. E., Ford, K., & Bova, C. A. (1996). Psychometrics of a brief acculturation scale for Hispanics in a probability sample of urban Hispanic adolescents and young adults. *Hispanic Journal of Behavioral Sciences, 18*, 29–38.

Pabón, E. (1998). Hispanic adolescent delinquency and the family: A discussion of sociocultural influences. *Adolescence, 33*, 132, 941–955.

Peñalosa F., & McDonagh, E. (1966). Social mobility in a Mexican-American community. *Social Forces, 44*, 498–505.

Petersilia, J. (1985). Racial disparities in the criminal justice system: A summary. *Crime and Delinquency, 31*, 15–34.

Poe-Yamagata, E., & Jones, M. (2000). *And justice for some: Differential treatment of minority youth in the justice system.* Building Blocks for Youth. Washington, D.C.

Pope, C. E., & Feyerhern, W. (1990a). Minority status and juvenile justice processing: An assessment of the research literature (Part 1). *Criminal Justice Abstracts, 22*, 327–335.

Pope, C. E. & Feyerhern, W. (1990b). Minority status and juvenile justice processing: An assessment of the research literature (Part 2). *Criminal Justice Abstracts, 22*, 527–542.

Poverty, welfare, labor. (2003) *Migration News*, 1–2. Retrieved October 10. 2003: www.http/migration.ucdavis.edu/mn.

Rodríguez, O., & Weisburd, D. (1991). The integrated social control model and ethnicity. *Criminal Justice and Behavior, 18*, 464–479.

Rodríguez, O. (1996). New immigrant Hispanic population: An integrated approach to preventing delinquency and crime. National Institute of Justice.

Sampson, R., & Lauritsen, J. (1997). Racial and ethnic disparities in crime and criminal justice in the United States. In M. Tonry (Ed.), *Ethnicity, crime and immigration: Comparative and cross-national perspectives.* Vol. 21. Chicago: University of Chicago Press.

Sabogal, F., Marín, G., Otero Sabogal, R., VannOss Marín, B., & Perez-Stable, E. (1987). Hispanic familism and acculturation: What changes and what doesn't? *Hispanic Journal of Behavioral Sciences, 9*, 397–412.

Scheier L. M., Botvinet, G. J., Díaz, T. & Ifill-Williams, M. (1997). Ethnic identity as a moderator of psychosocial risk and adolescent alcohol and marijuana use: Concurrent and longitudinal analyses. *Journal of Child and Adolescent Substance Abuse, 6*, 21–47.

Security: hearings, detention, visas. (2002) *Migration News*, 1–2. Retrieved September 9, 2002: www.http/migration.ucdavis.edu/mn.

Snyder, H. N., & Sickmund, M. (1999). *Minorities in the juvenile justice system.* Juvenile Justice Bulletin, U.S. Department of Justice, Office of Justice Programs, Office of Juvenile Justice and Delinquency Prevention, Washington, D.C.

Sommers, I., Fagan, J., & Baskin, D. (1992). Sociocultural influences on the explanation of delinquency for Puerto Rican youths. *Hispanic Journal of Behavioral Sciences, 15,* 36–62.

Spohn, C. & Holleran, D. (2000). The imprisonment penalty paid by young, unemployed black and Hispanic male offenders. *Criminology, 38,* 281–306.

Steffensmeier, D., & Demuth, S. (2001). Ethnicity and judge's sentencing decisions: Hispanic-Black-White comparisons. *Criminology, 39,* 145–178.

Steffensmeier, D., & Demuth, S. (2000). Ethnicity and sentencing outcomes in U.S. federal courts: Who is punished more harshly—white, black, white-Hispanic, or black-Hispanic defendants? *American Sociological Review, 65,* 705–729.

Strom, K. L. (2000). *Profile of state prisoners under age 18, 1985–97.* U.S. Department of Justice, Office of Justice Programs, Bureau of Justice Statistics, Washington, D.C.

Therrien, M., & Ramírez, R. (2000). *The Hispanic population in the United States,* United States Census Bureau, Current Population Reports, Series P 20–535. Washington, D.C.

Tonry, M. (1995). *Malign neglect: Race, crime, and punishment in America.* New York: Oxford University Press.

Unnever, J. D., & Hembroff, L. A. (1988). The prediction of racial/ethnic sentencing disparities: An expectation states approach. *Journal of Research in Crime and Delinquency, 25,* 53–82.

United States ex rel. Negron v. New York. (1970). 434 F.2d 386, 391 (2d Circuit Court).

U.S. Immigration and Customs Enforcement, Department of Homeland Security (2004). Available at http://www.ice.gov/graphics/enforce/imm/index.htm.

U.S. Immigration and Customs Enforcement, Department of Homeland Security (2004). Available at http://www.ice.gov/graphics/enforce/imm/imm_dro.htm.

U.S. Immigration and Naturalization Service (2002). *Office of Juvenile Affairs.* Fact sheet, August, 1, 2002, Office of Public Affairs. Available at http://www.ins.usdoj.gov.

U.S. Immigration and Naturalization Service (2000). *INS Juvenile detention and shelter care program.* Fact Sheet, September, 7, 2000, revised, Office of Public Affairs. Available at http://www.ins.usdoj.gov.

U.S. Office of the Inspector General (2001). *Unaccompanied juveniles in INS custody.* Report Number I-2001-009. Washington, D.C.

Urbina, M. G. (2004). Language barriers in the Wisconsin court system: The Latino(a) experience. *Journal of Ethnicity in Criminal Justice, 2,* 91–118.

Valentine S., & Mosley, G. (2000). Acculturation and sex-role attitudes among Mexican Americans: A longitudinal analysis. *Hispanic Journal of Behavioral Science, 22,* 104–113.

Vega, W. A., Gil, A. G., Warheit, G. J., Zimmerman, R. S., & Apospori, E. (1993). Acculturation and delinquent behavior among Cuban American adolescents: Toward an empirical model. *American Journal of Community Psychology, 21,* 113–125.

Villarruel, F. A., & Walter, N. E. (2002). *¿Dónde está la justicia? A call to action on behalf of Latino and Latina youth in the U.S. justice system.* Building Blocks for Youth. Michigan State University, Institute for Children, Youth, and Families.

Wall, J. A., Power, T. G., & Arbona, C. (1993). Susceptibility to antisocial peer pressure and its relation to acculturation in Mexican American adolescents. *Journal of Adolescent Research, 8,* 403–418.

Zapata, J. T., & Katims, D. S. (1994). Antecedents of substance use among Mexican American school-age children. *Journal of Drug Education, 24,* 233–251.

Zatz, M. (1984). Race, ethnicity, and determinate sentencing. *Criminology, 22,* 147–171.

CHAPTER THREE

BLACK YOUTH: DISPROPORTIONALITY AND DELINQUENCY

Everette B. Penn

INTRODUCTION

Over the last few decades, the disproportionate number of Black youths in the juvenile justice system has become a national issue. Black youths' delinquency has often been explained through the use of social disorganization and subcultural perspectives. Once Black youths have been placed in the juvenile justice system, disproportionate minority confinement (DMC) literature points to discriminatory practices by individuals that propel Black youths deeper into the system (Bishop & Frazier, 1988; Leiber, 2002; Bishop & Frazier; 1996).

A predominant theme in the juvenile justice literature is the disproportionate involvement of Black youths in the juvenile justice system. Defined as having origins in any of the Black racial groups of Africa (U.S. Office of Management and Budget, 1997), Black persons currently number 34,658,190 (12 percent of the U.S. population) (U.S. Census Bureau, 2002). Thirteen percent of those who are ten to seventeen years old in the general population are Black (U.S. Census Bureau, 2002). Because they fall under the jurisdiction of the juvenile justice system and because most states define acts committed by this population as delinquency (Jackson & Knepper, 2003), this age group is the focus of this chapter. When studying recent arrest and processing data for juveniles, it is apparent that Black youth comprise a disproportionate number of youth in the juvenile justice system (U.S. Department of Justice, 2002). This chapter examines Black youth delinquency and disproportionality through a historical analysis, a review of current statistics, and recent juvenile justice scholarship.

Overview of the History of
Black Youth in Juvenile Justice

The American juvenile justice system has its roots in the English system, which follows the doctrine of *"parens patriae,"* meaning "state as parent" (McShane & Williams, 2003). Within the British colonies of America, the state began to intervene in the lives of wayward children, who for centuries earlier had received the same harsh treatment as adults. Later, in the newly formed United States, the move for new ways of handling wayward youth became known as "child saving" (Platt, 1977).

The child-saving movement in the United States began during the late 1800's (Platt, 1977). Anglo-Saxon, Protestant, and middle- and upper-class White women worked to contain the "ills of the city" by preventing the children of the newly arrived European, immigrant, working class from leading wayward lives in a developing industrialized urban environment (Platt, 1977). Based on a medical approach to criminality, crime was believed to be a sickness that could be treated or cured. Houses of refuge and other institutions were built in order to treat wayward youth. Such facilities were open only to Whites, until there developed a need for someone to perform the household duties (Ward, 2001). Believing that the child-saving movement was not intended for Black children, Ward (2001) states: "[T]he rehabilitation of Black delinquents was a contradiction in terms" (p. 47). Just as the Black man was "invisible" (Ellison, 1952), so too was the Black child. As a group, Black children were seen as undeveloped adults who could perform the menial tasks of adults but were incapable of thinking or acting as developed adults in society. In the antebellum South the subordination of a Black child was vital in order to have a devalued Black adult who would act as a "good nigger" when older in order to continue the economic prosperity, political traditions, and cultural functions of the South (Ward, 2001).

Saving wayward Black youths was viewed as a waste of money because there was no use trying to reform them (Oshinsky, 1996). Thus, delinquent White boys were taught useful occupations, while delinquent Black boys were put to work on meaningless tasks in support of the institution (Mennel, 1973). Consequently, delinquent Black youths stayed in facilities longer than delinquent Whites, who gained skills that could be applied to apprenticeships in the community, thus aiding their reform and speeding their time of release (Ward, 2001).

The progressive work of the child savers culminated in 1899 with the creation of the Juvenile Court Act and the establishment of the first juvenile court in the nation—in Cook County, Illinois (Platt, 1977). Thus, the state became the "ultimate parent" prepared to protect the welfare of its children. The meager beginnings of this first juvenile court in the United States consisted of six paid probation officers, sixteen Chicago police officers, and thirty-six private citizens who at times supervised children on probation. Additionally, there was one woman who worked without pay. This "colored" woman had the task of taking charge of all of the "colored" children (Platt, 1977).

Through a benevolent philosophy, an informal system of juvenile justice developed in the United States. This system would be called into question in both the Kent case of 1966 and the Gault case of 1967, as well as several others. The United States Supreme Court deemed the informal practices of the juvenile justice system as unconstitutional since the child received the worst of both the juvenile and the criminal justice system (Kent, 1966). As a result of the Court's decision, juvenile justice courts across the country were required to formalize their processes, including improved record keeping and processing information. Such tracking methods provide a clearer picture of youths in the juvenile justice system. Contemporary data indicate that minority youths (particularly Blacks and Latinos) have more contact with the juvenile justice system than White youths. In fact, Black youths are the most disproportionately represented racial or ethnic group—especially in contact with police and in out-of-home placement (Walker, Spohn, & DeLone, 2004).

DISPROPORTIONATE MINORITY CONFINEMENT OF BLACK YOUTH

The study of disproportionate minority confinement (DMC) became a significant federal policy issue in 1988, when an amendment was made to the Juvenile Justice and Delinquency Prevention Act of 1974. DMC is defined as a situation in which

> the proportion of juveniles detained or confined in secure detention facilities, secure correctional facilities, jails and lockups [and] who are members of minority groups...exceeds the proportion of such groups represented in the general population. (Devine, Coolbaugh, & Jenkins, 1998)

In 1992, the Office of Juvenile Justice and Delinquency Prevention (OJJDP) created the DMC initiative, which required states seeking Juvenile Justice and Delinquency Prevention (JJDP) formula grants to determine if disproportionate minority confinement existed, to identify causes, and to develop and implement corrective strategies (Leiber, 2002). Previous literature on the subject had suggested that processing decisions are not racially and culturally neutral (Devine, Coolbaugh, & Jenkins, 1998). Findings from the DMC initiative indicated that disproportionate minority confinement does, in fact, exist and is most severe for Blacks at the intake and placement stages of the juvenile justice system (Leiber, 2002).

A key tool used to determine disproportionality is the "DMC Index Score" (Devine, Coolbaugh, & Jenkins, 1998). The score is compiled by dividing the percentage of youths from a specific racial or ethnic group that has had contact with the juvenile justice system by the population of that group below the age of 18. A score of one means a proportionate representation. A score of more than one indicates overrepresentation and a score of less than one indicates underrepresentation. When one evaluates the state of DMC for Black youths in the juvenile justice system, any percentage above 12 would produce a DMC Index Score above 1, thus indicating overrepresentation. Although the DMC Index Score was originally used to measure disproportionate confinement it is useful when examining disproportionality of any racial or ethnic group throughout the juvenile justice system. Below is a review of data concerning Blacks in the juvenile justice system. It provides a presentation of DMC among Black youths, as well as the precise points concerning which DMC is most prevalent.

Arrests

Like the adult criminal justice system, the juvenile justice system has several departure and decision points. Even before an arrest is made, the discretion shown by law enforcement personnel is one of most significant points in the system. In most jurisdictions the officer may choose to handle the case as he or she sees fit (Jackson & Knepper, 2003). The officer may decide to give a verbal warning or some other nonjudicial option that does not require the youth to be taken into custody. If the officer decides to take the youth into custody, an arrest may occur. The officer's decision is subjective and may be guided by numerous factors, including the nature of the offense, a youth's prior contact with the juvenile or criminal justice system, or the officer's beliefs about youths of a particular race or ethnic group.

A total of 1,558,496 arrests of persons under eighteen occurred in 2001 (U.S. Department of Justice, 2002). Of these youths, a total of 410,668, or 26.4 percent, were Black. More specific data on property crime and violent crime show that Blacks comprised 28.4 percent of property-crime arrests and 42.5 percent of violent-crime arrests. Moreover, Blacks represented 47.6 percent of those arrested for murder/nonnegligent homicide and 58.1 percent for robbery (U.S. Department of Justice, 2002).

Juveniles Detained Prior to Court Disposition

When an offense is serious or a youth fails to complete a diversion agreement, the juvenile is placed in temporary confinement (Jackson & Knepper, 2003). In 2000, prior to having their cases heard in court, 22.8 percent of Black youths were detained (U.S. Department of Justice, 2001). According to type of offense, 24 percent of Blacks were detained for violent cases and 19.5 percent for property offenses. For drug offenses, 34.6 percent of Black youths were detained (U.S. Department of Justice, 2001).

Petitioned and Waived Cases

A product of the *parens patriae* philosophy was that 56.9 percent of all juvenile cases were petitioned in 2000 (U.S. Department of Justice, 2001). Petitioning is a formal handling of a case, resulting in an official appearance in court and either a rendering of a disposition in juvenile court or a transfer to adult court for processing. Of those cases petitioned in 2000, 63.4 percent found the youths delinquent and 0.8 percent were transferred to adult courts (U.S. Department of Justice, 2001). Overall, 64.9 percent of Black cases were petitioned in 2000 (U.S. Department of Justice, 2001). Of those cases involving Black youths, 1.0 percent were transferred to adult proceedings (U.S. Department of Justice, 2001).

Adjudicated Cases

The judging of a delinquent child creates an adjudicated case. There are four outcomes of an adjudicated case: 1) placement outside of the home, 2) probation, 3) a fine or other court action, or 4) dismissal. In 2000, placement outside of the home occurred in 25.8 percent of the adjudicated cases; probation occurred in 57.7 percent; some type of fine, restitution, community service, or other service with little or no further court involvement occurred in 11.2 percent; and dismissal occurred in 5.2 percent (U.S. Department of Justice, 2001).

For cases involving Black youths in the same year, dismissal occurred in 5.8 percent, fines and community service in only 7.5 percent, probation in 57.2 percent, and placement outside of the home in 29.5 percent (U.S. Department of Justice, 2001). Overall, 108,931 juvenile offenders were placed in residential custody facilities. Blacks represented 42,963, or 39 percent, of the placements (U.S. Department of Justice, 2001). Such placements represented more than any other racial or ethnic group.

DMC Index Score and the Cumulative Disadvantage

According to the DMC Index Scores, as presented above, the score representing the total arrests of Black youths was 2.0. Arrests for property offenses produced an index score of 2.1 and for violent offenses, 3.2. In adjudicated cases involving Black youths, placement outside of the home produced an index score of 3.0. These high DMC Index Scores have received considerable national attention. For some, the issue is resolved by acknowledging that the DMC Index Scores do not take into account crime seriousness, prior juvenile record, or other legally relevant criteria (Walker, Sphon & DeLone, 2004). Thus, for some, high DMC Index Scores for Black youths can be simplistically explained by the youths' differences in offending (Feld, 1999). That is, since Black youths are arrested for more serious offenses than other youths, upon adjudication they require placement outside the home more often. But Pope and Feyerherm (1990) found that, of over forty published studies, two-thirds indicated that even after the seriousness of the offense, the prior record, and other legal factors were controlled, Blacks, along with other minorities, were treated more harshly by the juvenile and criminal justice systems.

Bishop and Frazier (1988) call the harsher treatment a "cumulative disadvantage" for minorities that starts out as a small risk factor in the beginning stages of the juvenile justice system. As youths advance through the system, race becomes a more pronounced variable, especially for Black youth (Panel on Juvenile Crime, 2001). To test this conclusion, the Panel on Juvenile Crime compared the risk of placement outside the home for White and Black youths. Some 7.2 percent of Blacks youth, as compared to 3.6 percent of White youths, were arrested (Panel of Juvenile Crime, 2001). Once arrested, 69 percent of Blacks were referred to juvenile court, as compared to 58 percent of Whites. As they were processed into the juvenile justice system, Blacks were more than three times as likely as Whites to be adjudicated and confined outside of the home (Panel of Juvenile Crime, 2001).

In order to fully understand the overrepresentation of Black youth in the juvenile justice system, it is useful to examine some theoretical frameworks which best explain why and how contact is made with the system. Once black youths are in the system, an analysis of recent research about the juvenile justice worker's perception of Black youths aids in determining the possible origin of the "cumulative disadvantage."

Theoretical Explanations of
Black Youth Criminal Activity

There are scores of theories that explain Black youth delinquency. Often they emphasize structural inequality in the wider society and an adaptation made by the individual to live a subcultural lifestyle. Thus, social disorganization (Shaw & McKay, 1942; Wilson, 1987) and a subculture perspective (Cloward & Ohlin, 1960; Wolfgang & Ferracuti, 1967; Anderson; 1994) provide a theoretical foundation that explains some Black youths' delinquent activity.

Social Disorganization

Broadly defined, social disorganization is based on the concept of stable, cohesive groupings in neighborhoods. When relationships are strong in neighborhoods, a social control exists, preventing delinquency and criminal activity (Shaw & McKay, 1942). Low income, physical deterioration of dwellings, and transient populations where extremes in standards of behavior exist are common characteristics of socially disorganized areas (Shaw & McKay, 1942). Through their research, Shaw and McKay (1942) discovered that socially disorganized areas had high percentages of foreign-born and newly migrated Black persons. They advise caution in relating delinquency to race or nationality by stressing that Blacks and immigrants have the least access to the necessities of life, thus making them least prepared for the competitive struggle (Shaw & McKay, 1942).

Black families living in socially disorganized areas can best be understood by reviewing poverty statistics. In 2001 the official poverty income level for a two-person household was $11,569 annually. As household size increases, so does the income that is considered to be the official poverty level (i.e., $14,128 for a family of three and $18,104 for a family of four [U.S. Census Bureau, 2002]). Furthermore, it is noteworthy that 30 percent of Black children are raised in poverty, while only 12.8 percent of White children live in the same economic condition (U.S. Census Bureau, 2002). Living in such poverty increases one's chances of living in areas that have elements of social disorganization: low economic status, a mixture of different ethnic groups, high residential mobility, and broken homes (Sampson & Groves, 1989).

Black poverty finds its roots in historical discriminatory practices (Frazier, 1968; Franklin & Moss, 2000), which resulted in an unskilled labor force unable to compete in the marketplace for adequate wages (Wilson, 1987). While other racial and ethnic groups developed businesses and moved on to more affluent neighborhoods that exhibited less violence, poverty, and crime, Blacks continued to come to urban areas, despite the change from a goods-producing environment that was once filled with manufacturing jobs for unskilled workers. Those that could move out of the cities did so in vast numbers. Many of those left behind existed in urban areas rotting with social decay and economic decline. While these external factors are important for understanding the roots of Black poverty, this discussion would be incomplete without presenting the economic impact of out-of-wedlock births.

In 2000, 68.5 percent of Black children were born out of wedlock, compared to 27.1 percent of White children (U.S. Census Bureau, 2002). When living arrangements are analyzed, 49 percent of Black children and 17 percent of White children live with mothers only (U.S. Census Bureau, 2002). The birth circumstances and the living situation of a child become important factors related to poverty because of the difference in income levels. When income levels for two-parent households are compared to those of one-parent, female-headed households, poverty becomes most apparent. On average, a Black female earns $16,282 annually, compared to the $16,652 of a White female (U.S. Census Bureau, 2002). Thus, when one parent is working, the income of a Black female raising a child would be almost equal to that of a White female in the same situation. However, the similarities end when both parents are working. The average annual salary of Black males, $21,466, is only 70 percent of the $30,240 average annual salary earned by White males (U.S. Census Bureau, 2002). A significantly lower income for Black males, combined with a slightly lower income for Black females, results in an average annual Black family income of $37,748, as compared to an annual average income of $46,892 for a White family. Thus, a Black family makes 80 cents to the dollar of a White family when both parents are working.

However, only 39 percent of all Black youths are raised in a household in which both parents are present, while 49 percent are raised by only a female parent. In contrast, 75 percent of White youths live in a family in which both parents are present (U.S. Census Bureau, 2002). The $16,282 annual income of Black females is 66 percent less than the $46,892 of the two working parents in a White household. Thus, choices, options, associations, contacts, and opportunities are quite different for the Black family, especially the child. Hawkins, Laub, Lauritsen, and Cothern (2000) state that there are higher levels of violence among the youths found in a female-headed household. Additionally, a correlation between the high number of female-headed households and delinquency has been attributed to the belief that such families are dysfunctional and unable to provide proper supervision for the children (Gottfredson & Hirschi, 1990). However, some caution must be given to this theoretical explanation. Not all youths in poverty or in female-headed households become delinquent. In fact, most do not. But what may occur is a complex mixing of structural pressures, dysfunctional adaptations, and personal choices leading to the promotion, acceptance, and toleration of a broad range of deviant and disruptive behaviors that becomes a subcultural lifestyle.

Subcultural Perspectives

The compounded elements that come from poverty and living in a socially disorganized environment make the choice of a subcultural lifestyle appealing and more available through cultural transmission (Shaw & McKay, 1942). Youths who believe they have little, if any, access to traditional opportunities (i.e., employment, upward mobility, middle-class lifestyle) retreat to another lifestyle that they perceive will bring material possessions and gains (Cloward & Ohlin, 1960). The subcultural lifestyle of Black youths is attributed to the mass exodus of middle- and working-class families from urban areas during the 1970's and 1980's. The departure of these families left a void and removed the "social buffer" which guards against elements of social disorganization in urban neighborhoods (Wilson, 1987). Thus, these "truly disadvantaged" Black children no longer saw or emulated practices of the main culture; instead a "code of the streets" subculture developed (Anderson, 1994; Wilson 1987).

The "streets" produce a culture which values physical toughness (Anderson, 1994; Canada, 1995; Prothrow-Stith, 1991). Physical ability, fighting, and various forms of violence are ways to win and keep respect. In these neighborhoods the Black youth's ability to fight and win is a valuable status symbol that gives the youth the "juice" (Anderson, 1990;1994). This violence results in serious injury or death, as displayed in the high number of victimized Black youths and arrests for assault, murder, and nonnegligent homicide (U.S. Department of Justice, 2001). Black youths who choose to follow this subculture are judged by their peers according to their toughness and ability to "get over"—which may include selling drugs, gambling, theft, and other delinquent and criminal activities (Anderson, 1990; Oliver, 2003; Reese, 2004)— rather than the more traditional criteria of school success, organizational involvement, and bonding to the community (Hirschi, 1969).

From the above literature, a plausible theoretical foundation emerges that explains Black youths' involvement in the juvenile justice system. A large number of Black youths live in poverty and socially disorganized urban areas. Within these areas constant portrayals of material success gained by illegal means cause a subculture to develop that places toughness and violence as paramount, because achieving success through legitimate means is seen as unobtainable. This lifestyle results in a disproportionate number of encounters with law enforcement officials. These encounters result in formal juvenile justice processing because of their severity, nature, and frequency.

Income disparities, living conditions, and a subcultural lifestyle are elements disproportionately found among Black youths. These elements provide an explanation for the high numbers of Black youths who enter the juvenile justice system. Changes in economic conditions, as well as personal choices that promote middle-class values, are responses that may lower the number of initial contacts of Black youths with the juvenile justice system. But the reality is that once Black youths enter the system, they are processed deeper into it than any other racial or ethnic group. A review of research on juvenile justice workers reveals possible causes of greater Black youth confinement.

BLACK YOUTHS AND JUVENILE JUSTICE WORKERS

The juvenile justice system offers its workers greater discretionary powers as compared to those in the adult system (Walker, DeLone, & Spohn, 2004). Although changes have occurred, the juvenile justice system still remains rehabilitative in its focus. Therefore, greater subjectivity is allowed to exist under the claim that actions in the juvenile justice system are done for the good of the youth. The practice of individual decision making provides an opportunity for the racial and ethnic beliefs of the juvenile justice worker to have a greater impact on the processing of Black youths (Walker, DeLone & Spohn, 2004). The perceptions of juvenile justice workers in the system have a dominating role in the processing of the youths (Ulmer & Kramer, 1998; Bridges & Steen, 1998). The socialization of each juvenile justice worker— from judge to child-care worker—creates a cumulative effect in which the sentencing of a particular juvenile is influenced by the individual belief system of the person with whom the youth comes in contact (Davis, Severy, & Kraus, 1993).

Frazier's and Bishop's (1995) interviews of justice officials show that the differences experienced by Black youths once inside the juvenile justice system can be partially explained by race. In their research, nearly two-thirds of the thirty-one juvenile judges, prosecutors, public defenders, and intake supervisors believed the race of a youth influenced disposition once he or she was in the system. These interviews also confirmed that, just as in the adult criminal justice system, money influences outcomes in the juvenile justice system. As discussed above, Blacks have significantly fewer economic resources as compared to Whites. Because of this relative lack of money, they are unable to hire a private attorney. The United States Supreme Court decision, *In re Gault* (1967), provided the right to counsel for adjudication and many misdemeanor offenses. But, generally speaking, studies examining legal representation for indigent offenders reveal a system that is overloaded and underfunded (Kerbs, 1999). Subsequent findings indicated that "hiring an attorney could provide more benefits to whites than to racial minorities, and representation by a public defender could have more negative consequences for racial minorities than for whites" (Walker, Spohn, & DeLone, 2004, p. 152).

The lack of money also prevents a family from being able to afford costly private treatment programs. The juvenile justice system provides needed services, such as drug treatment programs and other social and psychological services, but Black youths must settle for confinement since their families cannot afford to pay for the services. As one public defender stated: "There is economic discrimination. If parents can afford a private attorney or they can afford this or that private counseling, they get the best treatment" (Frazier & Bishop, 1995, p. 32).

Finally, Frazier's and Bishop's interviews concluded that female-headed households led criminal justice workers to believe that the home environment was unstable and incapable of proper supervision (Frazier & Bishop, 1995). However, DeJong and Jackson (1998) found that, even if Black youths lived with both parents, there was no difference in their dispositions—thus negating the belief that if Black families are headed by females their Black sons or daughters are treated differently in the juvenile justice system. Bridges and Steen (1998) provide additional support that the race of the youth is important. Their research found that even when age, gender, prior criminal involvement, and seriousness of offense are controlled, there still remains a perception that Black youths are more culpable, dangerous, less remorseful, and a greater threat to society than White youths.

Juvenile justice workers as members of society become receptors of images presented to them. These images in the media and throughout society portray Blacks in a negative way. As one intake supervisor states: "There is a perception all through the system that the nonwhite community needs more cleaning up. The perception that crime is Black becomes a self-fulfilling prophecy...." (Frazier & Bishop, 1995, p. 36). From these findings, one can conclude that race, specifically the Black race, is a pervasive influence in the processing of youths inside the juvenile justice system. The practice in which "invidious distinctions based on negative judgments about an entire group of people" (Walker, Spohn, & DeLone 2004, p. 17) takes place, and results in racial discrimination. The danger of discrimination in the minds of juvenile-justice workers is the creation of a domino effect in which being Black is the dominant variable. Thus, the best practices or the best treatment programs are not implemented for these youth; instead, a Black youth is perceived as more in need of supervision and control by the juvenile justice system.

Why Being Black Matters in Juvenile Justice

According to Mann (1993): "Anyone who claims that racism and discrimination are not pervasive in the United States today, and that these insidious practices have not existed throughout the history of this country, is out of touch with the reality of the American structure" (p. 23). Blacks' disproportionate involvement in both the juvenile and criminal justice systems can be understood in a historical context.

Blacks have not always been disproportionately involved in the juvenile and criminal justice systems. Before the Civil War, Blacks were underrepresented in crime statistics (Young, 1994). W. E. B. DuBois wrote in 1901 that slavery presented a system in which "there was no crime of any consequence among Negroes" (DuBois, 2002, p. 83). Since Negroes were considered "property," without the protections and privileges of citizens, their control and handling were at the whim of Whites. After the emancipation of Blacks from slavery, there was a great migration away from the South to northern urban areas, where Blacks sought decent wages (Frazier, 1939). As noted previously, this migration would later result in large numbers of northern Blacks living in socially disorganized areas (Wilson, 1987).

For the Blacks who stayed in the South, a convict lease system developed (DuBois, 2002). Administered by states, this system allowed private citizens to hire prison labor. Writing in 1901, DuBois found that over 70 percent of southern prisoners were Black. He also noted that Blacks were more easily convicted and received longer sentences (DuBois, 2002). The convict lease system resembled slavery since the forced labor of Blacks provided low-cost human capital to a White, southern, agriculture-based economy. The more prisoners there were incarcerated, the greater was the accessibility of a low-cost labor force for the South.

Contemporary justice practices no longer allow convict leasing, but a practice of labeling and stereotyping of Black youths has emerged—with perhaps more dangerous consequences. The stigmatizing of Blacks as a perceived serious threat to public safety is a phenomenon called "Blackophobia" (Gabbidon, 1994). Images of being robbed, assaulted, or otherwise victimized by Blacks are presented through the media, thus creating fear. A study of the media (which included local and network television, newspapers, broadcasts, and print news organizations from 1910 through 2001) determined that the reportage of Black crime was inaccurate. The proportion of crimes committed by Blacks is overreported, while Black victimization is underreported (Dorfman & Schiraldi, 2001). Blackophobia and the media's advancement of it become imbedded in the minds of police officers, court personnel, judges, and jury members, making them prejudiced when processing Black youth. Support for this conclusion comes from Free (1996), who discovered that skin color is a salient factor in determining an individual's social worth. Thus, perceived as worthless, Black youths face a harsher juvenile justice system. Worse yet, their perceptions of being worthless may become internalized and thus create further delinquency among them.

Black children become aware of their "inferior" status at a very young age. According to classic studies about Black children (some under the age of five), skin-color sensitivity led most to choose a white doll instead of a black doll (Clark & Clark, 1947; Morland, 1969). Many Black children learn early, through media and through a self-assessment of their own living conditions, that beauty, status, and success come with white skin (Kvaraceus, 1965). Even preschool children are aware that light skin is preferred over dark (Hopson & Hopson, 1992). The very heart of the differences between Blacks and Whites is found in many of the definitions of the words *black* and *white*. Many definitions of the word *black* are negative in connotation: "soiled," "wicked," or "evil"; "the opposite of white" (Merriam-Webster, Inc., 2003). Many definitions of the word *white* are positive in connotation: "pure," "clean," "spotless," "clear," and "of favorable appearance" (Merriam-Webster, Inc., 2003).

Even if a Black youth is able to overcome the internal negative feelings and the media's negative portrayal of being Black, as an adult he or she may have to overcome job discrimination. For example, in a recent study, hypothetical job candidates with identical resumes were sent to 1,300 job advertisers. The only difference was that some resumes had "White sounding names" (i.e., Brad, Matthew, Brendan, Carrie, Sarah, and Emily), while others had "Black sounding names" (i.e., Rasheed, Tyrone, Jamal, Kenya, Lakisha, and Aisha) (Hamilton, 2003). The research indicated that White-sounding names had a 50 percent greater callback rate. Additionally, discrimination held even when Black candidates had stronger credentials, such as better schooling, awards, and fewer gaps on the resume (Hamilton, 2003). Such discrimination affects the economic abilities of Blacks and could lead to their living in socially disorganized areas.

Thus, through media portrayals, some dictionary definitions, and individual beliefs, Black is viewed as inferior to White. This view is learned in childhood, and it is supported and reinforced in adolescence and adulthood. A "social distance" (Georges-Abeyie, 1989) emerges that moves many Blacks further away from the main culture because black skin is associated with dangerousness, criminality, ignorance, and untrustworthiness (Harvey, 1995; Tatum, 2000). "Being Black" becomes the variable that explains the cumulative effect for Black youths once they are inside the juvenile justice system. Discriminatory practices by individuals applied at various decision points throughout the system create insurmountable hurdles for Black youths to overcome in order to exit it. In the end, these hurdles produce an invisible wall that in its current state cannot be fully seen, avoided, destroyed, or changed.

CONCLUSION

As indicated above, Black youths are disproportionately involved in delinquency. Their disproportionate numbers have been explained by disparities in economic status and by choice of a lifestyle that involves criminal behavior rather than more socially acceptable practices. Yet, when all the variables are controlled, such as prior arrest, severity of crime, and living conditions, Black youths still remain disproportionately numerous in the various decision- and exit-points of the juvenile justice system. With a DMC Index Score as high as three, racial discrimination is left as the only viable reason for the disproportion. It is not discrimination institutionalized through law or system-wide practice; rather it is entrenched in the minds of police officers, judges, court personnel, child-care workers, and juries. It is discrimination that allows decision makers to believe that Black youths deserve harsher penalties because of the very characteristic they can never change—being Black.

In the future, juvenile justice research must seek the empirical data to support the "being Black" argument. This support will be difficult since being Black is often interwoven in many undesired social variables. With different offending rates established, the juvenile-justice worker is the key element of change. The challenge remains to demand that all persons in every part of the juvenile justice system base their decisions on facts and on the best interests of the youths as well as those of society. Those youths in need of supervision, who provide a real and constant threat to society, should receive the treatment available to them, even if it involves placement outside of the home. But this decision is only fair and just when the race or ethnicity of the youth does not enter the mind of the juvenile-justice worker who has contact with the youth in the juvenile justice system.

REFERENCES

Anderson, E. (1990). *Street wise: Race, class, and change in an urban community.* Chicago: University of Chicago Press.

Anderson, E. (1994, May). The code of the streets. *The Atlantic Monthly,* 80–94.

Bishop, D., & Frazier, C. (1988). The influence of race in juvenile justice processing. *Journal of Research in Crime and Delinquency, 22,* 309–328.

Bishop, D., & Frazier, C. (1996). Race effects in juvenile justice decision-making: Findings of a statewide analysis. *Journal of Criminal Law and Criminology, 86* (2), 392–413.

Bridges, G., & Steen, S. (1998). Race disparities in official assessments of juvenile offenders: Attributional stereotypes as mediating mechanisms. *American Sociological Review, 63,* 554–570.

Canada, G. (1995). *Fist, stick, knife, gun.* Boston: Beacon Press.

Clark, K., & Clark, M. (1947). Racial identification and preference in Negro children. In T. Newcomb & E. Hartley (Eds.), *Readings in social psychology.* New York: Holt.

Cloward, R., & Ohlin, L. (1960). *Delinquency and opportunity: A theory of delinquent gangs.* New York: Free Press.

Davis, T., Severy, L., & Kraus, S. (1993). Predictors of sentencing decisions: The beliefs, *personality variables, and demographic factors of juvenile justice personnel."* *Journal of Applied Social Psychology, 23,* 451–477.

DeJong, C., & Jackson, K. (1998). Putting race into context: Race, juvenile justice processing, and urbanization. *Justice Quarterly, 15,* 487–504.

Devine, P., Coolbaugh, K., & Jenkins, S. (1998). *Disproportionate minority confinement: Lessons learned from five states.* Washington, D.C.: United States Department of Justice, Office of Justice Programs, Office of Juvenile Justice and Delinquency Prevention.

Dorfman, L., and Schiraldi, V. (2001). *Off balance: Youth, race and crime in the news.* Retrieved July 25, 2001: http://www.building blocks for youth.org/media/media.html.

DuBois, W. (2002). "The spawn of slavery: The convict lease system in the United States." In S. Gabbidon, H. Greene, & V. Young (Eds.), *African American classics in criminology and criminal justice* (pp. 81–88). Thousand Oaks, CA: Sage Publications.

Ellison, R. (1952). *Invisible Man.* New York: Random House.

Feld, B. (1999). *Bad kids: Race and the transformation of the juvenile court.* London: Oxford University Press.

Frazier, C., and Bishop, D. (1995). Reflections on race effects in juvenile justice. In K. Leonard, C. Pope, & W. Feyerherm (Eds.), *Minorities in juvenile justice.* Thousand Oaks, CA.: Sage Publications.

Frazier, E. (1939). *The Negro family in the United States.* Chicago: University of Chicago Press.

Frazier, E. (1968). *E. Franklin Frazier on race relations.* Chicago: University of Chicago Press.

Franklin, J., & Moss, A. (2000). *From slavery to freedom: A history of African Americans* (8th ed.). New York: Knopf.

Free, M. (1996). *African Americans and the criminal justice system.* New York: Garland.

Gabbidon, S. (1994). Blackophobia: What is it, and who are its victims. In P. Kedia (Ed.), *Black on Black crime: Facing facts—Challenging fictions.* Bristol, IN: Wyndham Hall Press.

Gabbidon, S., Greene, H., & Young., V. (2002). *African American classics in criminology and criminal justice.* Thousand Oaks, CA: Sage Publications.

Georges-Abeyie, D. (1989). Race, ethnicity, and the spatial dynamic: Toward a realistic study of black crime, crime victimization, and criminal justice processing of blacks." *Social Justice, 16* (4), 35–54.

Gottfredson, M., & Hirschi, T. (1990). *A general theory of crime.* Stanford, CA: Stanford University Press.

Hamilton, K. (2003, June 18). What's in a name? *Black Issues in Higher Education, 28*–30.

Harvey, D. (1995). *Ethnicity, race, and crime: Perspectives across time and place.* Albany: State University of New York Press.

Hawkins, D., Laub, J., Lauritsen, J., & Cothern, L. (2000). *Race, ethnicity and serious and violent juvenile offending.* Washington, D.C.: United States Department of Justice, Office of Justice Programs, Office of Juvenile Justice and Delinquency Prevention.

Hirschi, T. (1969). *Causes of delinquency.* Berkeley: University of California Press.

Hopson, D., & Hopson, D. (1992). Implications of doll color preferences among black preschool children and white preschool children." In A. Burlew, W. Banks, H. McAdoo, & D. Azibo (Eds.), *African American psychology: Theory, research and practice* (pp. 183–189). Newbury, CA: Sage Publications.

In re Gault (1967). 387 U.S. 1, 87 S. Ct. 1428.

Jackson, M., & Knepper, P. (2003). *Delinquency and justice.* Boston: Allyn and Bacon.

Kent v. United States. (1966). 383 U.S. 541.

Kerbs, J. (1999). Unequal justice: Juvenile court abolution and African Americans. *Annals of the American Academy of Political and Social Science, 564,* 109–126.

Kvaraceus, W. (1965). *The Negro self-concept: Implications for school and citizenship.* New York: McGraw-Hill.

Leiber, M. (2002). Disproportionate minority confinement (DMC) of youth: An analysis of state and federal efforts to address the issue." *Crime and Delinquency, 40* (January 2002), 2–45.

Mann, C. (1993). *Unequal Justice.* Bloomington, IN: Indiana University Press.

McShane, M., & Williams, F. (Eds.) (2003). *Encyclopedia of juvenile justice.* Thousand Oaks, CA: Sage Publications.

Mennel, R. (1973). *Thorns and thistles: Juvenile delinquents in the United States, 1825–1940.* Lebanon, NH: University Press of New England.

Merriam-Webster, Inc. (2003). *Merriam-Webster's collegiate dictionary* (11th ed.). Springfield, MA: Author.

Morland, J. (1969). Race awareness among American and Hong Kong Chinese children. *American Journal of Sociology, 75,* 360–374.

Oliver, W. (2003). The structural-cultural perspective: A theory of black male violence. In D. Hawkins (Ed.), *Violent crime: Assessing race and ethnic differences.* Cambridge, UK: Cambridge University Press.

Oshinsky, D. (1996). *Worse than slavery: Parchman Farm and the ordeal of Jim Crow justice.* New York: Free Press.

Panel on Juvenile Crime. (2001). *Juvenile crime juvenile justice.* Washington, D.C.: National Academy Press.

Platt, A. (1977). *The child savers: Invention of delinquency* (2nd ed.). Chicago: University of Chicago Press.

Pope, C., & Feyerherm, W. (1990). Minority status and juvenile justice processing: An assessment of the research literature (Part I). *Criminal Justice Abstracts, 22,* 327–335.

Prothrow-Stith, D. (1991). *Deadly consequences.* New York: Harper Collins.

Reasons, C., Conley, D., & Debro, J. (2002). *Race, class, gender, and justice in the United States.* Boston, MA: Allyn and Bacon.

Reese, R. (2004). *American paradox: Young Black men* Durham, N.C.: Carolina Academic Press.

Sampson, R., & Groves, B. (1989). Community structure and crime: Testing social disorganization theory. *American Journal of Sociology, 94",* 774–802.

Shaw, C., & McKay, H. (1942). *Juvenile delinquency and urban areas.* Chicago: University of Chicago Press.

Tatum, B. L. (2000). Deconstruction of the association of race and crime: The salience of skin color. In M. W. Markowitz & D. Jones-Brown (Eds.), *The system in Black and White: Exploring the connections between race, crime and justice* (pp. 31–46). Westport, CT: Praeger.

Ulmer, J., & Kramer, J. (1998). The use and transformation of formal decision-making criteria: Sentencing guidelines, organizational contexts, and case processing strategies. *Social Problems, 45* (2).

United States Census Bureau. (2002). *Population and household economic topics.* Retrieved June 6, 2004: http://www.census.gov/population.html.

United States Department of Justice. (2002). *Sourcebook of criminal justice statistics.*Retrieved June 6, 2004: http://www.albany.edu/sourcebook.html.

United States Department of Justice. (2001). *Sourcebook of criminal justice statistics 2000.* Washington, D.C.: Government Printing Office.

United States Office of Management and Budget. (1997). Revisions to the standards for classification of federal data on race and ethnicity. *Federal register, 62* (October 30), 368–374.

Walker, S., Spohn, C., & DeLone, M. (2004). *The color of justice: Race, ethnicity, and crime in America.* Belmont, CA: Wadsworth.

Ward, G. (2001). Color lines of social control: Juvenile justice administration in a racialized social system, 1825–2000. Ph.D. diss., University of Michigan, 2001. (UMI 3029453)

Williams, F., & McShane, M. (1999). *Criminological theory* (3rd ed.). Upper Saddle River, NJ: Prentice Hall.

Wilson, W. (1987). *The truly disadvantaged: The inner city, the underclass and public policy.* Chicago: University of Chicago Press.

Wolfgang, M., & Ferracuti, F. (1967). *The subculture of violence: Towards an integrated theory in criminology.* London: Tavistock.

Young, V. (1994). The politics of disproportionality. In A. Sulton (Ed.), *African-American perspectives n: Crime causation, criminal justice administration and crime prevention* (pp. 69–81). Englewood, CO: Sulton Books.

CHAPTER FOUR

ASIAN AMERICANS AND JUVENILE JUSTICE[1]

N. Prabha Unnithan

People collectively referred to as "Asian Americans" in the United States represent a diverse set of cultures and ethnic backgrounds.[2] Asian Americans numbered 10,242,998 according to the 2000 census and comprised 3.6 percent of the U.S. population. Among the ethnic groups included in this category are Cambodians, Chinese, Filipinos, Indians, Japanese, Laotians, and Vietnamese. The Asian American population grew at an impressive rate of 48.26 percent between 1990 and 2000. They represent waves of migration to the United States at different historical periods. However, recent growth in the Asian American population is usually traced to amendments passed in 1965 to the Immigration and Nationality Act that eased earlier entry restrictions. In order of number, Chinese-Americans constitute the largest segment of the Asian American population, followed by Filipino-Americans, Indian-Americans and Japanese-Americans, respectively.

Fong and Shinagawa (2000) observe:

> Asian Americans are one of the fastest growing populations in the United States and one of the most diverse in terms of class, culture, political orientation, and social experience. Among their populations are some of the highest achieving ethnic groups in the U. S., as well as those deeply affected by discrimination, linguistic barriers, and cultural differences. (p. 1)

However, as this chapter will show, information and research about the interactions of Asian Americans with American criminal justice, in general, and

---

1. I thank my colleague, Dr. Joon Kim, for his help in preparing this chapter.
2. See Knepper (2000) for a focused discussion of shifts, changes, and problems in official statistical classifications of race/ethnicity.

with juvenile justice, in particular, is sparse and therefore difficult to categorize and describe. For example, in an official publication on youth violence from the American Psychological Association, Chen and True (1994) note that basic information about the involvement of Asians/Pacific Islanders in the criminal justice system is fragmentary: "There is a serious need for more data on the prevalence and incidence of violence among these youth, the nature and characteristics of risks involved, and the contributing factors" (p. 158). In the same volume, Becker, Barham, Eron, and Chen (1995) state that in future research, "wherever possible, fine grained distinctions should be made; for example, data should be collected not just on 'Asian Americans' but specifically on Chinese, Koreans, Japanese, Vietnamese, Thai, Cambodians, Pacific Islanders, and other subgroups" (p. 442).

ASIAN AMERICAN CRIME AND DELINQUENCY: NEGLECT AND THE NUMBERS

We can speculate on three mutually reinforcing reasons for the relative neglect of crime and delinquency among Asian Americans, in general, and among specific ethnic groups within that population. First, Asian Americans constitute a relatively minor proportion of the total arrests for various offenses in the United States. According to the numbers for the year 2001 from the *Sourcebook of Criminal Justice Statistics,* there were 103,750 arrests of Asians and Pacific Islanders for various offenses, which constituted 1.1 percent of the total arrests in the nation. This percentage is far below these groups' proportion in the U. S. population—3.6 percent. This low percentage has also been the case historically, as Kitano and Daniels (2001) point out:

> Yet scholarly studies conducted in the 1930s showed low rates of crime and delinquency among "Orientals" in California and statistics from the FBI fifty years later showed that arrests of Asian Americans for serious crimes remained well below their proportion in their population. (p. 194)

However, if we consider the above-mentioned percentage of 1.1 for 2001 as a criterion, we can see that Asians and Pacific Islanders are overrepresented in the following offenses: running away (4.2 percent); gambling (4.1 percent); and prostitution and commercialized vice (2.1 percent). Ten years ago, the *Sourcebook for Criminal Justice Statistics* for 1991 showed that the arrests of Asian Americans constituted 0.9 percent of the total arrests in the nation and that this subpopulation was overrepresented in running away, offenses against family and children, and gambling. If we focus on the number of Asians/Pacific Islanders arrested in 2001 who were below the age of eighteen and compare it to the number arrested in 1991, we see a slightly altered picture: While the number of Asian/Pacific Islander juveniles arrested in 2001 was 23, 228, or 1.5 percent of the total number of arrests, the three most serious offenses were murder and nonnegligent manslaughter (5.1 percent); running away (4.2 percent); and larceny (2.0 percent). Similar figures from ten years ago (in 1991, when the overall Asian American proportion of juvenile arrests was 1.6%) showed that the three offenses for which Asian American juveniles were proportionately more likely to be arrested were (in the following order) offenses against family and children, running away, and the catchall category of "other offenses." While there may be a turn toward more serious offenses in 2001 than in 1991, many of the above are generally considered less serious public-order offenses or status offenses. As a result, a second reason why relatively less attention is paid to Asian American criminality and delinquency is that Asian Americans are involved in less serious offenses.

Third, the impressive (although far from uniform) educational and occupational achievements of Asian Americans have garnered them the reputation for being a "model minority" (Fong, 2001). In addition to this positive image, Asian American students are perceived by teachers as conservative, highly conforming and inhibited (Sue & Sue, 1993); staying on task; cooperative; and possessing higher self-control (Feng & Cartledge, 1996). It is thus not surprising that this minority's low involvement in crime and delinquency, its perceived association with mostly less serious offenses and its (for the most part) high academic and professional achievements have been drawn together in mutually reinforcing ways and to such an extent that the words *crime, delinquency,* and *Asian Americans* are rarely strung together in one sentence. Therefore, a strong and consistent tradition of Asian American juvenile delinquency and justice research does not exist at this time.

The rest of this chapter will summarize the modest literature on the involvement of Asian American juveniles in crime and delinquency by describing major trends and lines of research and identifying gaps in our knowledge. We can divide the research on Asian American juvenile crime and delinquency into three main areas. The first has focused on the larger question of immigration and crime, using Asian Americans as the most recent case studies in a long-standing American tradition of inquiries into social mechanisms that help integrate new arrivals and that curb deviant behavior among their young. In particular, this line of research has explored questions about issues such as the nature and patterns of offending among the young of immigrant groups from Asia as well as the best mechanisms for explaining these issues. A second area of research has focused on issues related to the formation of Asian American gangs and resulting gang activities. In terms of the sheer volume of publications, this area has held perhaps the strongest research tradition, although some observers believe that the concerns which motivate such attention to gang activities are overblown and misplaced. A third set of research questions focus on a variety of related issues and concerns (lack of cooperation with the police, substance abuse, curfews, etc.). Let us turn to each of these areas and examine in detail the findings and contentions of the research.

ASIAN AMERICAN IMMIGRATION, JUVENILE CRIME, AND DELINQUENCY

Sellin's (1938) well-known formulation of "culture conflict" places emphasis on identifying behaviors that would be considered noncriminal (e.g., honor killing) in an individual's (i.e., an immigrant's) culture of origin but are nevertheless criminalized in the culture where that individual has settled. This "culture conflict" is an example of traditional criminological theorizing regarding the connection between immigration and crime. Such variations in conduct norms and the culture conflict that results serve as predictors of the likelihood of greater involvement in criminal activity by immigrants. How then can we explain the relatively low rates of crime and delinquency among various Asian American groups? Clearly, these low rates pose a challenge to earlier criminological assumptions regarding immigrant cultures as sources of deviance and crime especially when they are brought into contact with certain normative expectations of the dominant culture. At the same time, how do we explain the higher rates of crime and delinquency in some Asian American immigrant groups and not in others?

Following this traditional cultural approach, Kitano (1967) compares the familial, ethnic, and normative internalization of twenty-five Japanese-American delinquents with those of thirty-seven nondelinquent counterparts of similar extraction. He finds that the delinquents were more likely to come from "broken homes," had a greater amount of interaction with non-Japanese peers, and were unhappy with the manner of their upbringing. Kitano highlights the strength of the social control inherent in traditional Japanese socialization as an explanation for the overall lower rates of crime and delinquency among Japanese-American juveniles. Kim and Goto (2000), however, find that peer delinquency (as opposed to parental social support) is a better predictor of delinquency among Asian American high school adolescents on the West Coast. More recently, Lor and Chu (2002) report that Hmong children who experience less frequent interaction with their parents are more likely to become delinquent. Another factor that has contributed to the rise in Asian American delinquency involves the differences between female and male juveniles. The overrepresentation of males over females in the juvenile justice system exists in all racial and ethnic groups, but it is much higher among Asian Americans (Lorch & Chien, 1988).

"The majority of Asian Americans living below poverty are Southeast Asian refugees," notes Le (1993, p. 167). While many of those who came to the United States as refugee children from Southeast Asia were accompanied by parents and guardians, they nevertheless constitute a higher risk group for delinquency. Hopkins, Weinberg, and Clement (1994) examine juvenile delinquency among Southeast Asian refugees. They highlight several problems relating to acculturation to U. S. society, role reversal (i.e., children teaching adults about the ways of the new mainstream culture), the lack of parental guidance, and the aftermath of having moved from war-torn countries. They suggest that the juvenile justice system has to do a better job of taking these factors into account in attempting to prevent delinquency in this group. Long and Ricard (1997) explore the issue of continuing difficulties in acculturation and accommodation into American society and culture in their book-length ethnographic research. These difficulties were compounded by the fact that the neighborhoods where newly arrived Vietnamese-Americans settled were often inhospitable to them. Bankston and Zhou (1997) remind us of the complex interplay of culture and geographic location in their survey of 402 Vietnamese-American high school students. They find that while culturally these students are expected to work hard and respect elders, many of them have settled in low-income American communities where the young are influenced by the different cultures of disadvantaged youths around them. The result is the formation of two distinct social groups that Bankston & Zhou (1997) term "valedictorians and delinquents."

Waters (1999) has made the most sophisticated attempt at explaining crime among Asian American youths. He examines crime and delinquency among immigrant youths from Laos, especially the Mien and Lao subgroups. They are compared to immigrants in California who are Vietnamese, Chinese, and Korean (the last group was seldomly involved in gang activity). As noted above, traditional criminological explanations for crimes among immigrants have focused on the cultural baggage of differences brought by immigrants to their new places of residence. Waters, however, argues that the nature of the migration process (of settling in, adjusting to, and negotiating a place in the host society) can itself be a factor resulting in deviance and crime. Waters finds in his research that a migrant group is likely to experience spurts of youth-related crime if it has a large number of young at-risk males in the second generation, lower levels of group solidarity and socioeconomic status, and misperceptions of the host society's legal norms. The combination of all these characteristics is likely to increase the possibility that gang activity will develop. The absence of one or more of them (e.g., the fewer at-risk young males among Korean-American families, the strong Hmong organizational leadership resulting in enhanced social cohesiveness) will lessen the odds of the development of gang activity.

ASIAN AMERICAN GANGS AND GANG ACTIVITY

"A gang may be defined as a peer group of persons in a lower- , middle- , or upper-class community who participate in activities that are either harmful to themselves and/or others in society" (Morales, 1992, p. 105). The literature has documented the presence of these groups among various Asian American communities, with particular emphasis on Chinese- and Vietnamese-Americans. Huston (1995) provides a historical perspective on the emergence of Chinese secret societies and their connections to organized crime, and explores the consequences of their involvement with businesses and individuals living in various "Chinatowns" in North America. Huang and Wang (2002) trace the evolution of these original "triads" into organized crime groups and later into the development of street gangs. Joe (1994) notes that police, policy makers, and journalists have often promoted a conspiratorial view that connects such organized crime groups to Asian American street gangs. She contends, based on ethnographic interviews with former and current members of Asian gangs in San Francisco, that links between gang membership and organized crime exist mostly as individual and group associations, not as ongoing criminal conspiracies.

Asian street gangs became a major concern in the 1990s with alleged increases in their criminal and violent activities (Song & Dombrink, 1994; Wang, 1998; 2002a), including bank robberies (Wang 2002b) and home invasion robberies (Burke & O'Rear, 1990). Chin's (1996) interviews with former or active members of Chinese gangs in New York show that almost all respondents were involved in assaults and that 82 percent of them participated in "one or more robberies." While most research on Chinese gangs has focused on the cities of San Francisco and New York, Mark (2000) investigates the birth and development of Oakland, California's first Chinese gang, the Suey Sing boys, during the period 1968–1972. Wang (2000) asserts that membership in Asian gangs is increasing and will pose greater challenges both in terms of social scientific explanation and law enforcement response.[3] For example, using a survey of 603 businesses owned by Chinese in New York, Chin, Fagan, and Kelly (1992) report that 69 percent of them have been approached by Chinese gang members for purposes of extortion, while 54 percent have been actually victimized.

Glasser (1998) suggests that many such juveniles join gangs for a variety of reasons, including security, commonalities of language, and the problems of coping. Echoing ideas discussed in the previous section about the difficulties of adapting to a new society, Song, Dombrink, and Geis (1992) argue that Chinese and Vietnamese gang members are responding to a perceived "identity crisis" and, in the case of the Vietnamese, to biased law enforcement. Toy (1992) focuses on the changes in traditional family structures that result in peer group membership (i.e., gang membership) becoming the means of solving adjustment problems, particularly those involving victimization and psychological distress. (For another explanation that formally integrates various criminological theories, see Bankston and Caldas [1996]). Baba (2001) finds that Vietnamese gang members, compared to other ethnically similar delinquents, are likely to have been more involved in substance use and to have committed more status, nonviolent, and violent offenses.

However, not all researchers share the elevated concern about the presence and activities of Asian gangs. For example, Knox and McCurrie (1997) and McCurrie (1999) summarize research findings on Asian gangs as follows. They conclude that the Asian gang problem is a minor part of the overall gang problem in America and that there is very little that is unique when one considers the variety of individual and social characteristics of gang members as well as the organization of gangs. Further, most Asian gang members who come to the attention of this country's criminal justice system are not members of exclusively Asian gangs.

OTHER ISSUES

I am including, under this heading, research that does not focus on the major issues discussed above but that is sparked by other concerns related to various Asian American groups. Some scholars and law enforcement officials

---

3. For an elaboration of possible intervention strategies in dealing with Asian gangs, see Jan (1993).

have mentioned the general reluctance of Asian Americans to report crime to the police. (See, for example, Song [1992] on Chinese- and Vietnamese-Americans.) Also, Ho and Hendricks (2000) assert:

> Asian victims rarely report the crimes to the police because of misconceptions about the U. S. legal system. Asian Americans or immigrants generally attempt to avoid the legal system because they perceive law enforcement agencies, based on their experiences in their home countries, as political tools of suppression rather than enforcers of justice. (p. 201)

Among other matters, Pogrebin and Poole (1989) and Poole and Pogrebin (1990) explore this reluctance based on a field study in Aurora, Colorado, involving Korean-Americans. They recommend that police departments improve their outreach efforts toward Asian American communities and that they emphasize the importance of reporting crimes. While the reluctance to report crimes may stem from problems of mutual perception in police-community relations, Chin, Kelly, and Fagan (1993) report that as researchers they experienced a great deal of cooperation and "an unexpectedly high response rate from business owners" when studying the sensitive issue of gang extortion (see summary of study above).

While not specifically among juveniles, Sasao (1992) reviews and summarizes patterns of alcohol and other drug use among Asian Americans. Wells, Morrison, Gillmore, Catalano, Iritani, and Hawkins (1992) provide information regarding the early relationship between the initiation of substance use and delinquency among Asian Americans in a study of fifth graders from various racial backgrounds in Seattle, Washington. Nagasawa, Qian, and Wong (2001) point out variations among different Asian American ethnic groups in terms of marijuana use and delinquency. They find that Filipinos and Pacific Islanders are more likely to engage in both forms of deviant behavior than members of other Asian American ethnic groups. On a more hopeful note, Walker, Treno, Grube, and Light (2003) find that Asian American adolescents (surveyed in California in a study of all racial backgrounds) are likely to report lower rates of driving after drinking and of riding with drinking drivers.

Finally, two studies that pertain specifically to Asian Americans and the juvenile justice system should be mentioned. In one study, concerning the juvenile curfews that were imposed in many jurisdictions during the 1990s as a means of delinquency prevention, Hirschel, Dean, and Dumond (2001) found that the curfews in Charlotte, North Carolina, had negative effects on Asian (and Hispanic) youth in that they increased the number of their arrests. A second study, the innovative work of Zhang (1995) that examines the use of reintegrative shaming among Asian Americans in comparison to that among African-Americans, shows promise.

Summary and Conclusion

The major preoccupations of research on Asian American crime and delinquency have been to explain the impact of immigration and its aftermath in terms of these behaviors and to characterize gangs and gang activity (arguably, overemphasizing the latter).[4] Other criminal- and juvenile-justice issues have received scant attention. The next mainstays of available research appear to be on Chinese- , Vietnamese- , and Laotian-Americans. Korean- and Japanese-Americans have received some attention. Very little research has been conducted on crime and delinquency among other Asian groups living in the United States, such as Indians and Filipinos. Further, the involvement of Asian Americans and Asian American juveniles in particular offenses that are higher in number in proportion to those in the total population—offenses such as running away and gambling—have not been investigated in any great detail. Why, for example, have Asian American juveniles run away from home at higher rates than would be expected? How is police, prosecutorial, and judicial discretion exercised when the delinquent runaway happens to be an Asian American?

Concerning juvenile justice in particular, the gap in the literature about Asian Americans is especially worrisome. As noted earlier, not much is known about the experiences of such juveniles as they move through the juvenile justice system. What happens, for example, to Asian American juveniles who are apprehended after running away from home? How well do they respond to decisions and directives of the juvenile court regarding dispositions such as foster care placement, probation, juvenile training school, and so on. Do these dispositions tend to be more or less severe? How are families included in delinquency prevention and treatment? How are the needs (educational, cultural, religious, psychological) of juvenile offenders from Asian American ethnic groups met by correctional authorities? There are many such questions that can be raised, but, unfortunately, not many answers are currently available about an important and fast-growing segment of the American population.

---

4. It may be relevant to ask ourselves why only these two topics—the aftermath of immigration and gang activity—have been the major threads of research on Asian American crime and delinquency, as opposed to other possibilities mentioned later in this paper.

REFERENCES

Baba, Y. (2001). Vietnamese gangs, cliques, and delinquents. *Journal of Gang Research,* *8* (2), 1–20.

Bankston, C. L., III, & Caldas, S. J. (1996). Adolescents and deviance in a Vietnamese-American community. *Deviant Behavior, 17* (2), 159–181.

Bankston, C. L., III, & Zhou, M. (1997). Valedictorians and delinquents: The bifurcation of Vietnamese American youth. *Deviant Behavior, 18* (4), 343–364.

Becker, J. V., Barham, J., Eron, L. D., & Chen, S. A. (1994). The present status and future directions for psychological research on youth violence. In L. D. Eron, J. H. Gentry, & P. Schlegel (Eds.), *Reason to hope: A psychosocial perspective on violence and youth.* Washington, D.C.: American Psychological Association.

Burke, T. W., & O'Rear, C. E. (1990). Home invaders: Asian gangs in America. *Police Studies, 13* (4), 154–156.

Chin, K. L. (1996). Gang violence in Chinatown. In C. R. Huff (Ed.), *Gangs in America* (2nd ed.). Thousand Oaks, CA: Sage Publications.

Chin, K. L., Fagan, J., & Kelly, R. J. (1992). Patterns of Chinese gang extortion. *Justice Quarterly, 9* (4), 625–646.

Chin, K. L., Kelly, R. J., & Fagan, J. A. (1993). Methodological issues in studying Chinese gang extortion. *Gang Journal, 1* (2), 25–36.

Chen, S. A., & True, R. H. (1994). Asian/Pacific Island Americans. In L. D. Eron, J. H. Gentry, & P. Schlegel (Eds.), *Reason to hope: A psychosocial perspective on violence and youth.* Washington, D.C.: American Psychological Association.

Feng, H., & Cartledge, G. (1996). Social skills assessment of inner-city Asian, African, and European American students. *School Psychology Review, 25* (2), 227–238.

Fong, T. P. (2001). *The contemporary Asian American experience: Beyond the model minority* (2nd ed.). Upper Saddle River, NJ: Prentice Hall.

Fong, T. P., & Shinagawa, L. H. (2000). *Asian Americans: Experiences and perspectives.* Upper Saddle River, NJ: Prentice Hall.

Glasser, W. (1998). *Choice theory: A new psychology of personal freedom.* New York: HarperCollins.

Hirschel, J. D., Dean, C. W., & Dumond, D. (2001). Juvenile curfews and race. *Criminal Justice Policy Review, 12* (3), 197–214.

Ho, T., & Hendricks, C. (2000). Asian Americans and the criminal justice system. In J. E. Hendricks & B. D. Byers (Eds.), *Multicultural perspectives in criminal justice and criminology.* Springfield, IL: Charles C. Thomas.

Hopkins, J. A., Weinberg, L. A., & Clement, M. (1994). Southeast Asian refugee youth: Implications for juvenile justice. *Juvenile and Family Court Journal, 45* (2), 15–27.

Huang, H. L., & Wang, J. Z. (2002). From religious cult to criminal gang: The evolution of Chinese triads (Part I). *Journal of Gang Research, 9* (4), 25–32.

Huston, P. (1995). *Tongs, gangs, and triads: Chinese crime groups in North America.* Boulder, CO: Paladin Press.

Jan, L. (1993). Asian gang problems and social policy solutions: A discussion and review. *Gang Journal, 1* (4), 37–44.

Joe, K. A. (1994). The new criminal conspiracy: Asian gangs and organized crime in San Francisco. *Journal of Research in Crime and Delinquency, 31* (4), 390–415.

Kim, T. E., & Goto, S. G. (2000). Peer delinquency and parental social support as predictors of Asian American adolescent delinquency. *Deviant Behavior, 21* (4), 331–347.

Kitano, H. L. (1967). Japanese-American crime and delinquency. *Journal of Psychology, 66* (2), 253–263.

Kitano, H. L., & Daniels, R. (2001). *Asian Americans: Emerging minorities.* Upper Saddle River, NJ: Prentice Hall.

Knepper, P. (2000). The alchemy of race. In M. W. Markowitz & D. D. Jones-Brown (Eds.), *The System in black and white: Exploring the connections between race, crime and justice.* Westport, CT: Praeger.

Knox, G. W., & McCurrie, T. F. (1997). Asian gangs: Recent research findings. *Journal of Contemporary Criminal Justice, 13* (4), 301–308.

Le, N. (1993). Policy for a community 'at risk': The case of the South East Asian refugees. In LEAP Asian Pacific American Public Policy Institute (Ed.), *The state of Asian Pacific America: Policy issues to the year 2020* (pp. 298–304). Los Angeles: UCLA Asian American Studies Center.

Long, P. D. P., & Ricard, L. (1997). *The dream shattered: Vietnamese gangs in America.* Boston: Northeastern University Press.

Lor, N. P., & Chu, M. M. (2002). Hmong parents' perceptions of their youths' delinquency. *Journal of Social Work Research and Evaluation, 3* (1), 47–60.

Lorch, B. D., & Chien, C. Y. A. (1988). An exploration of race and its relationship to youth substance use and other delinquent activities. *Sociological Viewpoints, 4* (2), 86–100.

Mark, G. Y. (2000). Oakland Chinatown's first youth gang: The Suey Sing boys. *Free Inquiry in Creative Sociology, 28* (1), 31–40.

McCurrie, T. F. (1999). Asian gangs: A research note. *Journal of Gang Research, 6* (2), 47–51.

Morales, A. (1992). A clinical model for the prevention of gang violence and homicide. In R. C. Cervantes (Ed.), *Substance abuse and gang violence.* Newbury Park, CA: Sage Publications.

Nagaswa, R., Qian, Z., & Wong, P. (2001). Theory of segmented assimilation and the adoption of marijuana use and delinquent behavior by Asian Pacific youth. *Sociological Quarterly, 42* (3), 351–372.

Pogrebin, M. R., & Poole, E. D. (1989). South Korean immigrants and crime: A case study. *Journal of Ethnic Studies, 17* (3), 47–80.

Poole, E. D., & Pogrebin, M. R. (1990). Crime and law enforcement policy in the Korean American community. *Police Studies, 13* (2), 57–66.

Sasao, T. (1992). Substance abuse among Asian/Pacific Islander Americans. In R. C. Cervantes (Ed.), *Substance abuse and gang violence.* Newbury Park, CA: Sage Publications.

Sellin, T. (1938). *Culture conflict and crime.* New York: Social Science Research Council.

Song, J. H. L. (1992). Attitudes of Chinese immigrants and Vietnamese refugees toward law enforcement in the United States. *Justice Quarterly, 9* (4), 703–720.

Song, J. H. L., & Dombrink, J. (1994). Asian emerging crime groups: Examining the definition of organized crime. *Criminal Justice Review, 19,* 228–243.

Song, J. H. L., Dombrink, J., & Geis, G. (1992). Lost in the melting pot: Asian youth gangs in the United States. *Gang Journal, 1* (1), 1–12.

Sue, D., & Sue, D. W. (1993). Ethnic identity: Cultural factors in the psychological development of Asians in America. In D. R. Atkinson, G. Morten, & D. W. Sue (Eds.), *Counseling American minorities: A cross-cultural perspective*. Madison, WI: Brown and Benchmark.

Toy, C. (1992). Coming out to play: Reasons to join and participate in Asian gangs. *Gang Journal, 1* (1), 13–29.

Walker, S., Treno, A. J., Grube, W., & Light, A. M. (2003). Ethnic differences in driving after drinking and riding with drinking drivers among adolescents. *Alcoholism—Clinical and Experimental Research, 27* (8), 1299–1304.

Wang, J. Z. (2000). Asian gangs: New challenges in the 21st century. *Journal of Gang Research, 8* (1), 51–62.

Wang, J. Z. (2002a). A preliminary profile of Laotian/Hmong gangs: A California perspective. *Journal of Gang Research, 9* (4), 1–14.

Wang, J. Z. (2002b). Bank robberies by an Asian gang: An assessment of the routine activities theory. *International Journal of Offender Therapy and Comparative Criminology, 46* (5), 555–568.

Wang, Z. (1998). A special report of the NGRC: An update of Asian gang affiliation (A preliminary analysis of the 1996 survey in 17 states). *Journal of Gang Research, 5* (3), 53–59.

Waters, T. (1999). *Crime and immigrant youth*. Thousand Oaks, CA: Sage Publications.

Wells, E. A., Morrison, D. M., Gillmore, M. R. Catalano, R. F., Iritani, B., & Hawkins, D. J. (1992). Race differences in antisocial behaviors and attitudes and early initiation of substance use. *Journal of Drug Education, 22* (2), 115–130.

Zhang, S. X. (1995). Measuring shaming in an ethnic context. *British Journal of Criminology, 35* (2), 248–262.

CHAPTER FIVE

NATIVE AMERICAN YOUTH AND DELINQUENCY

Laurence Armand French

INTRODUCTION

Native Americans often receive the least amount of attention as compared to other racial and ethnic groups. Conceivably, this is a result of their relative isolation on reservations as well as their relative concealment among mainstream society. Nevertheless, their youth and delinquency issues are compelling and deserve specific attention. Before discussing some of these issues, the chapter begins with a historical background of Native American youths. This history presents over a century of federal policies that have targeted Native Americans and resulted in discriminatory practices. Following the historical material, the chapter contrasts the Native American ethos of harmony with the Protestant ethic. In addition to providing general information on Native American crime and delinquency, the chapter also provides a case study of Native American justice in the Navajo Nation, which is the largest tribe in the United States. The chapter concludes with a discussion of Native American gangs and an overview of prevention and intervention measures for Native American delinquency.

HISTORICAL BACKGROUND

Among Native Americans, "youth" as a stage in a person's development did not exist during pre-Columbian (aboriginal) times. In fact, it was absent in the tribal enculturation process. Native American cultures generally subscribed to a socialization process that involved three developmental stages: (1) infancy/childhood, (2) adulthood, and (3) eldership. The first stage allowed considerable freedom of behavior, while the second represented the time of life when one was considered a responsible member of the extended family (the clan). It was during this stage that one *counted coup*—which meant testing life in the raw, taking chances in order to demonstrate one's survival skills and abilities. The last stage was the most significant in that the elders (both men and women) were those who had tested life and survived. They were often afforded the most respect in aboriginal societies. They were both teachers of the children and valued advisors to all tribal members. The elders were also the tribal librarians in these nonliterate societies where tradition was passed on orally through myths and stories. This socialization process was common to North American Indian groups and still exists among those tribes that have been able to retain their language and significant cultural roots—notably, the Pueblo tribes, the Athapaskans (the Navajo and Apache), and other tribes of Alaska, western Canada, and the southwestern United States.

Indeed, this method of socialization continues to exist today in isolated, homogeneous folk societies. Many cultures, in the past and today, offer a clear transition from childhood dependency to mature adulthood, avoiding the intermediate step of adolescence. In the more stable cultural environments associated with folk societies, the transition between childhood and adulthood is usually marked by a distinctive rite of passage. Munn (1973) defined the social/cultural significance of this process:

> [R]itual is seen as a kind of adjustive procedure for settling the disturbance caused by the diachronic play of life change or movement across the backdrop of a structurally compartmented sociocultural space. The dynamism of life processes requires transition across the boundaries (e.g., from one status to another, from one temporal category or phase to another, etc.); this can be affected primarily by ritual action that dramatizes transition and thus articulates the various life processes requiring change with the static, positional ordering of sociocultural categories (p. 602).

The clearly defined transition between childhood and adulthood, usually at the onset of puberty, leaves little doubt as to the individual's identity, regardless of gender, and status vis-à-vis others sharing the same sociocultural environment. This process was used to avoid or correct deviance among isolated folk societies as well as among traditional Native American groups. However, the purpose of correcting deviant behavior was to maintain harmony, thus reflecting an informal method of restorative justice as opposed to formal restitution or retribution justice, as is often the case among Western and industrialized societies (French, 1977).

Prior to European contact, North American Indians were a varied lot, comprised of hundreds of separate social units further divided into a number of linguistic groups. Yet they shared a common metaphysical belief system, one based upon harmony with their natural environment. While myths of origin vary from group to group, they all share a similar theme—a cooperative, harmonious ethos, especially among their own people. Indeed, many native groups referred to themselves as "the people," a label that signifies strong in-group ethnocentrism. While they felt strongly about their own group, most American Indians had a rather humble perception of themselves within their total natural environment. They had considerable respect not only for powerful natural phenomena but for other living organisms sharing their ecosystem. They usually referred to their tangible natural environment as "mother earth" while viewing extraterrestrial elements, those interacting with earth, as constituting "father sky." Within the aboriginal "harmony ethos," order and control were dictated by folkways, mores, and customs, without the aid of formal institutions such as those within Western-type societies. Even so, traditional Indians were exposed to a complex system of socialization, one that involved all aspects of their existence and lasted for the duration of their lives. This folk-socialization process was transmitted orally from generation to generation.

Contradictory Federal Policies and Increased Indian Marginality

Five centuries of Euro-American contact, including complex, and often contradictory, policies toward the Indians have essentially destroyed the aboriginal traditionalism of Native Americans and along with it the smooth transition from childhood to adulthood. Briefly stated, these policies ranged from outright physical genocide, from first contact until the 1890s, to a more subtle process of cultural genocide, lasting from first contact until the present. Official U.S.-Indian policies included *Removal* (1830s–1880s); *Allotment* (1860s–1907); *Indian Reorganization* (1930s); *Termination/Relocation* (1950s–1970s); and the current policies of *Self-Determination/New Federalism*. Together these often contradictory policies served to create a marginalized Indian population—a social/cultural milieu where "being Indian" was seen as constituting inferior status within the larger, dominant U.S. society (French, 1994).

Official U.S.-Indian Policy

Removal involved using the U.S. Army to forcibly uproot tribes and march them off their traditional lands so that white settlers could claim them. Thousands died during these forced marches and while this process involved dozens of tribes, it is best illustrated by the Cherokees' 1838 removal known as the "Trail of Tears" and by the Navajos' removal in 1864 known as "The Long Walk." Tribes were removed regardless of their compliance with U.S. customs and laws. Most tribes were removed to Indian Territory, currently the state of Oklahoma. Following the Civil War, whites intruded into Indian Territory, causing the U.S. Congress to divide collectively held tribal lands into individual allotments, thus creating a large amount of surplus land for white settlers. Many Indian landholders were subsequently cheated out of their allotments in white courts, where their word meant little against that of the white settler. Finally, Indian Territory was dissolved by the U.S. Congress in 1907, when Oklahoma was recognized as a state (French, 1987).

Attempts at preserving Indian country began during the Depression years with President Roosevelt's administration. Indian Reorganization was essentially a form of federal paternalism where tribes were compelled to adopt U.S.-style governments with limited participation in their own governance. The federal government retained ultimate political, economic, and judicial authority over the nation's Indian wards. Then, in the 1950s, under the Eisenhower administration, efforts were again made to forcibly convert Native Americans from their traditional cooperative societies to those of Christians/capitalists. Under this plan tribes were to be treated as corporations and tribal members to be considered stockholders. This plan became the rationale for Termination—the termination of U.S. treaty obligations to the first Americans. The other side of this coin was the plan to entice young tribal members away from the reservations (Indian country) and into urban centers closer to the influences of the larger U.S. society. This process of Relocation resulted in large urban Indian ghettoes with increased psychocultural marginality and corresponding mental and physical health problems that continue today. Also during this period the federal government eliminated its treaty responsibility to protect Indians in Indian country: It unilaterally awarded certain states criminal and civil authority over tribes. Termination, Relocation, and state policing in Indian country all proved to be dire failures, even though remnants of these programs still exist—to the dismay of the tribes afflicted by these policies (French, 1987).

Self-Determination began in the 1970s, following passage of the Civil Rights Bills of the mid-1960s. The first application permitted tribal involvement in education in Indian country. Religious rights soon followed. While these policies provided tribes more say in tribal matters, they were again followed by attempts to diminish federal treaty responsibilities. Indeed, the New Federalism under President Reagan forced tribes to compete for federal monies via grants when, in fact, these monies were already guaranteed by treaty obligations. The impact of Self-Determination and the New Federalism continues today, with some tribes still fighting for more control over tribal matters. The massive lawsuit against the federal government over the mismanagement of $10 billion of Indian monies from the sale of tribal resources (Individual Indian Money or IIM fund) continues to the present (French, 1987; French, 1994; French, 2003; *Cobell v. Babbitt, Summers, and Gover,* 1996).

CONTRASTS IN ETHOS

Clearly, the United States judicial system is based upon the tenets of the Protestant ethic with its focus on individual, and not group, responsibility. Marked differences exist between the aboriginal Native American harmony ethos and the Protestant ethic. Individual culpability, competitiveness, and guilt—all critical to the Protestant ethic—were alien to the native harmony ethos. Group cooperation, not individual competitiveness, was the basic social value associated with aboriginal life. In order to insulate the individual from the internalization of excessive guilt or frustration resulting from complex avoidance networks, stressful conflict situations were conveniently resolved by aboriginal Native Americans through the use of real or imaginary third persons or objects, which took the form of fictional figures from their respective "creation" myths (French, 1994; Weber, 1958).

Elements of the harmony ethos exist even today in Indian country, especially among those tribes that still retain their language, including the largest Indian tribe in the United States—the Navajo. Characteristics of the harmony ethos that conflict with the dictates of the majority society, including the dictates of the criminal justice system, are the resentment of imposed authority; a hesitancy to command others; a reluctance to refuse requests made by others within the tribal clan; an obligatory hospitality and sharing with kinfolk; an impassivity regarding greetings and exchanges (including a lack of eye contact with others, notably nonclan members); a refusal, or unwillingness, to contradict others; and the absence of gestures in public speaking. Caught between the dictates of two different social systems, many Native Americans, notably youth now forced into the nontraditional developmental stage—adolescence—become marginalized. French (2003) coined this process of being torn between two worlds without fully belonging to either "psychocultural marginality."

The consequences of psychocultural marginality among Native Americans today are reflected in health and crime statistics. Native Americans have the highest addiction rate of any group in the United States, as well as one of the most difficult treatment records. The National Institute on Alcohol Abuse and Alcoholism found that alcohol is the major factor in five leading causes of death for American Indians—motor vehicle crashes, alcoholism, cirrhosis, suicide, and homicide (Gordis, 1994). This addiction has its greatest impact on Native American youths. In addition to alcoholism, notably fetal alcohol syndrome (FAS) and fetal alcohol effect (FAE), inhalation abuse is also rampant among this population. With this comes a host of morbid health and social issues, such as obesity, hypertension, Type II diabetes, child abuse, family violence, suicide, homicide, and a high accident rate, its causes including drunk driving. Moreover, the official federal reaction has traditionally been to incarcerate those charged with certain criminal offenses (e.g., drunk driving, child abuse) rather than treating them. With this approach, the government merely exacerbates these problems (French, 1994; French, 2003; Park, 1950; Sellin, 1938; Stonequist, 1937). The nature of this phenomenon is illustrated by the meaning of justice and the judicial processes among the Navajos—the largest U.S. tribe.

The Navajo Example

The Navajo Nation is the largest Indian tribe in the United States, covering some 25,000 square miles in an area of the Southwest that includes sections of three states: Arizona, New Mexico, and Utah. It is estimated to be the size of West Virginia and has close to half the enrolled members of American Indian tribes in the country. The Navajo Nation estimates its population to be over 160,000 enrolled members, with about 80 percent residing on the reservation. Another ten thousand non-Navajos also reside on the reservation. The tribe's complex social system revolves around the clan and the "Beauty Way"— the tribe's manifestation of the harmony ethos. The four original clans are the Towering House Clan, the One-Walks-Around Clan, the Bitter Water Clan, and the Mud Clan (Kluckholn & Leighton, 1946).

According to the Beauty Way, the purpose of justice is the restoration of harmony (Hozho). As in most Native American aboriginal belief systems, the Navajo view their world as divided into four quadrants, Mount Blanco protecting them from the east, Mount Taylor the southern barrier, Mount Humphrey defining the western boundary, and Mount Hespurus protecting them from the north. The four Navajo colors are white, yellow, blue, and black, with the first two representing the day and the latter two depicting the night.

There is a widespread conception within the Navajo Nation that it is an independent country. Officially, however, the Navajo Nation, like all federally recognized tribes constituting Indian country, falls under the supervision of the U.S. Government, mainly the U.S. Department of the Interior (Bureau of Indian Affairs, or BIA) and the U.S. Department of Justice (Federal Bureau of Investigation, or FBI). Indian health is served by the U.S. Department of Health and Human Services (Indian Health Services), while the U.S. Department of the Treasury serves as the manager of Indian trust funds. The U.S. Department of Education, in conjunction with the BIA, regulates many of the Indian schools, including the Johnson-O'Malley and Self-Determination schools.

The Navajo Nation has a two-level court system, consisting of district trial courts and the Navajo Nation Supreme Court. The Supreme Court serves as the appellate court for the district trial courts. There are seven judicial districts in the Navajo Nation; each has a district court, and five of the districts each has its own family court. Together, the district courts serve all 110 chapters of the Navajo Nation. The Navajo judiciary consists of seventeen judges, including fourteen trial judges and three members of the Supreme Court. Despite the tribe's claims of state or national autonomy, the Navajo Nation's courts are BIA Courts of Indian Offenses regulated by the United States' Annotated Title 25, "Indians."

Juvenile court judges are appointed in the same manner and have the same qualifications as judges of the trial courts and serve in the seven districts. Juvenile courts have original jurisdiction within the Navajo Nation concerning the following:

–any child who is alleged to have violated any Federal, tribal, state, or local law or municipal ordinance, regardless of where the violation occurred;
–any child who is neglected or dependent or is beyond the control of his/her parent, custodian, or school authorities;
–the determination of the custody of any child or the appointment of a guardian of the person of any child who comes within the purview of the court's jurisdiction under other provisions of this chapter;
–the determination of the legal parent-child relationship, including the termination of residual parental rights and duties as to a child who comes within the purview of the court's jurisdiction under other provisions of this chapter;
–judicial consent to the marriage of a child, the employment of a child, or the enlistment of a child in the armed forces, and to emergency medical or surgical treatment of a child who comes within the

purview of the court's jurisdiction under other provisions of this chapter;

–the treatment or commitment of a mentally defective or mentally ill child who comes within the purview of the court's jurisdiction under other provisions of this chapter. (French, 2003)

The juvenile court also has exclusive original jurisdiction to try all adults within the Navajo Nation for offenses committed against children. It is important to remember that tribal jurisdiction includes only enrolled members within the confines of the reservation. Navajo youths or adults arrested out of the tribal jurisdiction are not protected by the tribal laws of the reservation. Thus, a Navajo arrested in New York City is not protected by Navajo tribal law. The tribe, however, does have jurisdiction over enrolled members adopted by nontribal members, even if the parents of the child reside off the reservation. This overview of the Navajo judicial process, including that for children and youth, provides an illustration of the criminal justice system in Indian country. It should also be noted that, according to Public Law 280, those courts, some of whose original jurisdiction the federal government has unilaterally allocated to the state, have a more complex criminal and juvenile justice process.

French and Picthall-French's (1998) study on marginalized youth clearly showed that the Navajo were disproportionately at risk in comparison to their white, Hispanic (Mexican Americans), Mexican, and African-American counterparts. The National Institute on Drug Abuse (NIDA) 139-question Problem-Oriented Screening Instrument (POSIT) showed that Navajo girls were at highest risk, followed by Navajo boys. These findings clearly indicate a heavy reliance on substance abuse, notably alcohol and some inhalant abuse, as a form of escapism, and deficits in adequate mental health interventions. Poor family and peer relations, coupled with inadequate social skills and educational success, rounded out the profile for Navajo youths, ages twelve to nineteen.

A review of the total Navajo court data from the fiscal years 1998 to 1999 indicates that the vast majority of district court cases were for adult criminal activity (22,665) in comparison to 3,591 juvenile cases. Of the juvenile cases, 2,197 were for delinquency, making up 61 percent of the Navajo Family Court Children's cases. Children in need of supervision (CHINS) accounted for 768 cases, while 626 cases accounted for dependent children. Delinquency cases, on the other hand, made up 9 percent of those offenses that could be labeled as criminal activity. Not reflected in these data are the pretrial dispositions that exist on the Navajo Nation via the reinstatement of the traditional "peacemakers court" (French, 2003).

The Nature and Extent of
Delinquency in Indian Country

The most recent data on crimes in Indian country, notably those falling under federal jurisdiction, are provided in the February 1999 U.S. Department of Justice bulletin, *American Indians and Crime*. A quick review of these findings indicate the following:

> *Violent victimizations:* American Indians experience per capita rates of violence that are more than twice those of the U.S. resident population.
> *Murder:* The murder rate among American Indians is 7 per 100,000, a rate similar to that found among the general population. The rate of murder among blacks is more than five times that among American Indians.
> *Age:* Rates of violence in every age group are higher among American Indians than those of all races. Nearly a third of all American Indian victims of violence are between the ages of eighteen and twenty-four. This group of American Indians experiences the highest per-capita rate of violence of any racial group classified by age—about one violent crime for every four persons.
> *Sex:* Rates of violent victimization for both males and females are higher among American Indians than for all races. The rate of violent crime experienced by American Indian women is nearly 50 percent higher that that reported by black females.
> *Offender race:* At least 70 percent of the violent actions experienced by American Indians are committed by persons not of the same race—a substantial higher rate of interracial violence than that experienced by white or black victims.
> *Alcohol use by offender:* Of all races, American Indians as victims of violence were the most likely to indicate that the offender committed the offense while drinking.
> *Weapon use by offender:* More than 10 percent of American Indian nonlethal violence involved a firearm. American Indian murder victims were less likely to have been murdered by a handgun than victims of all other races.
> *Crimes reported to police:* American Indian victims of violence reported the crime to the police at about the average rate for all races.
> *Arrests for adults and youths:* American Indian arrest rates for violence among youths were about the same as the rates among white youths.

Violent-crime arrest rates for American Indian adults were similar to those for youths. Among other racial groups, arrest rates for adults were lower than those for youths.

Arrests for drug and alcohol offenses: The arrest rate among American Indians for alcohol-related offenses (driving under the influence, liquor law violations, and public drunkenness) was more than double that found among all other races, while drug arrest rates were lower than average. (Greenfeld & Smith, 1999)

Other studies indicate that American Indians are incarcerated at a 38 percent higher rate than other ethnic groups. Moreover, this problem is compounded when one considers incarcerated youths in Indian country. Depending on the tribe, youths can be held in federal, state, or local jails. And the rate of incarcerated Indian youths has risen some 50 percent between 1994 and 2000. Indeed, it is estimated that more than 70 percent of youths in federal custody on any given day are American Indians. At the local level (tribal, state, county, municipal) Indian youths are not always kept separate from adults as required by law. The Navajo Nation runs two of the eight facilities specifically designed for youth offenders in Indian country. Both holding and serving facilities are desperately needed in Indian country for both youthful and adult offenders. It is estimated that there are seventy-five jails serving fifty-seven of the 224 reservations under BIA influence. Ten of these are for juveniles only, while the remaining thirty-six facilities have selected juvenile-designated beds (Jorgensen & Wakeling, 1998). This situation is worst for incarcerated female juvenile offenders in Indian country, especially those in protective custody (Ditton, 2000; French, 2003).

NATIVE AMERICAN YOUTH GANGS

Gangs are a growing problem for Native American communities. The advent of the mass media into even the most rural reservation has contributed to the psychocultural marginality, especially among Native American youths. This has led to the emergence of Indian youth gangs. While a few Native American gangs were reported as early as the mid-1980s, they began to increase in large numbers during the 1990s. Strong cultural traditionalism in Indian country following the Wounded Knee II conflict of the mid-1970s most likely provided a sense of Indian pride and Pan-Indianism that was difficult to penetrate until the 1990s, when this Indian movement waned. Increased access to the mass media in Indian country during the late 1900s also contributed to the wide dissemination of gang activity among black and Hispanic youths that ultimately influenced marginalized Native American youth. Many of these gangs, notably those in the West, are affiliated with Hispanic gangs. This may be due to the fact that western Hispanic gangs are comprised mainly of Mexican American youths, many with mixed Spanish-Indian heritage. Another reason for the affiliation of Native American gangs with Hispanic ones is there is no historical antecedent for antisocial associations for Indian youths, given that no adolescent developmental stage existed during aboriginal times.

The available research on Native American gangs clearly links membership with marginality and a high level of substance abuse. Indian teen gang members are usually recruited in more concentrated areas, such as regional or boarding schools and areas of reservations located near urban centers. Native American gangs identify themselves by the common method of communication—graffiti. Indian teen gang members also follow traditional gang dress, modeling their attire on that of Hispanic and African-American gangs.

As would be expected, youth gangs exist on the country's largest reservation, that of the Navajo Nation. It is estimated that over half of the Navajo population is age nineteen or under. New Mexico, which contains a portion of the Navajo Nation, nineteen Pueblo Tribes, and two Apache reservations, has the second largest proportion of Native American youths in the United States. It is also the state with the highest proportion of Hispanics—namely Mexican Americans. This combination of a marginalized Indian teen population and a Hispanic population with a long history of family and community support for machismo expressions among its youths creates a close affiliation between the two populations. An added element is the widespread Pan-Indian custom of counting coup—the traditional method of experiencing life among Native Americans. Thus the marginalized phenotypical Indian youth quickly finds his/her identity needs, albeit transitory, met through gang membership, substance use, and the corresponding excitement provided by gang activity (Bachman, 1992; Flowers, 1988; French, 1982; French, 1994; Nielson & Silverman, 1996).

Prevention and Intervention of Delinquency in Indian Country

Clearly, the best preventive and intervention methods need to be tribal-centric, involving not only traditional tribal customs but also trained Native American professionals from that cultural group. Only since the mid-1980s has a cultural perspective been taken toward Native American social, health, and criminal justice issues. The premise is a need to foster a positive cultural ethnic identity before the root causes of addiction can be effectively addressed. A major focus of this approach should address youths in Indian country. As finally recognized by federal oversight agencies, the approach requires the integration of tribal-specific traditional spiritual approaches, including sacred sweats, vision quests, and the Navajo peacemakers judicial process. Past abuses in Indian country were devastating for Native American youths. Changes only came about with Congressional investigations and the passing of new federal laws. These changes occurred following the disclosure of rampant sexual exploitation of Indian youths, mainly by non-Indian federal employees.

An expansion of Indian Self-Determination relevant to child abuse in Indian country came with the *New Federalism* concept initiated in 1989. Congressional findings of chronic child abuse in Indian country, especially those abuses committed by non-Indian BIA teachers, provided a new impetus for tribal control of Indian education. The New Federalism also expanded child protection laws to include Indian country. The Final Report and Legislative Recommendations of the U.S. Senate's Special Committee on Investigations of the Select Committee of Indian Affairs also reviewed the potential for corruption and fraud in Indian country.

The Committee found that paternalistic federal control over American Indians had created a federal bureaucracy ensnarled in red tape and riddled with fraud, mismanagement, and waste. Worse, the Committee found that federal officials in every agency had known of the abuses but did little or nothing to stop them. Federal agencies had known, for example, that the hundreds of millions of dollars spent on the government's program to promote Indian economic development had been largely drained by shell companies posing as legitimate Indian-owned firms. The Bureau of Indian Affairs (BIA) did not need the Committee to discover that nineteen of the largest so-called Indian companies that garnered federal contracts were frauds. A BIA division chief had warned his superiors in an internal memo that the entire program was a "massive fraud (and) financial scandal." Yet, in thirty-one years, the BIA had discovered only two minor instances of possible fraud.

In federally run schools for Indians, BIA officials knew that school administrators had hired teachers with prior offenses for child molestation. Moreover, BIA knew its employees had failed to report or investigate repeated allegations of sexual abuse by teachers, in one case for fourteen years. Yet the BIA promoted negligent school administrators and, failing to require the protections from child abuse found in all fifty states, never fully adopted a system that required employees to report and investigate child abuse. Federal agencies responsible for protecting natural resources also neglected known problems. For instance, federal officials in Oklahoma admitted that Indian land was "wide open" to oil theft, yet for the past three years they have been unable to discover (or have ignored) any instances of it. They even ignored specific allegations against the nation's largest purchaser of Indian oil, which Committee investigators later caught repeatedly stealing from Indians.

The federal budget for Indian programs is $3.3 billion annually. Yet surprisingly little of these funds reach the Indian people. In fact, the total household income for American Indians from all sources, including the federal government, is actually less than the entire federal budget of $3.3 billion. Not only do American Indians suffer from this extreme waste, but year after year all American taxpayers must foot the bill for a limited budget from a negligent and unresponsive bureaucracy. The Committee also found that the BIA permitted a pattern of child abuse by its teachers to fester throughout BIA schools nationwide. For almost fifteen years, while child abuse reporting standards were being adopted by all fifty states, the Bureau failed to issue any reporting guidelines for its own teachers. Incredibly, the BIA did not require even a minimal background check into potential school employees. As a result, BIA employed teachers who actually admitted past child molestation, including at least one Arizona teacher who explicitly listed a prior criminal offense for child abuse on his employment form.

At a Cherokee Reservation elementary school in North Carolina, the BIA employed Paul Price, a confessed child molester, after his previous principal fired him for molesting seventh grade boys and warned BIA officials that Price was an admitted pedophile. Shocked to learn several years later from teachers at the Cherokee school that Price continued to teach despite the warning, Price's former principal told several Cherokee teachers of Price's pedophilia and notified the highest BIA official at Cherokee. Instead of dismissing Price or conducting an inquiry, BIA administrators lectured an assembly of Cherokee teachers on the unforeseen consequences of slander.

The Committee found that during his fourteen years at Cherokee, Price molested at least twenty-five students while the BIA continued to ignore repeated allegations, including an eyewitness account by a teacher's aide. Even after Price was finally caught and the negligence of BIA supervisors came to light, not a single official was ever disciplined for tolerating the abuse of countless students for fourteen years. Indeed, the negligent Cherokee principal who received the eyewitness report was actually promoted to the BIA Central Office in Washington, the same office that, despite the Price case, failed for years to institute background checks for potential teachers or reporting requirements for instances of suspected abuse. Another BIA Cherokee school official was promoted to the Hopi (Pueblo) Reservation in Arizona without any inquiry into his handling of the Price fiasco.

Meanwhile at Hopi, a distraught mother reported to the local BIA principal a possible instance of child sexual abuse by the remedial reading teacher, John Boone. Even though five years earlier the principal had received police reports of alleged child sexual abuse by Boone, the principal failed to investigate the mother's report or contact law enforcement authorities. He simply notified his superior, who also took no action. A year later, the same mother eventually reported the teacher to the FBI, which found that he had abused 142 Hopi children, most during the years of the BIA's neglect. Again, no discipline or censure of school officials followed. The BIA simply provided the abused children with one counselor, who compounded their distress by intimately interviewing them for a book he wished to write on the case. Sadly, these wrongs were not isolated incidents. While in the past year the Bureau has finally promulgated some internal child abuse reporting guidelines, it has taken the Special Committee's public hearings for the BIA to fully acknowledge its failure (U.S. Senate, 1989).

In 1990, the federal government for the first time established an Indian child protection statute. Title IV of Public Law 101-630 (Miscellaneous Indian Legislation) provided the "Indian Child Protection and Family Violence Prevention Act." The major elements of this act are to

1. require that reports of abused Indian children be made to the appropriate authorities in an effort to prevent further abuse;
2. authorize such actions as are necessary to ensure effective child protection in Indian country;
3. establish the Indian Child Abuse Prevention and Treatment Grant Program to provide funds for the establishment on Indian reservations of treatment programs for victims of child sexual abuse;
4. provide for the treatment and prevention of incidents of family violence; and
5. authorize other actions necessary to ensure effective child protection on Indian reservations. (Public Law 101-379, 1990)

One of the outcomes of this law was that Indian Health Services established a dozen Regional Youth Treatment Centers throughout Indian country serving as critical pretrial diversions for marginalized Native American youths with mental health problems that have the potential for expression in delinquency or criminal activity. And the U.S. Department of Justice established a Tribal Youth Program at the Office of Juvenile Justice and Delinquency Prevention (OJJDP). The OJJDP mandate is to support and enhance tribal efforts in preventing delinquency and to improve the juvenile justice system for American Indian and Alaska Native youths. These are promising initiatives, but only time will tell if the U.S. Government remains serious in its commitment to providing quality social, health, educational, and criminal justice services in Indian country.

REFERENCES

Bachman, R. (1992). *Death and violence on the reservation.* New York: Auburn House.

Cobell v. Babbitt, Summers, and Gover. (1996). U.S. District Court, District of Columbia, 30 F. Supp. 2d 24.

Ditton, P. M. (2000). *Jails in Indian country, 1998 and 1999.* Washington, D.C.: U.S. Department of Justice Programs, Bureau of Justice Statistics (NCJ 173410).

Flowers, R. B. (1988). *Minorities and criminality.* New York: Praeger.

French, L. A. (1977). A cultural perspective toward juvenile delinquency. *International Journal of Comparative and Applied Criminal Justice, 2* (Fall), 111–121.

French, L. A. (1982). *Indians and criminal justice.* Totowa, NJ: Allanheld Osmun.

French, L. A. (1987). *Psychocultural change and the American Indian: An ethno-historical analysis.* New York: Garland.

French, L. A. (1994). *The winds of injustice: American Indians and the U.S. government.* New York: Garland.

French, L. A. (2003). *Native American justice.* Chicago: Burnham, Inc.

French, L.A., & Picthall-French, N.E. (1998). The role of substance abuse among rural youth by race, culture and gender. *Alcoholism Treatment Quarterly, 16* (3), 101–108.

Gordis, E. (1994). Alcohol and minorities. *Alcohol Alert 23,* 1–4. (PH 347).

Greenfeld, L.A., & Smith, S.K. (1999). *American Indians and crime.* Washington, D.C.: U.S. Department of Justice, Bureau of Justice Statistics (NCJ 173386).

Jorgensen, M., & Wakeling, S. (1998). Fighting crime in Indian country. In John F. Kennedy School of Government (Ed.), *Indian Country Today.* Cambridge: Harvard University Press.

Kluckholn, C., & Leighton, D. (1946). *The Navajo.* Cambridge: Harvard University Press.

Munn, N. (1973). Symbolism in a ritual context. In J. Honigmann (Ed.), *Handbook of social and cultural anthropology.* Chicago: Rand McNally.

Nielsen, M. O., & Silverman, R. A. (1996). *Native Americans, crime and justice.* Boulder, CO: Westview Press.

Park, R. E. (1950). *Race and culture.* New York: Free Press.

Public Law 101–630. (1990). *Indian Child Protection and Family Violence Prevention Act, Title IV.* 25 USC 3210.

Sellin, T. (1938). *Culture, conflict and crime.* New York: Social Science Research Council.

Stonequist. E. (1937). *The marginal man.* New York: Russell.

United States Senate. (1989). *Part One — The executive summary: A new federalism for American Indians. Final report and legislative recommendations: A report of the Special Committee on Investigations of the Select Committee on Indian Affairs (101st Congress, 1st Session).* Washington, D.C.: U.S. Government Printing Office, Second Printing, 9–10, 60–101.

Weber, M. (1958). *The Protestant ethic and the spirit of capitalism.* New York: Charles Scribner's Sons.

Part II

Issues on Race
and Juvenile Justice

CHAPTER SIX

Domestic Violence, Crime, and Delinquency Among African-Americans

Lee E. Ross

Introduction

Victimization by violence is far too common among children in America.[1] Every year, three to ten million children witness domestic violence (Carter & Stevens, 1999). In New Haven, Connecticut, 39 percent of sixth, eighth, and

---

1. The author acknowledges that domestic violence is both a problem and a concern for the vast majority of Americans (regardless of race or socioeconomic status). While this chapter is primarily concerned with the effects of domestic violence on African-Americans (especially juveniles), the discussion relates to all children, regardless of race, color, or creed. Domestic violence is everywhere and everyone is vulnerable. No one is exempt. Therefore, it is difficult to conclude reliably which groups are more likely to *engage* in domestic violence. Research does suggest, however, that domestic violence in some communities is more likely to come to the attention of police than in other communities. Therefore, the disproportionate overrepresentation of African-Americans in domestic violence-related arrests should not suggest they are more prone to violence or more likely to choose violence. It mainly suggests that such violence among them is more likely to be detected. Studies that consistently report rates of black domestic violence as double those of whites (Straus & Gelles, 1990) do not explain *why* blacks are more likely to be arrested. Rather they focus on factors thought to condition the relationship between blacks and domestic violence (e.g., environmental stress and other issues of structural inequality). For further discussion, see Bent-Goodley, T. (2001) Eradicating domestic violence in the African-American community: A literature review and action agenda. *Trauma, Violence, & Abuse: A Review Journal, 2*, 316–330.

tenth grade students had seen someone shot at in the previous year (Schwab-Stone et al., 1999). Approximately four million adolescents have been victims of a serious physical assault, and nine million have witnessed serious violence during their lifetimes (Kirkpatrick & Saunders, 1997). In Miami, Florida, more than 90 percent of the high school students have witnessed community violence and 44 percent have been a victim of a violent crime (Berman, Kurtines, Silverman, & Serafini, 1996).

This chapter reviews the scholarship of African-American and mainstream researchers to explore the connections between exposure to domestic violence and juvenile delinquency among African-Americans. In an effort to understand the dynamics and consequences of domestic violence, a macrosociological approach is advocated. Using a hypothetical case study as a basis for analysis, the article concludes with a discussion of ideas designed to raise awareness of the effects of domestic violence and its plausible connections to involvement in the criminal justice system.

What Is Domestic Violence?

Many scholars have used different terms to describe domestic violence. Although violent injuries occur disproportionately to women and men commit more serious violent acts than women, both genders engage in violence (Buzawa & Buzawa, 1996). Consequently, gender-neutral terms are used in defining domestic violence, a term which is often a synonym for domestic assault, intimate partner violence, and intimate partner assaults between those who are now living together or who have previously cohabited. For purposes of this chapter, the definition is broadened to include any violence[2] that oc-

---

2. There is widespread disagreement on what constitutes *violence*. For example, the late Mahatmas Gandhi, widely known for his practices of nonviolent protest and civil disobedience, would regard violence as any attempt to impose ones will on another person. On a more practical level, most state statutes define violence as an individual act, usually a physical assault or threat of physical harm. This chapter broadens the definition by recognizing violence as nonphysical behaviors as well, such as name-calling, constant criticism, verbal harassment, psychological humiliation, and incidents of minor battering. In line with this, some researchers commonly employ a version of the Conflict Tactic Scale (CTS) as an appropriate strategy for determining the frequency of physical and psychological violence in the general population. For a description of the Conflict Tactics Scale, see Straus, M. A. (1989) *Manual for the conflict tactics scale.* Durham: University of New Hampshire, Family Violence Research Laboratory.

curs within families involving different combinations of family members. Given their foci on adult populations, some scholars maintain that the more age-restricted studies largely fail to report violence committed between teen partners, and also, especially, among siblings. But according to statistics these relationships can be quite violent (Buzawa & Buzawa, 1996). Even though parental violence against teens is at least as prevalent (Straus & Gelles, 1990), some researchers are reluctant to call it domestic violence per se, preferring instead more conventional terms like "child abuse" or "child maltreatment." Based on the prevalence and likelihood of youth exposure to domestic violence (whether experienced in the home, in the community, or through images from the media), the following section explains domestic violence as a significant problem confronting African-American youths.

THE EXTENT OF THE PROBLEM

As of 1999, black juveniles constituted 15 percent of the juvenile population (youths from birth to the age of 17), with the largest proportions of black juveniles residing in the District of Columbia (74 percent), Mississippi (45 percent), Louisiana (40 percent), South Carolina (36 percent), and Georgia (34 percent). During that year, approximately 30 percent of all cases in the criminal justice system involved African-American youths (Snyder & Sickmund, 1999). Given the widely acknowledged underreporting and limitations of official data, the actual involvement in juvenile delinquency and crime among African-Americans and others is, in all likelihood, much greater. While most research on juvenile delinquency focuses on males, female patterns of involvement are equally serious and have recently commanded increased research and scholarly attention.[3] In 1970, there were about 6,000 women in federal and state prisons; today there are nearly 100,000. During the 1990s, the

3. Although official measures do not suggest young black females are as involved in crime and delinquency as their male counterparts, there is still reason to be concerned, given their equal likelihood of exposure to violence within the household and community. Furthermore, if violence is learned behavior, females are also vulnerable to adopt violent tendencies in ways similar to males. In the case of domestic violence, Kathleen Daly has identified some distinct pathways to crime that [some] women might follow. *The harmed woman*, for example, suffered from abuse and neglect as a child, which in turn, caused her to act out and be labeled a "problem child." As an adult, this woman reacts to different situations with violence. *The battered woman*, in contrast, may not have a history of child abuse, but uses violence to defend herself against an abusive partner. For further discussion, see Kathleen Daly (1992). Women's pathways to felony court: Feminist

number of women incarcerated in this country doubled, while the total number of women in the nation increased by 30 percent (Bureau of Justice Statistics, 2000, p. 6). Furthermore, one study suggests that African-American females are largely overrepresented in the juvenile justice system as they comprise nearly half of all those in secure detention (Kakar, Friedemann, & Peck, 2002). As a matter of perspective, Caucasians comprise 65 percent of the juvenile population, but only 34 percent of Caucasian females are in detention. Comparatively, while seven of every ten cases involving white juvenile females are dismissed, only three of every ten cases are dismissed involving black juvenile females.

The social demographics of female crime and delinquency are almost indistinguishable from those associated with male crime and delinquency. For example, Chesney-Lind and Brown (1999) reported that young women in the correctional system are mostly poor, undereducated girls of color who have complex histories of trauma and substance abuse. Closely related to these, a more recent study (Kakar et al., 2002) examined the risk factors related to female delinquency and discovered that childhood maltreatment, parental incarceration, and school discipline problems were all significant.

Whether we refer to black males or black females, current trends suggest these numbers will not decrease anytime soon. In fact, a U.S. Department of Justice report predicts that between now and 2015 the population of juvenile minorities will experience substantial growth. Specifically, the number of black juveniles is expected to increase by 19 percent, Native American juveniles by 17 percent, and Asian/Pacific Islander juveniles by 74 percent, while white juveniles will increase by 3 percent. In addition, during this same period, juveniles of Hispanic ethnicity are expected to increase by 59 percent (Bureau of Justice Statistics, 2000, p. 6). If previous research is correct in its assertion that age is the strongest statistical determinant of criminal behavior (especially for young adults between the ages of sixteen and nineteen), it is entirely possible for rates of juvenile delinquency among African-Americans to worsen before getting better. Whether we examine annual Uniform Crime Reports, National Crime Victim Surveys, or self-reported surveys, crime data support the hypothesis that criminal activity has been and continues to be most pronounced among younger citizens (Steffensmeier & Streifel, 1991). In light of this hypothesis, we need to further our understanding of factors and driving forces behind juvenile delinquency within the African-American community. Among

---

theory of lawbreaking and problems of representation. *Review of Law and Women's Studies, 2,* 11–52.

a myriad of competing factors commonly used to understand violence in general, this chapter examines the neglected and often overlooked connection between exposure to domestic violence and juvenile crime.

African-American Research and Juvenile Delinquency

Although domestic violence has taken its toll on the African-American community, it has not received as much scholarly attention from African-American criminologists as one might expect. A cursory glance through a recent publication, *African American Classics in Criminology and Criminal Justice* (Gabbidon, Taylor-Greene, & Young, 2002), reveals only three academic works by African-American criminologists that touch on issues of juvenile delinquency among African-Americans. While some of the works are related indirectly to issues of juvenile delinquency, few are directly related. An earlier publication edited by Sulton (1994) also examined African-American perspectives on crime and justice. It, too, included three works on the topic of juvenile delinquency. None of these works, however, concerned the connections between domestic violence and juvenile delinquency.

Scholars within other disciplines—mainly sociologists—have, through modest efforts, produced some rather intriguing findings that deserve mentioning here. Some have examined issues of protracted poverty (Wilson, 1987), pathologies endemic to the black community (Frazier, 1948; Ogbu, 1991) a lack of personal responsibility (Steele, 1990), and even romanticized views of black culture thought to promote violence (Patterson, 1998). One of the more recent works relevant on this topic belongs to Cross (2003), a cultural psychologist, who traces the historical origins of youth delinquency and violence in black culture. His research contradicts earlier claims by "scholars of the black experience" who purported that contemporary problems in the black community can be traced in linear fashion to the legacy of slavery and past discrimination. For those who accept the notion that crime and delinquency go hand in hand with a pathogenic black culture, Cross (2003) takes a contrary stance in stating:

> Today, in similar fashion, we do violence to Black people in general, and Black males in particular, by accepting the fact that Blacks are genetically predisposed or culturally primed for involvement in crime, drug usage, and drug trafficking. (p. 77)

Cross maintains that Blacks exited slavery with the type of social capital, family attitudes, and positive achievement motivation that could have readily facilitated their rapid acculturation to American society. Therefore, it is important, Cross implies, to dismiss this "pathogenic" misconception of black culture so that it does not serve as an excuse for individual behaviors. Consequently, Cross's stance forces others, regardless of their circumstances or social conditions, to take personal responsibility for their actions.[4]

Mainstream Research into Juvenile Delinquency

Aside from African-American scholars, mainstream Caucasian researchers have spent considerable time exploring this issue as well. Based on the literature, studies of the effects of domestic violence have focused on the role of family-oriented and sociologically based theories. Individual level variables have been used to explain why a particular family might explode into violent behavior (Buzawa & Buzawa, 1996). The contributions of psychological and social psychological variables are thrown into the mix as family-oriented theorists have focused their attention on the characteristics of family structure that explains higher levels of domestic violence. Special characteristics of a family are also reliable predictors of future violence.

Other theorists have adopted a "subculture of violence" approach to explain the concentration of violence in some communities (Wolfgang & Ferracuti, 1982). Proponents of this view have postulated that minority groups develop a system of values that somehow condones violence and physical aggression. Rounding out the literature are feminist perspectives where macrolevel analyses are used to show how structural violence is used against women in Western society. For example, Dobash and Dobash (1979) assert that despite the contemporary ideology of spousal equality, marriage still institutionalizes the control of wives by husbands through the structure of husband and wife roles. All of these perspectives, however general, imply consequences for children who are immersed and trapped in social environments characterized by violence and by attitudes that espouse the use of violence to resolve conflict.

---

4. Taking responsibility for individual behavior is a key component of most social programs designed to remedy problems of repeated violent behavior. Programs that focus on issues of anger management highly emphasize the universal principle that *violence is a choice.* If they are correct, it is only logical to assume that people can also choose nonviolence when attempting to resolve personal conflicts.

Effects of Violence on Children

Whether at home, in school, or on the streets, too many American children witness and experience violence that leaves them psychologically scarred. These wounds, if left untreated, place a child at greater risk for symptoms of anxiety, depression, and a tendency toward criminal and violent behavior of his or her own. In what can only be described as a sad and vicious cycle, exposure to violence can be psychologically toxic. Moreover, some scholars suggests that exposure may produce disruptions in interpersonal relationships, problems with aggression, conduct disorder, and truancy. Furthermore, cognitive, psychological, and physical issues related to learning and teaching have been documented (Straus, 1992). Given the indirect connections among low academic performance, school dropout rates, crime, and delinquency, those most vulnerable should receive special concern, especially African-Americans.

Experiences of violence in childhood and of witnessing violence between caretakers have been explored as factors in predicting subsequent violence in adult intimate relationships. Several studies have found that the impact of *witnessing* parental violence in childhood is a stronger predictor of violence in adulthood than the *direct experience* of childhood violence (Eitle & Turner, 2002; Hotaling & Sugarman, 1986; McGee, 2003; Pagelow, 1984). One study reported that 45 percent of male batterers had witnessed their father beating their mother (Finkelor, Hotaling, & Yllo, 1988). Other studies suggest that social behavior in the child and adolescent is linked to the use of physical violence in the family setting (Lewis, Shanok, & Balla, 1979; Jaffe, Wolfe, Wilson, & Zak, 1986).

Family structure is one of the most important models in the learning of antisocial patterns of behavior and has been described as one of the major socialization agencies in children (Osuna, Alarcon, & Luna, 1992). Krutchnitt and Dornfield (1993) found that youths exposed to more family violence initiate delinquent activities at an earlier age and engage in more frequent and serious offending than those with less violent backgrounds. For instance, some researchers found that 50 to 70 percent of men who had been battered as children now batter their own children (Osuna, Alarcon, & Luna, 1992).

According to Bandura (1973), some social behaviors are the result of learning from aggressive models of behavior, together with the destabilizing role of these models during the child's development. To that end, some researchers have explored the "age of onset," or the age in which a youth begins delinquent behavior, as a consistent predictor of future criminal behavior. Perhaps it is only reasonable, then, to infer that a child's exposure to violence, in whatever manner, shape, or form, precedes the age of onset for certain violent juvenile offenses. If this inference is plausible, it is important to consider whether exposure to violence and victimization by it, combined with other factors, pave the way for future violent behavior. One way to assess the hypothesis, aside from empirical research, is to explore possible scenarios of how violence in the household affects children who might witness parents/guardians and dating couples physically abusing each other. Moreover, what happens when family members are arrested for domestic battery and charged with disorderly conduct? Does the "cycle of violence"[5] become self-perpetuating and create other victims (e.g., children) in the process? To provide answers, the following case study is used to explore the effects of witnessing and experiencing violence and its possible connection to crime and delinquency.

DOMESTIC VIOLENCE: A CASE METHOD APPROACH[6]

Michael, an only child, is ten years old and resides in a two-bedroom apartment with his mom and stepfather. Both parents have violent histories, having been physically abused as children. His stepfather, abandoned at birth, spent fourteen years in and out of different foster homes, where his guardians

---

5. Theoretically, for women caught in battering relationship, the abuse is inflicted in a repeated cycle made up of three phases: tension building, battering incident, and honeymoon. The tension-building phase involves a gradual increase in tension. This is characterized by the batterer engaging in behaviors such as name-calling and other forms of psychological humiliation. Phase two is the battering incident when physical violence is used against the victim. Often this is accompanied by severe verbal abuse. In the honeymoon phase batterer feels sorry for the behavior and acts apologetically and lovingly. The batterer may shower the victim with gifts and apologies and promises not to act this way again. A batterer's loving behavior reinforces the victim's hope that the batterer can change. This often encourages the victim to stay in the relationship. The Cycle of Violence was recognized and documented by Lenore Walker in her 1984 book, *The battered woman syndrome*. New York: Springer Publishing Company, Inc.

6. This hypothetical case is intended to reflect the characteristics and circumstances surrounding the lives of those who experience and are affected by domestic violence. Beyond its potential to inform our understanding of domestic violence, a case method approach has tremendous pedagogical value in teaching courses in the social sciences, especially in criminal justice and legal studies. Key questions provide a basis for analysis of each case. The casebook approach is also known to create a lively interactive classroom environment based on discussion and dialogue among students and professors. For an applied example of the casebook approach, see Carolyn Boyes-Watson. (2003). *Crime and justice: A casebook approach.* Boston: Allyn & Bacon.

were described as physically abusive, mean, and outright cruel. Both of Michael's parents had extensive juvenile records, ranging from simple possession to assault and battery. His mother spent three years in a juvenile detention center for aggravated assault, while his stepfather was incarcerated for ten years for involuntary manslaughter. Chemically dependent and living off public assistance, they are often delinquent with the monthly rent, sometimes opting to spend their last dollars on alcohol and other drugs to feed their chemical dependencies.

Michael's parents generally get along, except when drinking. Then, accusations fly as each take turns bringing up the past. His mother—aggressive and very controlling—rarely backs down from a fight. His stepfather is physically stronger and has beaten her severely on two separate occasions, once after accusing her of cheating—after she caught him cheating. As the walls are paper thin, Michael—along with a few neighbors—has either witnessed or heard most of their violent encounters. He is angry with his mother for tolerating his stepfather and has internalized anger with himself for being too little to protect his mother. Neighbors have called police on several occasions when the stepfather was arrested. Unable to afford bail, he would become extremely apologetic while begging her to borrow money to post bail. Understandably, Michael often feared the return of his stepfather, wondering if he would be his next victim. During warmer weather, Michael prefers to hang out at his friends' crib to escape his situation. As colder weather sets in, he finds himself stuck in the midst of all "the drama and the trauma." School is a welcome relief, but Michael has been disciplined on three separate occasions, once for slapping another classmate. On other occasions, he cursed at teachers and disrupted classes.

This case study provides a glimpse into the intricacies of a difficult situation, one that would challenge most research scholars in this area. How does this violence affect Michael? What lessons of violence are learned and communicated, and what will he take from these encounters into the future? Interventions, if any, would depend on one's understanding of its causes. As a reader, you are encouraged to understand and consider ways to address this issue. For instance, it might appear reasonable to contend that violence in Michael's home is a by-product of economic pressures. Other experts would likely label Michael's situation as an example of an intergenerational transmission of violence. (In other words, violence is transmitted, through learned behavior, from one generation to the next.) Would the reality of absolute poverty and relative economic inequality come into consideration? Clearly, answers are not easy to come by, as some would even define Michael's predicament as a "relationship problem" beyond the scope of most social interventions (e.g., criminal justice systems and child welfare agencies, among others).

SOCIAL CONSEQUENCES

The task of understanding Michael's predicament is difficult at best. Prior research suggests that the children of incarcerated parents are five times more likely to end up in jail themselves; about half of those in juvenile justice facilities have also had a parent behind bars. Furthermore, 78 percent of women behind bars are mothers; 64 percent of men, fathers. In effect, the children of incarcerated parents are more likely to end up in jail themselves (Johnston, 1995; Reed & Reed, 1997). In short, the situation portends the possibility of delinquency and violence for Michael and other children who share his circumstances.

Ostensibly, connecting juvenile delinquency to domestic violence is anything but easy, given a wider variety of delinquent behaviors. Nonetheless, researchers have examined the potential influence of variables ranging from an intergenerational transmission of violence to psychological maladjustment. In the process, these attempts at understanding domestic violence have assumed different levels of analysis among myriad theoretical positions. These have been, for the most part, quite adequate from a methodological standpoint. Whether the exploration considered single or multiple factors, all hold some degree of legitimacy and relevance that promotes a greater understanding and appreciation of this problem. For purposes of our discussion, it is important to note that these (and most) understandings of violence are best understood from a macrosociological point of view. The importance of this distinction is discussed in the following section.

A MACRO-SOCIOLOGICAL APPROACH

How are children like Michael affected by the daily rituals of witnessing violence in real life or through the media, as well as experiencing it firsthand? At times, answers to this and similar questions are somewhat dependent on the methods used to produce them. Social scientists have many innovative approaches and research strategies to examine hypothesized relations between domestic violence and juvenile delinquency. Given the broad nature of the social sciences, the number of theoretically relevant variables yielding explanations is virtually limitless. One quantitative approach is to correlate some measure of juvenile delinquency (i.e., usually through self-report surveys) with some measure of prior exposure to domestic violence. Paying strict attention to the correlation of the variables, clarifying their temporal sequence, and ruling out alternative explanations, partial and assumed causal relationships emerge. A qualitative approach is then employed to further define and clarify initial findings. Rarely, if ever, will a social scientist emerge with a comprehensive model capable of fully explaining certain outcomes (i.e., the occurrence of violence in a school setting). Circumscribed by research limitations, researchers often retreat to more conservative grounds where fewer variables are considered and even fewer theoretical models employed.

In a similar vein, some authors have adopted an ecological framework to explore connections between youth violence and exposure to violence in childhood (Belsky, 1980; Bronfenbrenner, 1977; Johnson-Reid, 1998). This approach suggests that individuals exist within a multilevel ecosystem. Johnson-Reid (1998) described the levels in terms of microsystems, mesosystems, and exosystems, since each—dynamic in nature—can affect the individual both directly and indirectly. The microsystem encompasses exposure to violence within the home environment; the mesosystem level includes violence within the community; and the exosystem level refers to violence exposure through the media" (p. 160). One distinguishing feature of this approach is its emphasis on a broad, social-learning concept of violence rather than an intergenerational transmission of violent behavior.

LEGAL AND SOCIAL INTERVENTIONS

Domestic-violence calls represent a significant portion of calls for service in all jurisdictions. If responding to domestic violence is dangerous for police, imagine what it must be like for Michael to live with it on a daily basis. Just as constant danger is a major source of stress for police, living with domestic violence is also stressful for children.

Is it the responsibility of the criminal justice system to protect Michael from further violence? Historically, the response of law enforcement to crime in African-American communities has been characterized as resulting in either underenforcement or overenforcement. In the context of domestic violence, some question the wisdom of arrest policies in situations when the arrest of at least one party involved in a domestic altercation (usually the presumptive primary physical aggressor) is mandated. In jurisdictions where police retain and use their discretion not to arrest persons involved in domestic violence incidents, relationship violence might be regarded as "expected" to some degree. For example, Hawkins (2002) asserts that the stereotypical views of criminal justice decision makers regard violence as normal in the black community. Such views result in an unwillingness to intervene in family violence and a failure to prevent future violence. Moreover, given the mistaken tendency to view black violence as normal, the legal response toward crime victims is uneven. This uneven response represents a devalued status of black victims and contributes to further violence within black communities. When violence is viewed as normal, lower-class blacks, for example, are more likely to suffer when decision makers question the likelihood of discovering viable solutions and effective interventions to ameliorate such conditions (pp. 208–209).

Consequently, the willingness of victims to seek help from law enforcement and criminal justice agencies is somewhat dependent on their prior relationship and interactions with police. In fact, one study reported that African-American women were 1.5 times less likely to call the police compared with white women (Joseph, 1997). It is therefore reasonable to assume that the social legacy of police action and inaction in African-American communities has, perhaps, biased the efforts and perceptions of all parties involved. It must be confusing for victims to question the efficacy of calling police when they so desperately need help—confusing especially for female victims, knowing that either filing charges or having charges dropped could possibly further endanger her safety when her abuser is released. Since domestic battery is a repetitive event, victims usually know what happens and what to expect from the system. After "doing the math," some rule out the need for police intervention when considering the social and economic costs involved. Compounding matters further, many victims experience what is regarded as a "honeymoon phase" between each violent episode (when minds change, broken hearts are mended, and promises are kept). This is also the phase when victims are most likely to request that arrest charges be dropped and restraining orders amended. Social and economic dependencies are equally important to consider, particularly among victims whose self-esteem may have been damaged from all the abuse. Given the confluence of these realities, this author would not expect African-American women to involve the police (and the system) in their predicaments. Maybe this is why, more times than not, a third party will call police to intervene. For Michael, this entire scenario suggests that violence isn't the only thing that is learned. When his mother and other victims are afraid to seek help, children, like Michael, learn that violence works. Consequently, if violence works for others, it can also work for Michael to resolve personal conflicts. Ever mindful that violence is a choice, however, we realize it is not the only option. With that in mind, this chapter concludes with a discussion of viable alternatives to violence.

ROLE OF EDUCATION

Various researchers have offered many useful insights into the problem of domestic violence in American households. Many, including this writer, hold the position that the criminal justice system cannot solve social problems of this nature. Most of the responses of the "system" are reactive and punitive, rather than proactive and restorative. Therefore, at this juncture, it may be prudent to consider other avenues in the hope of eventually solving this problem.

When we consider all the forces associated with domestic violence, we quickly recognize the need for a broad, comprehensive response. As we have seen, child abuse and neglect, a culture of violence, economic and social injustice, easy access to weapons, witnessing violence, and experiencing it all increase the likelihood of violence. Media-related violence is highly influential and a familiar accomplice to violent behavior. Likewise, television, movies, music, and interactive games are powerful—and often violent—learning tools. Some would argue that Michael learns as much violence from these media as he does from witnessing his parents. Who is to say which is more influential? For example, popular video games, such as *Freedom Fighter, Def Jam Vendetta, and Grand Theft Auto: Vice City,* provide ample opportunity for children to learn and further reinforce violent behaviors and tendencies. Given the highly complex and variable nature of factors that contribute to violence, a one-size-fits-all model is probably not the most effective intervention, since there are "different strokes for different folks." If we admit to the inherent difficulties of defining this problem and to the inability to control the exposure of violence among children, perhaps the best we can hope for are educational programs that enable a greater understanding and appreciation of the devastation that violence has on children. In short, we need to be more sensitive to the impact of violence on children. But where do we begin?

The existing literature, widely scattered, has proposed many excellent provisional solutions to the problems of domestic violence, in particular, and of violent behavior, in general. For African-Americans, for example, there is no substitute for a good education, one that begins within the family. According to Oliver (2002), one way to reduce social problems (e.g., domestic violence) among African-Americans is Afrocentric socialization. In Michael's case, this solution requires a greater social responsibility on the part of those closest to him to help him appreciate the value of education, especially as it related to his own self-identity and his place in the world. Such an action could conceivably attenuate the effects of white racism and historical patterns of discrimination; it would also further the development of an Afrocentric cultural ideology (or world view) that could be used to promote, unite, and mitigate the adverse effects of racial pressures. Citing Welsing's (1974) codes for behavioral conduct, the advice put forward by Oliver (2002) appears particularly useful. For those seeking a rudimentary understanding of violence, it all relates to "respect" of self and others. So one way to establish a foothold for solving this problem is to stop trying to diminish others through personal attacks. These can assume various abuses toward one another, such as name calling, cursing, squabbling, gossiping, being discourteous, fighting, and killing. Theoretically, to cease personal attacks gives one a greater sense of dignity and power (Oliver, 2002).

To complement these educational efforts, considerable work is required to improve the quality of parent-child relationships, whether the work involves increasing positive parenting practices or limiting a child's exposure to inappropriate social programming. As responsible adults, we need to model better behavior for children, and we need to instill in them the value of developing social skills to resolve conflicts in a peaceful manner. Borrowing from a well-established cliché, this author has argued elsewhere that if you are not part of the solution, you are part of the problem. There are alternatives to violence, and it is incumbent on adults—not children—to find them. Otherwise, violence, once confined to a family setting, in one way or another conceivably winds it way into the criminal justice system.

REFERENCES

Bandura, A. (1973). *Aggression: A social learning analysis.* Englewood Cliffs, NJ: Prentice Hall.

Belsky, J. (1980). Child maltreatment: An ecological integration. *American Psychologist, 35,* 320–335.

Berman S., Kurtines, W., Silverman, W., & Serafini, L. (1996). The impact of exposure to crime and violence on urban youth. Retrieved October 10, 2003: http://www.info.med.yale.edu/chldstdy/CDCP/violence/statistics.html.

Bronfenbrenner, U. (1977). Toward an experimental ecology of human development, *American Psychologist, 32,* 513–531.

Bureau of Justice Statistics. (2000). *Prisoners in 2000.* Washington D.C.: U.S. Department of Justice.

Buzawa, E. S., & Buzawa, C. G. (1996). *Domestic violence: The criminal justice response.* Thousand Oaks, CA: Sage Publications.

Carter, L., & Stevens, C. (1999). The future of children: Children and domestic violence, 9 (3). Retrieved October 10, 2003: http://www.info.med.yale.edu/chldstdy/CDCP/violence/statistics.html.

Chesney-Lind, M., & Brown, M. (1999). Girls and violence: An overview. In D. J. Flannery & C. R. Huff (Eds.), *Youth violence: Prevention, intervention, and social policy* (pp. 171–199). Washington, D.C.: American Psychiatric Press.

Cross, W. E. (2003). Tracing the historical origins of youth delinquency & violence: Myths and realities about black culture. *Journal of Social Issues, 59* (1), 67–83.

Dobash, E., & Dobash, R. P. (1979). *Violence against wives.* New York: Free Press.

Eitle, D, & Turner, R. J. (2002). Exposure to community violence and young adult crime: The effects of witnessing violence, traumatic victimization, and other stressful life events. *Journal of Research in Crime and Delinquency,* (May), 214–237.

Finkelor, D., Hotaling, G. T., & Yllo, K. (1988). *Stopping family violence: Research priorities for the coming decade.* Newbury Park, CA: Sage Publications.

Frazier, E. F. (1948). *The Negro family in the United States.* (Rev. ed.). New York: Dryden Press.

Gabbidon, S. L., Taylor-Greene, H., & Young, V. D. (Eds.). (2002). *African American classics in criminology and criminal justice.* Thousand Oaks, CA: Sage Publications.

Hawkins, D. (2002). Devalued lives and racial stereotypes: Ideological barriers to the prevention of family violence among Blacks. In S. L. Gabbidon, H. Taylor-Greene, & V. D. Young (Eds.), *African American classics in criminology and criminal justice* (pp. 201–211). Thousand Oaks, CA: Sage Publications.

Hotaling, G. T., & Sugarman, D. B. (1986). An analysis of risk markers in husband and wife violence: The current state of knowledge. *Violence and Victims, 1* (2), 101–124.

Jaffe, P., Wolf, D., Wilson, S., & Zak, L. (1986). Similarities in behavioral and social maladjustment among child victims and witnesses of family violence. *American Journal of Orthopsychiatry, 56,* 142–146.

Johnson-Reid, M. (1998). Youth violence and exposure to violence in childhood: An ecological review. *Aggression and Violent Behavior, 3* (2), 159–179.

Johnston, D. (1995) Effects of parental incarceration. In K. Gabel & D. Johnston (Eds.), *Children of incarcerated parents.* New York: Lexington Books.

Joseph, J. (1997). Women battering: A comparative analysis of Black and White women. In G. K. Kantor, & J. L. Jajinski (Eds.), *Out of darkness: Contemporary perspectives on family violence* (pp. 161–169). Thousand Oaks, CA: Sage Publications.

Kakar, S., Friedemann, M., & Peck, L. (2002). Girls in detention: Results of a focus group discussion: Interviews and official records review. *Journal of Contemporary Criminal Justice, 18* (1), 57–73.

Kirkpatrick, D., & Saunders, B. (1997). Prevalence and consequences of child victimization. National Center For Children Exposed to Violence. Retrieved on October 10, 2003: http://www.info.med.yale.edu/chldstdy/CDCP/violence/statistics.html.

Kruttschnitt, C., & Dornfield, M. (1993). Exposure to family violence: A partial explanation for initial and subsequent levels of delinquency. *Criminal Behavior and Mental Health, 3,* 61–75.

Lewis, D. O., Shanok, S. S., & Balla, D. A. (1979). Perinatal difficulties: Head trauma and child abuse in the histories of seriously delinquent children. *American Journal of Psychiatry, 136* (4), 419–423.

McGee, Z. (2003). Community violence & adolescent development: An examination of risk and protective factors among African-American youth. *Journal of Contemporary Criminal Justice,* (August), 293–314.

Ogbu, J. U. (1991). Low performance as an adaptation: The case of Blacks in Stockton, California. In M. A. Gibson & J. U. Ogbu (Eds.), *Minority and schooling* (pp. 249–285). New York: Grand Publishing.

Oliver, W. (2002). Black males and social problems. In S. L. Gabbidon, H. Taylor-Greene, & V. D. Young (Eds.) *African American classics in criminology and criminal justice* (pp. 245–259). Thousand Oaks, CA: Sage Publications.

Osuna, E., Alarcon, M., & Luna, A. (1992). Family violence as a determinant factor in juvenile maladjustment. *Journal of Forensic Sciences, 37* (6), 163–166.

Pagelow, D. M. (1984). *Family violence.* New York: Praeger.

Patterson, O. (1998). *Rituals of blood: Consequences of slavery in two American centuries.* Washington, D.C.: Civitas/Counterpoint.

Reed, D. F., & Reed, E. L. (1997). Children of incarcerated parents. *Social Justice, 24* (3), 152–175.

Schwab-Stone, M., Chen, C., Greenberger, E., Silver, D., Lichtman, J., & Voyce, C. (1999). No safe haven II: The effects of violence exposure on urban youth. National Center For Children Exposed to Violence. Retrieved October 10, 2003: http://www.info.med.yale.edu/chldstdy/CDCP/violence/statistics.html.

Snyder, D., & Sickmund, M. (1999). Population of counties by age and gender: 1990–1999 and Estimates of the population of counties by age, sex, and race/Hispanic origin: 1990–1999. U.S. Bureau of the Census. [machine-readable data files].

Steele, S. (1990). *The content of our character: A new vision of race in America.* New York: St. Martin's Press.

Steffensmeier, D., & Streifel, S. (1991). Age, gender, and crime across three historical periods. *Social Change, 69,* 869–894.

Straus, M., & Gelles, R. (1990) How violent are American families: Estimates from the national family resurvey and other studies. In M. Straus & R. Gelles (Eds.), *Physical violence in American families: Risk factors and adaptations in 8,145 families* (pp. 95–112). New Brunswick, NJ: Transaction.

Straus M. (1992). Children as witnesses to marital violence: A risk factor for lifelong problems among a nationally representative sample of American men and women. In D. F. Schwartz (Ed.)., *Children and violence: Report of the twenty-third Ross Roundtable on critical approaches to common pediatric problems* (pp. 98–104). Columbus, Ohio: Ross Laboratories.

Sulton, A. T. (Ed.). (1994). *African American perspectives on crime causation, criminal justice administration and crime prevention.* Englewood, CO: Sulton Books.

Welsing, F. (1974). The conspiracy to make Black males inferior. *Ebony, 29,* 84–93. (Cited in Oliver, 2002.)

Wilson, W. J. (1987). *The truly disadvantaged: The inner city, the underclass, and public policy.* Chicago: University of Chicago Press.

Wolfgang, M., & Ferracuti, F. (1982). *The subculture of violence: Towards an integrated theory in criminology* (2nd ed.). London: Tavistock.

CHAPTER SEVEN

REDUCING MINORITY YOUTH GANG INVOLVEMENT

Marilyn McShane and Frank P. Williams III

INTRODUCTION

What to do about youth gangs seems to dominate all discussions dealing with the subject of gangs. For the remainder of this discussion, we will refer to youth gangs as "gangs"—an approach which may sound reasonable, until one realizes that there is no precise definition of "a gang," no precise explanation of the causes of gangs, and no consensus on whether gangs are really different from, and independent of, other social- or crime-related problems (Thompson, Young, & Burns, 2000). As Cohen (1955) found many years ago while reviewing the criminological research on delinquency, the research clearly demonstrates that delinquent acts are commonly committed in the company of others. Therefore, it may be that gang behaviors primarily consist of "normal" delinquent acts. Two important questions, then, are: What constitutes *gang* delinquency, and why should the actions of gangs be identified and treated differently from "normal" delinquency? Only if gang delinquency is of a significantly different variety of delinquency or derived from a significantly different cause of delinquency should we begin to discuss methods of preventing or intervening in gang formation or behavior.

Here, one is reminded of the story of the Asian youth visiting his American friends and discovering how envious they were that he could eat all their favorite Chinese food at every meal. Somewhat perplexed, he reminded them that in China the natives just call it "food." Similarly, we are forced to wonder why the descriptor "gang crime" is placed at the forefront of the list of juvenile offenses and is therefore distinguished from them. Is a robbery any less or more of a robbery because a gang member commits it? Is an act of vandalism, theft,

111

or drug dealing enhanced or diminished when it becomes a "gang crime"? What is the specific purpose of applying the term "gang related" when describing, counting, or developing strategies for juvenile crime prevention? One possible answer is that the term "gang related" is applied not because it describes a crime committed by a juvenile, but because the term implies it is somehow important to us that the crime was committed by a gang member. If our perception of the crime is the reason, then gang-related crimes are different from others merely because we wish to identify them as different.

On the other hand, if gang crime is somehow truly different from non-gang crime, is it more serious? Many who advocate special programs, resources, and law enforcement measures argue that gang crime is more serious and should be a priority of juvenile crime intervention efforts. Indeed, it was fear of gang crimes that drove crime policy during the 1990s (Lane & Meeker, 2000). Gangs were associated with violent crime, particularly homicide and crimes involving weapons and drugs. We do not deny the reality that research has found gang membership and length of gang membership to be associated with higher levels of juvenile violence (Esbensen & Huizinga, 1993; Thornberry, Krohn, Lizotte, Smith, & Tobin, 2002). However, it is pronouncements by governmental authorities about the pervasiveness of violent and criminal gang activity with which we are most concerned. Such associations of gangs with violence and crime are not new. A history of such pronouncements has lasted over two hundred years in the United States alone. The recent movie *The Gangs of New York* illustrates the turn-of-the-twentieth-century reality of both gang violence and minority status. Large numbers of homeless children in nineteenth-century London similarly grouped into violent gangs as a protection and survival technique. Because gangs are not a new phenomenon, a brief history of gangs might contribute to a better understanding of the larger issues concerning them today.

Gangs:
A Story of Poor Immigrant Youths

Gang activity has been historically documented as early as the fifteenth century in Europe and has been part of American youth culture since the nineteenth century (Shelden, Tracy, & Brown, 2001). An important point lost to much of the public today is that gangs have been associated most commonly with immigrant status and are formed largely as a reaction to threats from other groups. The history of the emergence of gangs seems to suggest that they are a collective response to urbanization and, more recently, to industrialization associated with developing nations. Gang development is, without exception, a response to social and cultural adjustment by members of minority groups (frequently immigrants) and the poor and powerless in a society. Gangs emerged in the United States primarily during the industrial era, from 1850 to 1920, with its correspondingly large immigration and population shifts. These observations continue to hold true today: Gangs are most visible during periods of rapid population change. And, rather than having a stable presence, gangs are best characterized by a cyclical history.

We offer two well-known studies of gangs to demonstrate the makeup of twentieth-century gangs. When Thrasher (1927) conducted his famous study of Chicago gangs in the early 1900s, he found 1313 different gangs of which fewer than 10 percent had identities that were African-American (7 percent) and White/African-American (2.8 percent). An obvious observation is that youths from dominant social groups (primarily viewed as the white, Anglo-Saxon population) are generally not involved in gangs. When such youths are involved, the participants are almost always members of fringe groups. According to Miller's (1958) later study of delinquent youths in Boston, the predominant ethnic identities of the gang youths were Polish, Irish, and Italian. According to the views of such researchers as Thrasher and Miller, juveniles are drawn into social groups by neighborhood areas that reflect the identities, disorder, and disorganization of their residents. Indeed, it seems that the more disorganized the neighborhood is, the more likely it is that gangs will form. In part, this is due to a lack of conventional activities and facilities, such as recreational playgrounds, in which neighborhood children can spend their time. Without these advantages, playgroups tend to evolve into more structured and potentially deviant cliques, crowds, clubs, and, ultimately, gangs (Pelz, 2003).

Written accounts well before Thrasher's study provide vivid details of vicious gang wars that threw major cities into turmoil, as beatings, assassinations, and the maiming of innocent bystanders resulted from power struggles and turf battles. While many claim that gangs have become more violent, it is more likely that gangs have simply adopted the technology and organization of contemporary society and reflect current crime trends in general. The modern era of gangs is characterized by an increased access to and lethality in weaponry and by a greater degree of entrepreneurial organization. It can be easily argued that gangs have merely followed the times. Today's degree of concern with gangs in part reflects the changes in and the expansion of the definition a gang and its members.

Definitions of a Gang and of Gang Membership

Identifying gangs and gang members would seem to be an easy task. Moreover, such a process identifies those who should be the focus of arrest and prosecution, prevention and reduction efforts, and even those we should merely "watch." The gang identifier is, then, a very important consideration, and one can rightfully assume that, given the current three-decade-old concern with gangs, the issue has already been resolved. Unfortunately, however, no one definition has been developed that satisfactorily captures the concept of a "gang." Legal definitions vary from state to state; jurisdictional twists are common within states; and even sociological frameworks are diverse. Many would define gangs as consisting of as few as three people; others would label Boy Scout troops as gangs; and still others would define virtually any organized gathering of youths where some might engage in illegal activity—such as fraternity parties—as gangs. If we are unable to settle on a definition of what constitutes a gang, how can we determine who is a gang member?

When gang members are officially identified, mistakes frequently occur in the testimonies of "gang experts," who are most often police officers with "specialized training" in the area of gangs. These experts usually testify via an affidavit, often a boilerplate document, that the gang exists and that the person sought is a member of that gang. According to Gomez (2003), these affidavits are "considered sufficiently reliable to satisfy the admissibility requirements for expert opinions" (p. 76). Of course, this "reliability" begs the question of how such experts become experts and where they get their information. We know from numerous examples that such experts commonly have vested interests in using expansive definitions of what constitutes a gang. As a result, gang members are frequently identified by clothing or association with other "known" gang members—both of which criteria facilitate the identification of the largest possible number of gang members. These methods of identification also facilitate the identification of minorities as gang members.

Police often claim they are merely focusing on reported crimes or calls for service that seem to draw in minorities according to locations (frequently known as "hot spots"). Controversy extends from counting and identifying gang youths to arresting, charging, and sentencing these offenders and involves police, courts, and corrections officials, as well as the media and public interest groups. Thus, information based on law enforcement reports of gang activity can be rather suspect. Controversy also occurs when there is something to be gained by a particular location from its having large numbers of gang members.

Zatz (1985; 1987), for instance, accused Phoenix police of exaggerating a gang problem, particularly a Chicano gang problem, in order to acquire federal funds for gang suppression units within law enforcement. Similarly, Las Vegas police campaigned heavily statewide for antigang legislation, claiming that they were "outgunned and outstaffed" by gangbangers (McCorkle & Miethe, 1998; 2002). A division of the Los Angeles Police Department (LAPD), in order to gain access to substantial federal funding, invented data to show a false connection between gangs and illegal drugs (Williams, 2003). The National Institute of Justice some years later asked that its money be returned. Critics have also charged the LAPD with constructing and maintaining a grossly overinflated gang database that came to represent part of the racism problems underlying the agency. California continues to receive criticism over the Street Terrorism Enforcement and Prevention Act, which seemed to foster excessive law enforcement responses to youth activity in predominantly minority neighborhoods (Jackson & Rudman, 1993). Finally, some argue that the presence of gangs can be established by the presence of graffiti. While there are indeed identifiable gang graffiti, there are also, confusingly, non-gang graffiti—those of middle-class high school kids, of taggers, and even of true graffiti artists (Ferrell, 1993).

Some have suggested that the solution to problems created by official definitions is to rely on self-report studies (surveys or interviews where the respondents report on their opinions or behaviors) to compile either lists of gang members or estimates of the extent of gang membership. As one might quickly guess from an interview of a wannabe, such self-reports can be suspect. Bjerregaard's (2002) critique of self-reported gang membership offers a convincing argument that the way in which both *gang* and *membership* are defined is crucial to estimates of gang membership. However, social science research has not settled on a best definition of either term and therefore estimates are quite varied.

In examining the various approaches to defining gangs and gang members, Winfree, Fuller, Vigil, and Mays (1992) and Esbensen, Winfree, He, and Taylor (2001), have demonstrated that various definitions produce important differences in the way we discuss, account for, and even exhibit concern about gangs. They have also argued that the definition issue is by no means a trivial one. We cannot establish the effect of gang intervention, prevention or suppression programs without a common approach to what we are "treating." Moreover, any attempt to establish and assign "cause" is doomed to failure. Thus, in the comments concerning gang intervention and reduction programs below, one would do well to keep in mind that there is no uniformity among the programs or evaluations in what they consider to be the target population. Indeed, some programs designed to reduce gang involvement can ensure their success by targeting juveniles so far out on the periphery of gangs that it would be unlikely they would ever become true gang members.

GANGS, MORAL PANIC, AND THE STEREOTYPING OF MINORITY YOUTHS

Laws concerning gangs, as do many other laws, disproportionately impact minority populations. As conflict theorists would argue, this lack of parity is yet another way in which powerlessness (among the young, the poor, and a minority population) results in disproportionate representation in the criminal and juvenile justice system. The clustering of gang activity with other perceived criminal problems (violence, illegal drugs, robbery, graffiti) draws disproportionate law enforcement efforts to high crime areas that are primarily located in minority neighborhoods. In low income, densely populated areas, residents may have fewer life choices so that routine daily activities and close family ties alone may meet criteria for prosecution under some of the new antigang legislation around the nation. However, it is also true that residents of those neighborhoods frequently ask the police to "do something" about the local gang presence. Neither of these situations, a greater likelihood of prosecution and requests for police action, are mutually exclusive. The dilemma is that virtually any group of people would prefer to live in tranquility, but making requests of authorities toward that end produces the latent function (Robert Merton's term is the "unanticipated consequences of social action") of greater scrutiny by authorities—which inevitably results in higher crime rates (in the forms of both reported and observed crimes) for that group. This double-edged sword creates substantial problems for minority neighborhoods and their children.

The public's fear of gangs is often not only dramatized but perhaps even created by the media. As Thompson et al. (2000) found in their analysis of over 4,400 newspaper articles about gangs, the stories "presented readers with fear provoking images of families torn apart, schools turned into battle grounds, and communities paralyzed with fear" (p. 427). The emotions raised by these descriptions often translate into demands for tough action against gangs (Katz, Webb, & Armstrong, 2003), a sentiment to which law enforcement organizations easily respond.

In an ironic twist, their own fear of gangs (and of their allegedly sophisticated weaponry) may make police officers more prone to use deadly force in interactions with gang members, resulting ultimately in greater numbers of violent encounters—shootings of members, for example. If there is little public outcry condemning these shootings, then the label "gang member" can take on symbolic value. Put another way, a "gang member" (so labeled) involved in subsequent confrontational shootings could decrease public outcry. While the likelihood is very small, police could take an extreme position in which they would call all suspects in police shootings "gang members." Much more likely is that police *sometimes* use gang member status as a way to defuse anticipated reactions to a shooting. And, with certainty, there are some neighborhood groups who believe police use gang member status to defuse such reactions, whether the status is true or not. Consequently, some members of minority groups accuse police of hiding behind "gang-related" homicide to justify shooting youths.

While we have been building a case that perceptions of gangs, gang violence, and fear of gangs have been somewhat exaggerated, we should make it clear that gangs do pose problems for neighborhoods and that, on the whole, they do commit a greater proportion of more serious and violent acts. Our argument here is not that gangs are innocuous, but that exaggerated views and sensational claims can produce stereotypes that result in self-fulfilling prophecies. Among the public, media sensationalism has contributed to an exaggerated fear of gangs and virtually all gang-related phenomena. In turn this has affected both public and police reaction to gangs and, ultimately, even the behavior of gang members themselves. None of the terror, overreaction, and behavior are particularly beneficial for minority youths and their communities. What, then, can or should be done to reduce these problems for minority youths?

INTERVENTIONS: PROGRAMS, LAWS, AND LESSONS

In fairly recent years, various intervention and prevention mechanisms have been suggested and implemented to reduce the amount of crime attributed to gangs. Ironically, however, these gang intervention initiatives are often developed using the same assumptions, components, and practices as the delinquency intervention initiatives have used for the last one hundred years. As a result, recent educational, recreational, mentoring, group counseling, family support and community rebuilding programs (to name a few) were initially developed and used as general delinquency prevention approaches, not gang prevention and reduction efforts. Perhaps the main difference between general delinquency and gang interventions is that both legal and programming approaches for gang prevention and reduction usually have specific foci: targeting certain community areas; targeting activities such as loitering, drug sales, or prostitution; or targeting particular gang members or potential recruits.

A substantial number of research studies and program evaluations have been done, but, in general, the program results have remained questionable and the evaluation methodologies were poorly constructed. In many cases these measures were often evaluated in the context of overall reductions in area crime rates and were less likely to be compared in terms of effectiveness to other non-gang related juvenile crime prevention/intervention mechanisms. As a result, much of what is known about preventing or reducing gang involvement is anecdotal; Esbensen and Osgood (1999) even refer to the current state as one of a "paucity" of research. We focus below on two major types of strategies, legal and programmatic, but we focus less on the evidence of their efficacy.

Legal Approaches

Most gang initiatives have been either legal (remedial) or programmatic (preventative). Legal approaches have either relied on the enforcement of existing laws or resorted to creating new laws specifically targeting gangs. The problem with new laws is that they must pass through complex layers of judicial review. Many jurisdictions, aware that today's more conservative courts allow more infringement on individual rights in order to fight gangs, have instituted tough restrictions on the activities and associations of youths thought to be involved with gangs.

Beginning in 1988 with the California Street Terrorism Act, communities across the country sought creative legislation to combat not only the criminal activities of gang members but all of their umbrella activities as well. In addition to widening the net of what conduct constitutes criminal gang activity (loitering, recruiting new gang members, tattooing minors), authorities have increased the scope of who is subject to gang-related crime enforcement to include parents, siblings, landlords, and persons aspiring to join gangs. Although the burden to keep these laws constitutional would seem significant, it appears that most jurisdictions favor adopting a statute, regardless of its constitutionality, and enforcing it until such time as a case develops and is successful at a higher level of appeal that may strike the statute down. The California Supreme Court has upheld city regulations in the form of gang abatement injunctions that ban gang members from associating on street corners, driving, walking, or gathering together and from harassing anyone who has complained about them. Civil libertarians worry about the ways that curfews and gang abatement injunctions criminalize otherwise legal conduct and about the potential for biased enforcement, particularly in lower-income neighborhoods.

In 2000, California passed two revisions to the penal code that again widened the net for gang-related offenders. In one, a defendant need not be a member of a gang in order to be charged with a gang-related crime (gang affiliation). In the second, (gang conspiracy) the statute allows a gang member to be charged with any crime committed by a fellow gang member. Thus, one need not even participate in an actual crime to be prosecuted for that offense. The elements of these offenses include simply 1) active participation in a gang; 2) knowledge of a criminal street gang's crimes; and 3) the commission of a felony to aid and abet a gang. However, the gang conspiracy revision reduces this third element to prohibiting one from benefiting from a gang's crimes (de Vries, 2003).

Criminal law approaches to reducing gang violence and the spread of gang activity tend to be expensive in that they rely on an intensive law enforcement presence and aggressive court/prosecution efforts. A more fiscally conservative approach to gang intervention may be the use of civil litigation. Almost universally, civil litigation relies on public nuisance laws. Some communities have sued gangs and gang members (Stewart, 1998); others have held landlords liable for providing shelter for "criminals" (Lieberman, 1996); and yet others have placed locks on buildings or seized property used by gang members or in areas of gang activity (Bratton, 1995). The justification for these measures appears to lie in the new problem-oriented policing tactics as explained by the "broken windows" theory of Wilson and Kelling (1982), which postulates a causal relationship between minor public-order crimes and more serious crime and gang activity. Perhaps the primary reason for using civil litigation is its speed relative to criminal proceedings (Harvard Law Review, 2000). There are, as yet, no research reports on the effectiveness of nuisance litigation on existing gangs and the prevention of gangs. However, there are serious constitutional concerns, particularly in that such litigation is being applied primarily to minority groups.

Other law enforcement initiatives have been legally oriented in that they use interagency planning and partnerships to increase surveillance and supervision of offenders and high crime areas. In Operation Night Light, Boston area probation officers teamed with police to conduct surprise visits on probationers between the hours of 7:00 P.M. and midnight. Combined with a problem-oriented policing effort to reduce weapons violence in Boston (Operation Ceasefire), the project's evaluation indicated a significant decrease in the number of youth homicides in areas noted for gang activity (Braga, Kennedy, Piehl, & Waring, 2001). However, there may have been less success in antitrafficking aspects of the Gun Project because gun ownership did not seem to diminish, as did the use of weapons in the study area.

COMMUNITY PROGRAMS

There are several different kinds of programs which communities may sponsor to decrease gang violence among youths. Such programs address the same factors that appear related to other types of juvenile crime: lack of parental supervision and of healthy recreational resources, access to weapons, drug experimentation, and unemployment. Also, such programs are based on traditional delinquency theories that advocate role models, social bonding, and legitimate opportunity structures. Boys Clubs and Girls Clubs, YMCAs and YWCAs, Big Brothers and Big Sisters all target the prevention of initial gang membership by providing alternatives to recruitment by gang members.

Other programs have been developed to specifically target the development and spread of gangs in urban and suburban areas, and even rural areas. GREAT (Gang Resistance Education and Training) is a national curriculum used in fourth to seventh grades and similar to DARE, a drug education program. Trained law enforcement personnel participate in an effort to reduce negative attitudes and images of the police. Building self-esteem, motivation, and goal-setting behaviors are stressed as ways to insulate youths against the pressures they face from peer gang members. A national evaluation report by Esbensen and Osgood (1999) suggests that the students completing the GREAT program had lower rates of delinquent behaviors, although there is some question about whether those behaviors were gang-related. Another program, Cities in Schools (CIS), has also sought to lower dropout rates among teens, reduce school violence, and give inner-city youths access to more after-school activities. While these programs are often presented to entire classes, some focus on high-risk children, such as those in alternative settings where disciplinary issues have already resulted in the youth's removal from mainstream schools.

Many concerned parents, schools, churches, and communities work together to initiate after-school and weekend programs, such as midnight basketball games, teen concerts and game rooms outside the context of a national curriculum. However, the funding opportunities provided by federal efforts often compel local leadership to adopt wholesale messages and platforms regardless of their appropriateness or realistic appeal to their constituents. In one of the more street-level approaches, outreach workers in New York interact directly with gang members in aggression replacement training that will hopefully reconnect youths to their neighborhoods and family networks through more pro-social gang identities (Shelden et al., 2001). The rationale behind this approach is that the gang relationships will probably not be severed, so changing the nature and outlook of the gang is the most realistic route. It is possible that as youths age and mature, these programs will give them a face-saving way to make the transition into more responsible roles in their community. Other programs, such as Operation Kids CAN (Care About Neighborhoods), structure neighborhood clean-up projects, gardening, and graffiti removal to help instill pride and territorial protective interests in participating youths that may deter later criminal activity.

One of the debates in antigang programming is which youth should be prioritized for access to the limited resources available. Some programs target the very young on the premise that early interventions may have more success than later efforts that may have to compete against gang activity. Others, like Chicago's Gang Violence Reduction Program, focuses on older members from seventeen to twenty-four years old. In many areas it is too difficult to verify who is involved in gangs and to what extent they are involved, so the programs focus on both at-risk and gang-involved youth. This is the model followed by the Riverside, California and the Bloomington/Normal, Illinois Comprehensive Community-Wide Approach to Gang Prevention, Intervention, and Suppression.

In a nationwide evaluation of these youth gang prevention, intervention, and suppression programs Spergel, Curry, Chance, Kane, Ross, Alexander, Simmons, and Oh (1994) found that most communities engaged in suppression activities. Organizational responses within the community were less frequent and the creation of opportunities for youth directly in the community was least likely to occur. It is not surprising that the most expensive, albeit arguably the most potentially viable, options are those least likely to be pursued today. Many communities have formed task forces, but their composition and mandate have often been politically motivated, and few have done more than discuss problems. While some culturally sensitive programs and approaches have been tried, particularly for drug abuse prevention (Lovett, 2003), they have been few and poorly funded. Moreover, they have not been evaluated in any meaningful way. Thus, we do not know whether such programs are successful or, if they work, whether they could be successfully applied outside of the specific environment in which they were applied. For poor and minority communities this lack of focus is particularly disheartening.

CONCLUSIONS

Primarily because of their foci on middle-class values and behaviors, most programs designed to reduce youth gang involvement have either failed to achieve any lasting effects or frequently have had no effect at all. In short, these efforts reflect many others designed to deal with "social problems" in that they fail to take into account the needs and subcultures of minority communities and urban neighborhoods. Measures taken to address gang violence have done little to assist low-income and predominantly minority communities with the problems they face in providing safe and productive living and working environments for their residents. Simply enacting laws to increase prosecutions and penalties do little to address the root causes of youth crime, whether inside or outside the context of a gang. Drawing an ever wider net of youth into the criminal justice arena for an ever wider array of newly created offenses is counterproductive. In addition, these punitive policies have contributed to developing a larger gang culture that now transcends neighborhoods. What were once localized gangs are now well established in prisons and, as their members come and go, their membership and loyalties are no longer tied to geographical areas. This unforeseen consequence of spreading gang influence will likely have serious implications for future gang development.

If we are to have an effective reduction of the numbers of minority youth entering the criminal and juvenile justice systems, a much greater degree of sensitivity to neighborhood and cultural conditions is needed. Programs must be oriented toward the critical conditions that contribute to gang formation and the attraction of gangs to youthful residents. Because gangs develop and retain popularity for their ability to provide youth with a sense of belonging, protection, and status—the same attractions over the past few hundred years—the conditions creating this attractiveness must be dealt with. This means, among other things, that jobs must be available, education must be meaningful, neighborhood isolation must be reduced, and political power must be dispersed.

The real question is whether we can afford to continue treating the symptoms of such inattention to our urban neighborhoods as a law enforcement problem. If the answer to this question is in the affirmative, then we will continue to have neighborhoods that spawn gangs and youthful involvement in crime, just as those same neighborhoods spawn a sense of futility and hopelessness. Moreover, we will continue to pay economically for that solution in the form of an ever increasing criminal and juvenile justice system with its attendant financial burden. We will also continue to pay socially with an ever increasing class of people who are more and more disenfranchised in society and ever more angry about their position. In other words, such an affirmative answer is rather shortsighted, both economically and socially. The youth involved would not constitute just a year or two of high and ultimately unproductive costs; indeed, the high costs would be spread in a multiplicative fashion across their lifetimes. In fact, it would actually be cheaper to develop programs to improve lives in our urban neighborhoods now than to pay across the lifetimes of affected youths.

References

Bjerregaard, B. (2002). Self-definitions of gang membership and involvement in delinquent activities. *Youth & Society, 34* (1), 31–54.

Bjerregaard, B. (2003). Antigang legislation and its potential impact: The promises and pitfalls. *Criminal Justice Policy Review, 14* (2), 171–192.

Braga, A., Kennedy, D., Piehl, A., & Waring, E. J. (2001). Measuring the impact of operation ceasefire. In National Institute of Justice, *Reducing gun violence: The Boston gun project's operation ceasefire* (Part II, pp. 55–68). Washington, D.C.: National Institute of Justice.

Bratton, W. J. (1995). The New York Police Department's civil enforcement of quality-of-life crimes. *Journal of Law and Policy, 3* (2), 447–464.

Cohen, A. K. (1955). *Delinquent boys: The culture of the gang.* New York: Free Press.

de Vries, L. (2003). Guilt by association: Proposition 21's Gang Conspiracy Law will increase youth violence in California. *University of San Francisco Law Review, 37,* 191–226.

Esbensen, F., & Huizinga, D. (1993). Gangs, drugs, and delinquency in a survey of urban youth. *Criminology, 31,* 565–589.

Esbensen, F., & Osgood, D. W. (1999). Gang Resistance Education and Training (GREAT): Results from the national evaluation. *Journal of Research in Crime and Delinquency, 36,* 194–225.

Esbensen, F., Winfree, L. T., Jr., He, N., & Taylor, T. J. (2001). Youth gangs and definitional issues: When is a gang a gang, and why does it matter. *Crime and Delinquency 47,* 105–130.

Ferrell, J. (1993). *Crimes of style: Urban graffiti and the politics of criminality.* New York: Garland.

Gomez, P. (2003). It is not so simply because an expert says it is so: The reliability of gang expert testimony regarding membership in criminal street gangs: Pushing the limits of Texas Rule of Evidence 702. *St Mary's Law Journal, 34,* 581–623.

Harvard Law Review (2000). Developments in the law: The paths of civil litigation. *Harvard Law Review, 113* (7), 1172–1875.

Katz, C. M., Webb, V. J., & Armstrong, T. A. (2003). Fear of gangs: A test of alternative theoretical models. *Justice Quarterly, 20,* 95–130.

Jackson, P., & Rudman, C. (1993). Moral panic and the response to gangs in California. In S. Cummings & D. Monti (Eds.), *Gangs* (pp. 257–276). Albany: State University of New York Press.

Lane, J., & Meeker, J. W. (2000). Subcultural diversity and the fear of crime and gangs. *Crime and Delinquency, 46,* 497–521.

Lieberman, S. G. (1996). Note: Drug dealing and street gangs—the new nuisances: Modernizing old theories and bring neighbors together in the war against crime. *Washington University Journal of Urban and Contemporary Law, 50,* 235–264.

Lovett, M. D. (2003). Culturally specific programming. In M. McShane & F. Williams (Eds.), *Encyclopedia of Juvenile Justice* (pp. 95–98). Thousand Oaks, CA: Sage Publications.

McCorkle, R., & Meithe, T. (1998). The political and organization response to gangs: An examination of a "moral panic" in Nevada. *Justice Quarterly, 15,* 41–64.

McCorkle, R., and Meithe, T. (2002). *Panic: The social construction of the street gang problem.* Upper Saddle River, NJ: Prentice Hall.

Miller, W. B. (1958). Lower-class culture as a generating milieu of gang delinquency. *Journal of Social Issues, 14,* 5–19.

Pelz, B. (2003). Gangs, juvenile: History and theories. In M. McShane & F. Williams (Eds.), *Encyclopedia of juvenile justice* (pp. 167–174). Thousand Oaks, CA: Sage Publications.

Shelden, R., Tracy, S., & Brown, W. B. (2001). Youth gangs in American society. (2nd ed.). Belmont, CA: Wadsworth.

Spergel, I. A., Curry, G. D., Chance, R., Kane, C., Ross, R., Alexander, A., Simmons, E., & Oh, S. (1994). *Gang suppression and intervention: Problems and response.* Washington, D.C. U.S. Department of Justice, Office of Justice Programs, Office of Juvenile Justice and Delinquency Prevention.

Stewart, G. (1998). Black codes and broken windows: The legacy of racial hegemony in anti-gang civil injunctions. *Yale Law Journal, 107* (7), 2249–2279.

Thompson, C., Young, R. L., & Burns, R. (2000). Representing gangs in the news: Media constructions of criminal gangs. *Sociological Spectrum, 20,* 409–432.

Thornberry, T. P., Krohn, M. D., Lizotte, A. J., Smith, C. A., & Tobin, K. (2002). *Gangs and delinquency in developmental perspective.* New York: Cambridge University Press.

Thrasher, F. (1927). *The gang: A study of 1313 gangs in Chicago.* Chicago: University of Chicago Press.

Williams, F. P., III., & McShane, M. (2004). Youth, drugs, and delinquency. In P. Benekos and A. Merlo (Eds.), *Controversies in juvenile justice and delinquency* (pp. 69–88). Cincinnati, OH: Anderson Publishing.

Wilson, J. Q., & Kelling, G. L. (1982). The Police and neighborhood safety: Broken windows. *Atlantic Monthly, 249* (3), 29–38.

Winfree, L. T., Jr., Fuller, K., Vigil, T., & Mays, G. L. (1992). The definition and measurement of "gang status": Policy implication for juvenile justice. *Juvenile and Family Court Journal, 43* (1), 29–37.

Zatz, M. S. (1985). Los Cholos: Legal processing of Chicano gang members. *Social Problems, 33,* 13–30.

Zatz, M. S. (1987). Chicano youth gangs and crime: The creation of a moral panic. *Contemporary Crises, 11,* 129–158.

CHAPTER EIGHT

RACE, ETHNICITY, AND THE APPLICATION OF THE DEATH PENALTY TO JUVENILES: A HUMAN RIGHTS PERSPECTIVE

Daniel E. Georges-Abeyie

INTRODUCTION: THE JUDICIARY; SEPARATE AND UNEQUAL JUSTICE

The bombing of the World Trade Center in New York City on September 11, 2001 resulted in the assertion of a mythological racial and ethnic unity through the slogan "United We Stand", which implied that, at that time, there was a sudden "melting pot" assimilation of the masses. Presumably, this unity would result in future racial and ethnic impartiality in judicial and correctional system processes in response to adult crime and juvenile delinquency. The reality is that neither process had ever turned a blind eye to race and ethnicity in the adjudication of adult and juvenile offenders, a reality borne out previously in the statistical data which resulted in the primary holding in *Coker v. Georgia* (433 U.S. 584 [1977]). This landmark case found the imposition of capital punishment to be disproportionately severe as a response to the forcible rape of an adult female in which there were no concurrent offenses that aggravated the severity of the criminal offense. The statistical data in *Coker v. Georgia* also found that execution as a judicial response to the forcible rape of an adult female was almost exclusively reserved for Black males who, allegedly, forcibly raped White females. The dual standard in the imposition of the death penalty for the forcible rape of an adult female was "part and parcel" of a racial and ethnic reality that applied to juvenile offenders, mentally defective, or dysfunctional, adult Black and criminal offenders. This decision thereby negated the concept of *parens patriae*, which is the provision of protection and guidance by the state for those unable to appropriately care for themselves or to engage in rational, law-abiding behavior. In fact, the dual standard in the judicial process was, and continues to be, "part and parcel" of a greater dichotomy and differential, which has been the norm in racial and ethnic relations within the internationally recognized borders of the United States of America. (The law within a country's borders is referred to as the *jure gentium*.) This pattern is aptly depicted in the outstanding documentary *Shadow of Hate* (Guggenheim & Shields, 1995), which notes a pattern of dual and unequal justice and brutal extrajudicial treatment of White and non-White racial, ethnic, and religious minorities, including Catholics and various Protestant Christian sects, Jews, Native Americans, diasporac Africans, Latinos, Japanese, and Chinese immigrants.

The dichotomy in American criminal and noncriminal justice procedures and outcomes is the manifestation both of the internal conflict which exists among American general valuations and of the difference between fact and fiction, between general valuations and specific valuations, and between conceptualizing and actualizing general and specific valuations. The dichotomy is manifested, in part, by social and cultural factors associated with *petit apartheid*, a term which can be used to designate the informal, unofficial, de facto mores and norms of the nation. Such actions result in the transmutation of discretion into discrimination within the U.S. criminal justice and juvenile justice systems and in the actualization of social distance. Thus, the gross bias and differential in the application of the death penalty to non-White youths, in general, and to Black youths, in particular, is the expected manifestation of racist, "ethnophobic," and xenophobic U.S. mores and norms, which have frequently devalued non-White life and attributed primitive, animal-like, characteristics to non-Whites, in general, and to persons of African descent, in particular. This gross differential in the application of the death penalty to alleged and adjudicated non-White, mentally defective or dysfunctional, adult and juvenile offenders has frequently been so severe a violation of *jure gentium*, human rights law, and human rights standards in general that it now constitutes a gross violation of generally recognized international legal standards (referred to as *jus cogens* standards) which are binding on all nation-states. Thus, the United States has been immersed into the ranks of pariah nation-states (i.e., outcast nation-states which routinely violate such standards). That the United States continues to execute juvenile and adult criminal offenders, regardless of their mental health, places it among a decreasing number of nation-states which have utilized capital punishment for crimes nonpolitical and crimes not considered crimes against humanity.

The Execution of Juveniles:
The Jure Gentium, Jus Cogens, and
Human Rights Contexts

Amnesty International (2003b) notes that the worldwide movement to abolish the death penalty increasingly establishes the United States as a pariah nation-state. As this human rights organization observes: "Over half the countries in the world have now abolished the death penalty in law or practice. Amnesty International's latest information shows that 76 countries have abolished the death penalty for all crimes, with another 15 countries having abolished the death penalty for all crime except wartime crimes. Considering they have not carried out a death sentence in over a decade, another 21 countries can be considered abolitionist in practice" (p. 1). Indeed, according to the organization:

> [P]rogress [has been made] toward worldwide abolition of the death penalty[,] with more than three countries a year on average [having] abolished the death penalty for all crimes in the past decade. Over 35 countries and territories have abolished the death penalty for all crimes since 1990. They include countries in Africa…the Americas… Asia…and Europe. (p. 1)

Concerning actual death sentences and executions for 2002, Amnesty International (2003b) notes that at least 1,526 prisoners were executed in 31 countries and at least 3,248 people were sentenced to death in 76 countries. It also notes that "81 percent of all known executions took place in China, Iran, and the USA, [with] [s]eventy-one people…executed in the USA" (p. 2). Of special pertinence to this chapter is the use of the death penalty against child offenders, in general, and against non-White, including Negroid, child offenders, in particular. Amnesty International (2003b) states: "International human rights treaties prohibit anyone under 18 years at the time of the crime from being sentenced to death or executed." Nevertheless, over 110 countries still do so, the United States leading the way with thirteen such executions since 1990 (p. 2). In addition, Amnesty International (2003a) observes that the execution of juveniles under U.S. correctional jurisdiction persisted in 2003 and that a racial and ethnic disproportionality persisted in these executions: "Napoleon Beazley, T. J. Jones, and Toronto Patterson…[were] executed in Texas on May 28th, August 9th, and August 28th, respectively, for murders committed when they were 17 years old" (p. 267). This disturbing trend constitutes systemic and systematic racial and ethnic bias.

"PETIT APARTHEID" IN THE U. S. CRIMINAL JUSTICE SYSTEMS: THE PERSISTENCE OF RACIAL AND ETHNIC BIAS AS APPARENT AGGRAVATING FACTORS IN THE APPLICATION OF THE DEATH PENALTY TO JUVENILE OFFENDERS

The persistence of racial and ethnic bias as apparent aggravating factors in the adjudication and sentencing of non-White adult and juvenile offenders, in general, and of Black offenders, in particular, is apparent in the application of the death penalty under each state's jurisdiction and the two U.S. federal jurisdictions, military and civilian. The apparent, persistent impact of race and ethnicity on the application of the death penalty is noted by the National Coalition to Abolish the Death Penalty (NCADP) (2003b), which found two out of three children sent to death row are people of color. In addition, the Coalition points out, African-American youths (males and females) are the ones most likely to receive the death penalty; in the past, moreover, Native Americans as young as ten were executed. The NCADP (2003a) also observes that over 67% of the kids on death row are Black/Latino.

Amnesty International, perhaps the world's best-known human rights organization, along with acclaimed South African human-rights activist, Archbishop Desmond Tutu, concurs with the NCADP's assertion that race is a factor in death penalty sentencing and execution of Black juveniles, in particular, and of non-White juvenile offenders, in general. Amnesty International (2003d) points out Archbishop Tutu's "appeal for clemency for child offender Napoleon Beazley, an African-American child offender sentenced to death by 12 White jurors in 1995" (p. 24) and quotes the well-known activist: "Americans do not seem to think about the concrete, visceral impact that executions have on the African-American community in cases like Napoleon's, where there seem to be many indications that race was a factor in his sentencing.... I beg you, think of the degrading effect of Napoleon's sentence, under such circumstances, on the African-American community in general and the Grapeland community and his family in particular" (p. 24). Amnesty International also observes: "Nearly two-thirds of the 80 plus child offenders on death row in the USA are from ethnic or racial minorities" (pp. 24–25).

Thus, what is the documented reality of the disproportionate application of the death penalty to Black and other non-White minority child offenders in the twentieth and twenty-first centuries? According to Streib (2002), there have been 365 executions during the current era (1973–2002). Of these, twenty-one were of persons who were juveniles when they committed their crimes (p. 3). The twenty-one executions are listed below in Table 1 (Streib, 2002, p. 4), which has been amended by this author to note alleged mental retardation and mental illness based upon information provided by Amnesty International (2002c, pp. 100–102; 2002b).

Streib (2002) observes that, according to NAACP-LDF (2002), "Only 43% of executed juvenile offenders have been White, while 56% of executed adult offenders have been White" (as cited, p. 5). Streib also notes: "Race of victim is almost exactly the same for executed juvenile offenders (80% White victims) and for executed adult offenders (81%)" (p. 5). Thus, the race of the victim appears to be a significant factor in the application of the death penalty to both adult and juvenile offenders—a factor frequently cited by Amnesty International, the National Coalition to Abolish the Death Penalty, and other human rights organizations. This disproportion in the race of the homicide victims of the executed is frequently cited as proof that the execution of minorities in the United States is an American tradition which devalues the lives of people of color (Hawkins, 1983).

Thus, the disparate and apparently racially and ethnically discriminatory application of the death penalty to minority juvenile offenders indicates a more comprehensive problem: the disparate application of the most severe criminal justice sanction to minority offenders regardless of adult or juvenile status or the mental health of some of these minority juvenile offenders. Put succinctly, the racially and ethnically biased application of the death penalty in the United States has become judicial discretion transmuted to deadly discrimination. Such a transformation can be seen in the forms of both "grand apartheid" (official statute-enforced discrimination) and "petit apartheid." It has originated from the limited perception among the majority in the United States of the biological, cultural, and behavioral characteristics and mores of non-White racial and ethnic minorities, in general, and Negroids, in particular, resulting in the continuation of social distance, in practice, and not in the hyperbolic rhetoric of the post-September 11 slogan, "United We Stand."

Table 1.   Executions of Juvenile Homicide Offenders, January 1, 1973, through December 31, 2002

Name	Date of Execution	Place of Execution	Race & Sex of Offender/Victim	Age at Crime/Execution	Mental State
1. Rumbaugh, C	9-11-1985	TX	WM/WM	17/28	Bipolar disorder
2. Roach, J.T.	1-10-1986	SC	WM/WM/WF	17/25	IQ 60-70. History of mental illness
3. Pinkerton, J.	5-15-1986	TX	WM/WF, WF	17/24	
4. Prejean, D.	5-18-1990	LO	BM/WM	17/30	IQ 71-76, Schizophrenia
5. Garrett, J.	2-11-1992	TX	WM/WF	17/28	Mental illness, severely abused sexually and physically
6. Harris, C.	7-1-1993	TX	BM/WM	17/31	IQ 77, brain damage
7. Lashley, F.	7-28-1993	MS	BM/BF	17/29	Alcohol & drug use
8. Cantu, R.	8-24-1993	TX	LM/LM	17/26	Borderline mental retardation, IQ 70-80
9. Burgher, C.	12-7-1993	GA	WM/WM	17/33	Low IQ, mentally ill, brain damage, physically abused
10. Cannon, J.J.	4-22-1998	TX	WM/WF	17/38	IQ 79, brain damage, mental illness, borderline mental retardation, sexual abuse by male relatives
11. Carter, R.A.	5-8-1998	TX	BM/LF	17/34	IQ 74. Diagnosed as having retardation, brain damage
12. Wright, D.A.	10-14-1998	VA	BM/BF	17/26	Borderline mental retardation, mentally ill
13. Sellers, S.R.	2-4-1999	OK	WM/WM, WM, WF	16/29	Paranoid Schizophrenia, Multiple Personality Disorder
14. Thomas, C.	1-10-2000	VA	WM/WF	17/26	Alcohol & drug abuse
15. Roach, S.E.	1-19-2000	VA	WM/WF	17/23	"Particularly immature" for his age, "poor impulse control"
16. McGinnis, G.C.	1-25-2000	TX	BM/WF	17/27	Severely abused physically and sexually at home
17. Graham, G.L.	6-22-2000	TX	BM/WF	17/36	
18. Mitchell, G.L.	10-22-2001	TX	BM/WM	17/33	IQ 75, Drug abuse & addiction
19. Beazley, N.	5-28-2002	TX	BM/WM	17/25	
20. Jones, T.J.	8-8-2002	TX	BM/WM	17/25	
21. Patterson, T.	8-28-2002	TX	BM/BF	17/24	IQ 78

Source: Streib, V. L. (2002). The Juvenile Death Penalty Today: Death Sentences and Executions for Juvenile Crimes. Jan. 1, 1973–Dec. 31, 2002.

Why Non-White Racial and Ethnic Adult and Juvenile Offenders Face State-Sanctioned Homicide at a Disparate Rate within the Jure Gentium Borders of the United States

The much acclaimed, multipart documentary *Africans in America* (Bagwell, Bellows, & Chin, 1998) documents the devaluation in the American colonies of non-White life, in general, and of African-American life, in particular. It notes that in its lowlands and Sea Islands, the colony of South Carolina adopted the slave plantation structure and management scheme of Barbados, where the brutalization of adult and juvenile Negroids was the norm. In Barbados it was believed that it was less expensive to continuously import slaves and to work them to death than to provide a humane plantation environment where intergenerational enslavement was the norm. Thus, the expected death rate among South Carolinian Negroid slaves was one death for every three slaves within a three year period—a truly horrific death rate which clearly signified a devaluation of the life of Negroid homo sapiens in a colony marked by "grand apartheid" in virtually every facet of life, including the adjudication of adult and juvenile criminal offenders (Bagwell, Bellows, & Chin, 1998). "Grand apartheid" is defined as de jure oppression in the form of de jure racism manifested in [legal] master-initiated-and-administered beatings, burnings, mutilations, and executions (Milovanovic & Russell, 2001). The antebellum era of "grand apartheid" was followed by the current era of "petit apartheid." As noted earlier, this form of apartheid is defined as the informal, de facto mores and norms that permeate the American criminal justice system and that result in the transmutation of judicial discretion into discrimination via such realities as harsh sentences for minorities and lenient sentences for Whites; jury nullification, allowing the conviction of non-Whites based upon limited, or nonexistent, evidence and the exoneration of Whites based upon the same, or similar, evidence; the abrogation of due process for minority defendants; and the adjudication of minority juvenile offenders, many of whom are mentally deficient, resulting in harsh sentences rather than treatment by appropriate governmental agencies under the legal concept of *parens patriae*. It is also important to note that "grand apartheid" was part of the law of the land beginning with the original thirteen colonies and the nation-state they evolved into.

The primary question for the criminal justice scholar is, "Why 'grand apartheid' and 'petit apartheid'?" And the related question, "Why has judicial discretion become transmuted into lethal discrimination in the forms of disparate sentencing and execution of minority adult and juvenile offenders?" The answer is as simple and as accurate as the primary thesis of Michael Moore's 2002, Oscar-winning documentary *Bowling for Columbine*, which contends that the United States was founded upon racial, ethnic, religious intolerance, and fear. More specifically, the racial and ethnic intolerance noted in *Bowling for Columbine* (Moore, 2002); in *Shadow of Hate* (Guggenheim, 1995); in *Africans in America* (Bagwell, 1998); in *Racism, Empiricism, and Criminal Justice* (Georges-Abeyie,1990, pp. 11–14, pp. 25–34); in *Petit Apartheid in the U.S. Criminal Justice System* (Georges-Abeyie, 2001, pp. ix–xiv); and in the excellent text *Strangers to These Shores: Race and Ethnic Relations in the Untied States* (Parrillo, 2003) is the result of vast social distance in the American milieu because of general valuations and individual valuations and norms, some of which are contradictory in that they reject the basic premise of cultural and biological pluralism while recognizing U.S. racial and ethnic diversity. This reality, which acknowledges social distance and the limited assimilation of some racial and ethnic minorities, is further analyzed below. One should note, however, that the racial and ethnic diversity that was so much a part of colonial America and the early United States was diversity built largely on the forced migration of millions of Negroid African slaves and an institution (i.e., slavery) enforced by a complex system of laws and police power which governed virtually every aspect of the lives of those enslaved in order to mitigate the possibility of slave insurrections (Bagwell, Bellows, & Chin,1998). The reality for the African slaves brought to the shores of the Western Hemisphere was that of "grand apartheid," which was later modified by amendments to the United States Constitution, by case law, and by various legislative acts. In addition, a complex potpourri of discriminatory mores and related norms created vast social distance and the limited assimilation of Negroid and other non-White racial and ethnic minorities.

SOCIAL DISTANCE, ASSIMILATION OF NEGROIDS AND OTHER NON-WHITE MINORITIES, AND THE DISPROPORTIONATE EXECUTION OF NON-WHITE JUVENILE AND ADULT OFFENDERS

What is "social distance" and how has it influenced the sentencing of Negroid and other racial and ethnic minorities? Parrillo (2003) defines social distance as "the degree of closeness one desires in interaction with members of a particular group" [even one's own identity group] (p. 600). Put another way, social distance simply means how close one group feels toward another group. In 1926 Emory Bogardus devised a measurement scale which has been modified and used repeatedly since then to rank various nationality groups in the United States (Parrillo, 2003). The scale included questions which examined the level of "social distance" a group feels toward another group.

Unfortunately, identity variables have been modified since Bogardus developed the original scale. Nonetheless, the use of the original variables revealed a remarkable consistency in the attribution of social distance to thirty nationality groups, with those groups most phenotypically Caucasoid manifesting the lowest social-distance scores and those with darkest skin coloration and the least Caucasoid features manifesting the highest social-distance scores. Specifically, northwestern European Whites and White U.S. Americans manifested the lowest social-distance scores; southern and eastern Europeans manifested middle-range social-distance scores, and non-Whites manifested the highest social-distance scores when the scores were computed for nationality groups in 1926, 1946, 1956, and 1966. In 1926, Negroes ranked 26th, with a score of 3.28, and U.S. Whites ranked 2nd, with a score of 1.10; in 1946, Negroes ranked 29th, with a score of 3.60, and U.S. Whites ranked 1st, with a score of 1.04; in 1956, Negroes ranked 27th, with a score of 2.74, and U.S. Whites ranked 1st, with a score of 1.08; in 1966, Negroes ranked 29th, with a score of 2.56, and U.S. Whites ranked 1st, with a score of 1.07 (Bogardus, 1968, p. 152). Owen, Esiner, and McFaul (1981), using a replication of the original Bogardus scale, notes social distance scores in 1977 and 2001. In 1977, Negroes ranked 17th, with a score of 2.03, and U.S. Whites ranked 1st, with a score of 1.25; in 2001, African-Americans ranked 9th, with a score of 1.34, and U.S. Whites ranked 1st, with a score of 1.07 in 2001. The results of the study showed a dramatic decrease in the alleged social distance manifested by Negroes/African-Americans, although the nationality groups with the lowest social distance scores, in general, continued to be U. S. Whites and northwestern Europeans (p. 89).

Nonetheless, sentencing data indicate that Black and Latino adult and juvenile offenders, whether mentally competent or mentally deficient because of retardation, psychosis, and other mental-health disabilities, are disproportionately sentenced to "state sanctioned homicide" (the term utilized in officially sanctioned executions). Thus, one must question the reliability and validity of social-science studies which indicate a dramatic decrease in the social distance manifested by Negroid and other racial and ethnic minorities, including that of Latinos and Native Americans. The social distance manifested by Negroids and other racial and ethnic minorities may in fact remain elevated. What may have changed is the willingness of researchers to overtly express racial and ethnic bias in scientific surveys which purportedly objectively measure social distance/bias toward Negroids and some specific non-White ethnic minorities—an astute observation voiced by former Health and Human Services Secretary Patricia Harris. More troubling than faulty studies noting bias or the lack thereof (faults perhaps due to inconsistency in the identity groups utilized) would be the actual decrease in social distance manifested by Negroids and other racial and ethnic minorities when the propensity to disproportionately sentence and execute Negroid and other racial and ethnic minorities continues to be evident via death penalty data.

The U.S. preconceptions of Negroids and other racial and ethnic minorities: (1) that they do not belong; (2) that they do not contribute to the national development or to the social welfare of the nation-state; (3) that they are a threat to national security; and (4) that they are atavistic, as noted in the documentary *Shadow of Hate in America* (Guggenheim and Shields, 1995), remain a U.S. social reality, as manifested by the tepid, racially bifurcated public response to the beating of Rodney King by the Los Angeles police and, more recently, by the relatively little public response to the beating of 350-pound, five-foot-nine-inch Mr. Jones by the Cincinnati police in the fall of 2003. In fact, the response to the beating of Mr. Jones did not include major street demonstrations or the mass petitioning of U.S. government officials or major mass media coverage of outraged citizens outside of the African-American community.

According to Williams (1970), the "Basic American Values are the foundation of our beliefs, behaviors, definitions of social goals, and life expectations [including] contradictory values—freedom and individualism but external conformity, democracy and equality but racism and group superiority, nationalism but individualism—and these may spark divisions among people" (p. 35). The author of this work contends, based upon his observation of North American norms and mores, that the "The Basic American Values" also include the following, which are not cited by Williams: the belief in racial and ethnic distinctiveness, the appropriateness of violence as redress of a wrong, the right to eliminate those perceived as threats or as atavistic, the right to eliminate those who threaten one's way of life, the right to use racial and ethnic epithets when among one's own identity group, and the right to demonize those perceived as different or as a threat. This author also contends that the impact of negative valuations is enhanced by the limited assimilation of the targeted identity group. Gordon (1964) notes seven assimilation subprocesses/variables, i.e., Cultural/Behavioral, Structural, Marital, Identificational [involving the development of a sense of peoplehood based exclusively on the host society], Attitude Receptional [involving the absence of prejudice], Behavior Receptional [involving the absence of discrimination], and Civic [involving the absence of value and power conflict]. All but the most naïve social analyst would not concur with Gordon who noted that Negroids, in particular, and other racial and ethnic groups in the United States, in general, have experienced limited assimilation in terms of most of these sub-processes/variables, thereby widening their social distance and enhancing their status as worthy of special treatment by the U.S. criminal justice system, a treatment which includes their elimination as a threat by the targeted application of the death penalty. Thus, the disproportionate application of the death penalty to non-White juvenile offenders, in general, and Negroid juvenile offenders, in particular, even those with serious mental defects, should not surprise any objective analyst of the U.S. adult or juvenile justice systems.

CONCLUSION

The U.S. persistence in the application of the death penalty against adult offenders, much less against juvenile offenders, places the nation increasingly at odds with the world community of nation-states. Amnesty International and other human rights organizations view the death penalty as an egregious violation of human rights, as noted under *jure gentium* human rights law, such as Article Three and Article Five of the *Universal Declaration of Human Rights* proclaimed and adopted by the General Assembly of the United Nations on December 10, 1948. The world community of nation-states has adopted four international treaties providing for the abolition of the death penalty in all but the direst circumstances, such as those during a war. One treaty, the *Second Optional Protocol to the International Covenant on Civil and Political Rights*, passed by the United Nations General Assembly in 1989, is of worldwide scope; the other three treaties are regional.

Amnesty International (2002a) states: "The use of the death penalty against child offenders is prohibited under leading international instruments of worldwide or regional scope relating to human rights and the conduct of armed hostilities 'international humanitarian law'" (p. 1). Thus, the United Nations and regional intergovernmental agreements all prohibit the execution of child offenders under the age of eighteen.

One should note that when the United States ratified the *International Covenant on Civil and Political Rights* in 1992, it entered a reservation to Article 6, which prohibits the use of the death penalty for those who were under the age of eighteen at the time of the crime. Numerous European countries have voiced their objections to this U.S. reservation on the grounds that it is incompatible with the Covenant's objective. Moreover, the United Nations *Convention on the Rights of the Child [Article 37 (a)], 1995,* states: "Neither capital punishment nor life imprisonment without possibility of release shall be imposed for offenses committed by persons below 18 years of age." According to Amnesty International (2003c), "the United States and Somalia are the only countries in the world that have not ratified this Convention" (p. 1). The *jure gentium* prohibition under international human rights law against the execution of the mentally ill or the retarded is also virtually unchallenged other than by the United States and a few other pariah nation-states, which either refuse to recognize the prohibition or exercise reservations while signing treaties which prohibit such executions.

Nonetheless, even with international as well as other national prohibitions against the execution of juvenile, mentally ill, and mentally retarded offenders, the continued disparate sentencing and execution of Negroid, and other non-White, juvenile and adult offenders in the United States continues to be the natural outcome of these minorities' limited assimilation and vast social distance. It also continues to be the natural outcome of contradictory valuations and of the dissonance which exists between general basic valuations and specific valuations as well as of the dissonance between valuations and the actualization of valuations. Put simply, the actions of people frequently conflict with their democratic, nonracist valuations. Beliefs (valuations) and actions conflict especially when fear and perceived vested interest create a "we" and [a historic] "them" (or "those people") reality. When "those people" suffer considerable social distance based upon alleged atavism and phenotypic difference coupled with the myths of "not belonging" and of 'threat," one should expect a targeted response by both the adult and the juvenile justice systems, which may include capital punishment and the negation of the concept of *parens patriae.* Unfortunately, disdain for, or ignorance of, *jure gentium* by state and federal prosecutors has resulted in the violation of *jus cogens* standards prohibiting the execution of mentally ill and mentally defective inmates as well as juvenile offenders, regardless of their race. Mentally defective and mentally ill inmates, who are similar to juvenile offenders under international human rights law, are reserved protections similar to those for offenders considered under the *parens patriae* concept of U.S. jurisprudence. However, the social distance which exists between Black juvenile offenders, many of whom are mentally ill and/or mentally defective, and the officers of the court and the juries, which judge the offenders, results too frequently in their executions. The execution of Black juvenile offenders is the probable logical consequence of the aforementioned disdain, which has placed the United States within the ranks of pariah nation-states that treat minority juvenile offenders, especially Black juvenile offenders, as undeserving of mercy and thus as criminals rather than as persons under the protection of *parens patriae*.

REFERENCES

Amnesty International. (1998). *Fair trials manual.* London: Amnesty International Publications.

Amnesty International. (2002a). *Children and the death penalty: Executions worldwide since 1990.* (Publication No. AI Index: ENGACT 50/007/2002). Retrieved June 2003: http://www.amnestyusa.org.

Amnesty International. (2002b). *United States of America arbitrary, discriminatory, and cruel: An aide-memoire to 25 years of judicial killing, January 2002.* Publication No. AI Index: AMR 51/003/2002). Retrieved June 2003: http://www.amnesty usa.org.

Amnesty International. (2002c*). United States of America indecent and internationally illegal: The death penalty against child offenders, September 2002.* (Publication No. AI Index: AMR 51/143/2002). Retrieved June 2003: http://www. amnestyusa.org.

Amnesty International. (2003a). *Amnesty International report 2003.* New York: Amnesty International Publications.

Amnesty International. (2003b*). Facts and figures on the death penalty, April 2003.* (Publication No. AI Index: ACT 50/005/2003). Retrieved June 2003: http://www. amnestyusa.org.

Amnesty International. (2003c). *Fact sheet, death penalty facts.* Retrieved June 2003: http://www.amnestyusa.org/abolish/juveniles.html.

Amnesty International. (2003d). *United States of America death by discrimination the continuing role of race in capital cases, April 2003.* (Publication No. AI Index AMR 51/046/2003). Retrieved June 2003: http://www.amnestyusa.org.

Bagwell, O., Bellows, S. (Producers), & Chin, M. (Director of Photography). (1998). *Africans in America.* Boston: WGBH Video.

Bogardus, E. S. (1968). Comparing racial distance in Ethiopia, South Africa, and the United States. *Sociology and Social Research, 52,* 152.

Coker v. Georgia, 433 U.S. 584 (1977).

Convention on the Rights of the Child (Article 37 (a)), 1995; The Convention on the Rights of the Child was adopted by the UN General Assembly in 1989 and entered into force in 1990.

Georges-Abeyie, D. E. (2001). Foreword—Petit apartheid in criminal justice: "The more 'things' change, the more 'things' remain the same." In D. M. Iovanovic and K. K. Russell. (2001). *Petit apartheid in the U.S. criminal justice system: The dark figure of racism.* Durham, North Carolina: Carolina Academic Press, ix–xiv.

Georges-Abeyie, D. E. (1990). Criminal justice processing of non-white minorities. In B. D. MacLean and D. Milovanovic. (1990). *Racism, empiricism, and criminal justice* (pp. 25–34). Vancouver, Canada: The Collective Press.

Georges-Abeyie, D. E. (19990). The myth of a racist criminal justice system? In B. D. MacLean and D. Milovanovic. (1990). *Racism, empiricism, and criminal justice.* Vancouver, Canada: The Collective Press, 11–14.

Gordon, M. (1964). *Assimilation in American life.* New York: Oxford University Press.

Guggenheim, C. (Producer), & Shields, C. (Editor). (1995). *Shadow of hate in America.* Montgomery, AL: Teaching Tolerance for the Southern Poverty Law Center.

Hawkins, D. F. (1983). Black and white homicide differentials: Alternatives to an inadequate theory. *Criminal Justice and Behavior, 10,* 407–440.

International Covenant on Civil and Political Rights was adopted in 1966 by the UN General Assembly and entered into force in 1976.

Johnson, C., Smith, P., & WGBH Series Research Team. (1998). *Africans in America: America's journey through slavery.* San Diego: Harcourt. (Accompanies the video *Africans in America.*)

MacLean, B. D. & Milovanovic, D. (1990*). Racism, empiricism, and criminal justice.* Vancouver, Canada: The Collective Press.

Milovanovic, D., & Russell, K. K. (2001). *Petit apartheid in the U.S. criminal justice system: The dark figure of racism.* Durham, North Carolina: Carolina Academic Press.

Moore, M. (Producer), & Moore, M. (Director). (2002). *Bowling for Columbine.* GermanIconolatry Productions, Inc. and VIF Babelsberger Filmproduktion Gmbh & Co. Zweite KG.

NAACP-LDF. (2002). *Death row U.S.A.* New York: NAACP-LDF.

National Coalition to Abolish the Death Penalty. (2003a). Fact Sheet: *The Ku Klux Klan love the death penalty!* Retrieved June 2003: http://www.ncadp.org/html.

National Coalition to Abolish the Death Penalty. (2003b). Fact Sheet 1: *America's shame—killing kids.* Retrieved June 2003: http://www.nacdp.org/html/fact1.html.

National Coalition to Abolish the Death Penalty. (2003c). Fact Sheet 2: *Executing minorities: An American tradition.* Retrieved June 2003: *http://www.ncadp.org/ html/fact2/html.*

Owen, C. A., Eisen, H. C., & McFaul, T. R. (1981). A half-century of social distance research: National replication of the Bogardus Studies. *Sociology and Social Science Research, 66,* 89; and unpublished data.

Parrillo, V. N. (1985). *Strangers to these shores.* (2nd ed.). New York: John Wiley & Sons.

Parrillo, V. N. (2003). *Strangers to these shores.* (7th ed.). Boston: Allyn and Bacon.

Reid, S. T. (2004). *Criminal law.* (6th ed.). New York: McGraw-Hill.

Second Optional Protocol to the International Covenant on Civil and Political Rights, aiming at the abolition of the death penalty, was adopted by the United Nations General Assembly in 1989 and entered into force in 1991.

Streib, V. L. (2002). *The juvenile death penalty today: Death sentences and executions for juvenile crimes January 1, 1973–December 31, 2002. Retrieved* June 2003: http:// www.law.onu.edu/faculty/streib.

United Nations. (2002) *Report of the UN special rapporteur on extrajudicial, summary or arbitrary executions.* (United Nations Document No. A/51/457, paragraph 115*).* New York: United Nations.

United Nations Human Relations Commission. (1995). (United Nations Document No. CCPR/C/79/Add.50, 7 April 1995, paragraph 16). New York: United Nations.

Universal Declaration of Human Rights, adopted and proclaimed by the General Assembly, *United Nations Resolution 217 A (III) of December 1948.*

Williams, R. M. (1970). *American society: A sociological interpretation.* (3rd ed.). New York: Knopf, 1970.

Chapter Nine*

Disproportionate Minority Confinement (DMC) of Youth: An Analysis of State and Federal Efforts to Address the Issue

Michael J. Leiber

Since the mid-1990s, states participating in the Federal Formula Grants Program have been required to determine whether disproportionate minority confinement (DMC) exists in secure facilities, identify the causes, and develop and implement corrective strategies. DMC, a core requirement of the Juvenile Justice and Delinquency Prevention Act of 1974, as amended, consists of four interrelated stages: identification, assessment, intervention, and monitoring. The objective of the present research is to examine compliance with the identification and assessment stages of the DMC mandate. More specifically, the inquiry focuses on the extent of minority overrepresentation in states' juvenile justice systems and assessments of its causes. The discussion concludes with an examination of the politics and practical limitations that affect implementation of the DMC requirement.

Introduction

In 1992, the issue of disproportionate minority youth confinement (DMC) was included as a core requirement of the Juvenile Justice and Delinquency

* The following article first appeared in *Crime and Delinquency*, 48 (1), pp. 3–45. Copyright 2002 © by Michael Lieber. Reprinted by Permission of Sage Publications, Thousand Oaks, CA.

Prevention Act of 1974, as amended, along with the deinstutionalization of status offenders, the removal of juveniles in adult jails, and the separation of juveniles from adults in institutions. Beginning with fiscal year 1994 funds, states participating in the Federal Formula Grants Program were required to determine whether disproportionate minority confinement exists, identify the causes, and develop and implement corrective strategies (Federal Register, 1991, p. 22969; Hsia, 1999). States failing to make progress or at least show a good-faith effort toward this endeavor risked losing one fourth of their formula grant funds for that year and having to direct the remaining three fourths toward achieving compliance.[1]

The main objective of the present research is to examine the DMC mandate and state efforts to comply. The research focuses on two key components of the mandate: identification of the extent of minority overrepresentation in states' juvenile justice systems and assessment of the causes of DMC. The discussion centers on the politics and the practical limitations that surround and hinder the implementation of the DMC requirement as well as the learning curve experienced by the Office of Juvenile Justice and Delinquency Prevention (OJJDP), individual states, and the country as a whole in the past decade. The DMC requirement, however, is first discussed in greater detail followed by a brief discussion of the historical factors that influenced and shaped the focus of the mandate.

Although a considerable amount of freedom is allowed in addressing DMC, states have to indicate in their application for formula grants how they are progressing on this issue within the context of four interrelated phases or stages: the identification phase, the assessment phase, the intervention phase, and the monitoring phase (U.S. Department of Justice, 1990; 2000). The first phase is descriptive and involves the identification of the number and proportion of minority youth in arrests, secure detention facilities, secure correctional facilities, jails, and lockups. All figures should have distinguished between White versus other specific racial and ethnic groups. Statewide and county or jurisdictional breakdowns were also to be given. Where quantifiable documentation was not available, states were to provide a time-limited plan of action, not to exceed six months, that included the development and implementation of a system for

---

1. The Formula Grants Program is a federal incentive for states to comply with the mandates of the Juvenile Justice and Delinquency Prevention Act. The amount of federal money awarded to an individual state, based on the number of persons in the state age 17 and younger, can be significant. For example, in 1998, California received $7,839,000, Florida received $3,026.000, and Oklahoma received $779,000 (Office of Juvenile Justice and Delinquency Prevention, 1998).

the ongoing collection, analysis, and dissemination of information to determine whether disproportionate minority confinement is present.

If a determination had been made from Phase 1 that disproportionate minority representation exists, the state is required to conduct an assessment to investigate the specific reasons for this situation. The assessment phase attempts to address why minority overrepresentation exists. Assessments are expected to, at a minimum, explain differences between Whites and minorities in arrest, diversion, adjudication, and court disposition, including differences for secure detention and other incarceration and waiver of youth to adult court. Because of financial concerns, information can be provided on at least three counties in the state where minorities have the highest concentration of the youth population at risk. In addition, if there is more than one minority group that represents at least 1% of the statewide or county population, separate data should be presented for each group. If a completed assessment has not occurred, the state is required to submit a time-limited plan of action indicating how and when the assessment will be completed.

The third and fourth stages of the DMC requirement entail specific interventions and/or programs to reduce disproportionate minority overrepresentation and ongoing monitoring or systematic tracking of overrepresentation over time. The monitoring stage also includes the evaluation of intervention strategies to address DMC.

A Systems Perspective Focus

The traditional explanations for minority overrepresentation in both the juvenile and criminal justice systems have been differential offending and/or selection bias (e.g., Farrington, Loeber, Stouthamer-Loeber, Van Kammen, & Schmidt, 1996; Hindelang, 1978; Hindelang, Hirschi, & Weis, 1981). Between 1983 and 1992, juvenile arrests for all violent crime increased by 82% for Whites and 43% for African Americans, with the greatest change for robbery and homicide (e.g., Bilchik, 1999; Hawkins, Laub, Lauritsen, & Cothern, 2000). The dramatic rise in violent juvenile crime during this time and arrests for involvement in drugs were factors that contributed to minority overrepresentation in the juvenile justice system (e.g., Tonry, 1995) and could have easily directed the DMC initiative toward differences in the participation of these behaviors. Those involved in bringing attention to minority youth overrepresentation in the juvenile justice system as an issue, however, focused instead on selection bias and, specifically, the inequitable use of confinement for Whites and minorities.

As discussed by Feyerherm (1995), Congress, the Coalition for Juvenile Justice, the National Council of Juvenile and Family Court Judges, and concerned individuals (e.g., Ira Schwartz of the Center for the Study of Youth Policy and Barry Krisberg of the National Council on Crime and Delinquency) echoed this sentiment in flushing out disproportionate minority youth confinement as both a national and a state issue. For example, in 1987, Congressman Tauke, at a hearing before the House Subcommittee on Human Resources, stated that "minority juveniles are disproportionately incarcerated and we need to determine if a dual juvenile justice system is emerging" (p. 3).

In their third and fourth annual reports, *An Act of Empowerment* and *A Delicate Balance,* as well as at their spring conference held in 1988, the Coalition for Juvenile Justice (1987; 1989) focused on issues of minority youth in confinement and the differential processing of children of color. The theme of selection bias is also found in the title of the coalition's ninth annual report, *Pursuing the Promise: Equal Justice for All Juveniles* (Coalition for Juvenile Justice, 1993) and in the text, as in the statement, "Consistent with the mandates of the Juvenile Justice and Delinquency Prevention Act, the Coalition is primarily concerned with problems directly related to the juvenile justice system itself and, in this case, its potential for 'selection bias'" (p. 9).

The adoption of a systems perspective appeared to be the result of a reliance on the information provided by the Children in Custody Census of juvenile detention, correctional, and shelter facilities (Krisberg et al., 1987; see also Snyder & Sickmund, 1995). Data from the Children in Custody Census revealed the presence of minority youth overrepresentation and increased reliance on confinement that had been occurring since the late 1970s. Krisberg et al. (1987), for example, were among the first to show that the proportion of minority youth in public correctional facilities increased by 26% from 1979 to 1982 even though the number of minority youth arrested declined during these same years. Krisberg et al. (p. 184) also found that African American males were almost four times more likely than White males to be incarcerated in detention centers and training schools during this time.

Between 1985 and 1989, increases in minority youth overrepresentation were quite pronounced in delinquency referrals to juvenile court, petitioned cases, adjudicated delinquency cases, and delinquency cases placed outside the home (e.g., McGarrel, 1993). During this time period, the proportion of African American and Hispanic youth detained increased by 9% and 4%, respectively, while the proportion of White youth declined by 13% (Krisberg, DeComo, & Herrera, 1992, p. 2). In the 1990s, African American youth represented 41% of those held in detention, 46% in public long-term facilities, and 52% waived to adult court (Snyder & Sickmund, 1995, p. 91). In 1995, minorities made up 68% of the detention population compared with 65% in 1991 and 53% in 1983 (Sickmund, Snyder, & Poe-Yamagata, 1997, p. 42). The minority population in public long-term facilities (i.e., training schools) in 1995 was 68% compared with 69% in 1991 and 56% in 1983 (Sickmund et al., 1997, p. 42). Minority youth outnumbered White youth in public facilities by more than two to one. In private facilities, White youth slightly outnumbered minority youth (Sickmund et al., 1997, p. 42). One must keep in mind that minority youth made up 30% of the general juvenile population age 10 to 17. Of minority youth, African Americans represented 15%, Hispanics represented 12%, Native Americans represented 1.2%, and Asians represented 3.3%.

A review of the literature also suggests that research by Huizinga and Elliott (1987) and Pope and Feyerherm (1990a; 1990b; 1992) was influential in shaping the direction of the DMC requirement. Huizinga and Elliott (1987) used six waves of data from the National Youth Survey covering the years 1976 to 1983 and information from arrest records to assess the relationship between race, offending patterns, and the likelihood of arrest.

In an earlier study (Elliott & Ageton, 1980) involving the first year of the data (1976), African Americans were found to be disproportionately among the high-frequency offenders. With the exception of that year, Huizinga and Elliott (1987) found few consistent differences between delinquency involvement and racial groups for the years 1977 to 1980. Furthermore, Huizinga and Elliott reported that African Americans were apprehended and charged with more serious crimes than Whites involved in the same kinds of offenses. In their conclusion, the authors stated that "further investigation of the relationship of race to arrest and juvenile justice system processing is required if reasons underlying the differences in incarceration rates are to be more fully understood" (p. 221). Both Schwartz and Krisberg referred to these findings in their testimony before Congress prior to the passage of the DMC mandate in 1988.[2]

In 1988, Pope and Feyerherm (1990a; 1990b; 1992) received funding from OJJDP to conduct a literature review of research involving the study of the influence of race on case processing and outcomes within juvenile courts. For the years 1970 through 1988, Pope and Feyerherm found that roughly two thirds of the studies reported minority youth, primarily African Americans, received the more severe outcomes relative to White youth. In the more so-

---

2. That is, Schwartz's 1986 testimony and Krisberg's 1988 testimony before the House Subcommittee on Human Resources.

phisticated research, they found evidence of both direct and indirect race effects. The influence of race on decision making was not always present across the entire system or more or less pronounced at one particular stage in the juvenile justice system. Pope and Feyerherm, however, did find that a substantial body of research showed that the greatest disparity between racial groups occurred at intake and detention. There was also evidence that racial differences may accumulate and become more pronounced as minority youth go further into the system.

The Children in Custody data and the research by Huizinga and Elliott and by Pope and Feyerherm set the stage and agenda for addressing DMC within the context of the equitable usage of secure confinement for minority youth. Although the DMC requirement centered on confinement in secure settings or the back end of the system, the intent of the requirement was to focus on decision making at all stages in the system leading to confinement (Feyerherm, 1995). The emphasis on fairness in case processing and outcomes for minority youth lessened the concern as to why minority youth get into the system and, therefore, made the issue of minority criminality an unnecessary controversy (Feyerherm, 1996).

With a few exceptions (e.g., Bilchik, 1999; Hamparian & Leiber, 1997b; 1997a; Poe-Yamagata & Jones, 2000; Pope & Leiber, in press; Pope, Lovell, & Hsia, in press), information regarding state responses and progress toward compliance with DMC is lacking. Even the studies that have addressed DMC for the most part often use the requirement as a vehicle to highlight research conducted in one or a few states (e.g., Church, 1994; Devine, Coolbaugh, & Jenkins, 1998; Hsia & Hamparian, 1998; Kempf-Leonard, Pope, & Feyerherm, 1995; Leiber, 1994; Mann, 1994; Roscoe & Morton, 1994; Welsh, Harris, & Jenkins, 1996). Thus, little information is available concerning findings nationwide.[3]

The lack of research to the DMC requirement is puzzling and provides the impetus for the present study. The DMC initiative is a federal requirement for the 55 states and territories receiving formula grant funds (Bilchik, 1999, p. 10), and the absence of research into the topic raises the following questions: (a) What are states doing to comply? (b) What has been found? (c) What fac-

---

3. Until recently, the state assessment reports were not kept in a central location by the Office of Juvenile Justice and Delinquency Prevention (OJJDP). Information for this research was obtained from Community Research Associates, an agency that at one time had the Formula Grants Training and Technical Assistance contract with OJJDP. Also, OJJDP researchers, and some individual states generously provided copies of studies, Three-Year Plans, and Annual Plan Updates.

tors have had an impact on the implementation of the requirement? The present research addresses these three questions.

As of September 2001, most states that participate in the Formula Grants Program are implementing intervention strategies and policies following compliance with the identification stage and assessment studies conducted in the early to mid-1990s. A small number of states are in the process of an evaluation of the intervention activities and even fewer are at the monitoring stage (Devine et al., 1998; U.S. Department of Justice, 2000). Thus, the present research provides a comprehensive review of the information as reported by the states for the identification stage and primarily the first assessment reports and/or the State Three-Year Plans and Annual Plan Updates.[4] The review of the identification stage is based on 43 states and the District of Columbia. The evaluation of the assessment studies is drawn from 40 states.

The discussion of the results is organized around the identification and assessment stages of the DMC requirement. For the identification stage, documentation is required that indicates the extent to which minority youth are disproportionately arrested; confined in secure detention or correctional facilities, jails, or lockups; or transferred to criminal court. States calculate an index value of disproportionality to assess the extent of overrepresentation or underrepresentation for each of these outcomes.

The index value is arrived at by dividing the percentage of minority juveniles represented at each point by the percentage of minority juveniles in the state's total juvenile population at risk for secure confinement. An index value greater than 1.00 indicates that minorities are overrepresented. For example, an index value of 2.00 would mean that minority youth are represented at a rate twice their representation in the total at-risk population (usually defined as age 10 to 17). The greater the index number, the greater the amount of disproportionate representation. Conversely, an index less than 1.00 indicates that minorities are underrepresented. The information provided is as reported by the state, and no attempt was made to validate the accuracy of the disproportionate index value.

The review of the state assessment studies will present information on the study sites, the racial/ethnic groups involved, the decision-making stages investigated, the analytical procedures employed, research results, and the existence of race effects. The model for reviewing the assessment studies paral-

---

4. The State Three-Year Plans and the Annual Plan Updates outline and describe the state's juvenile justice system, problems and issues, juvenile population needs, and the state's plans to address the core Juvenile Justice and Delinquency Prevention Act mandates and beyond.

lels Pope and Feyerherm's (1993) method of review of research conducted on race and decision making. A race effect is defined as the presence of race differences at any decision point and involves a lenient and/or more severe outcome once relevant legal (e.g., crime severity, type of crime) and extralegal (e.g., age, family structure) factors are considered.

Results

The Identification Stage

The states' reporting of the index values for each decision-making point differentiated by minority, African American, and Hispanic is provided in Appendix A through Appendix C.[5] Before discussing the results, it must be noted that data limitations are evident and should be kept in mind. Information, for example, varied in the extent to which index values are presented for each of the eight categories. In addition, some of the states did not differentiate among minority groups and therefore failed to report identification information on African Americans and Hispanics. Another data limitation is that the data reported by the states are not for a uniform period. Some of the data are from the late 1980s, and some from the period between 1990 and 1996. Consequently, the time frame from which the data were collected needs to be considered when arriving at conclusions regarding the extent of DMC within a state and when making state comparisons on the issue. Despite these shortcomings, an examination of the data from the identification stage allows for several summary conclusions.

First, minority youth overrepresentation was evident in every state reviewed (see Appendix A). The extent of minority overrepresentation also was not limited to any specific region of the country. For example, Alabama reported slight overrepresentation at arrest (1.2), secure detention and secure corrections (1.3), transfer to adult court (1.4), and probation (1.1). Underrepresentation of minorities was reported in adult jails (.8) and adult lockups (.0). In comparison, the index values were much higher for minorities in Minnesota for arrests (1.8), secure detention (6.7), secure corrections (5.2), and adult jails (2.8).

Second, minority youth overrepresentation existed at all of the decision points. In fact, minorities were on average greater than 2 to 2.5 times their

---

5. Due to space limitations and lack of information, data are not presented for Native Americans and Asian Americans but are available upon request from the author.

percentage of the at-risk youth population (i.e., secure detention, 2.63; secure corrections, 2.64; adult jails, 2.01; adult lockups, 2.16; transfers to adult court, 2.55; and probation, 2.03). The exception was for arrests, but minority youth were still on average overrepresented (1.38).

Third, the decision point where minority youth overrepresentation was greatest varied by state. In Iowa, the index values were highest for secure detention (7.9) and secure corrections (6.6), whereas in Massachusetts the greatest overrepresentation was for minority youth placed in adult jails (4.7) and transferred to adult court (5.0). In Wisconsin, the highest index values were for adult lockups (6.8) and secure corrections (5.5).

Fourth and last, differentiating among minority groups indicated that overrepresentation existed for African Americans (see Appendix B) and Hispanics (see Appendix C). Also, African American youth overrepresentation was greater at each of the decision points than overrepresentation of Hispanic youth. For example, the average index was 3.23 for detention for African Americans compared with 1.41 for Hispanics. For secure corrections, the average index was 3.32 for African American youth, whereas for Hispanic youth the average index was 1.90.

In summary, the results from the identification stage confirmed trends seen in aggregate form from the Children in Custody series (e.g., Krisberg et al., 1987; Snyder et al., 1995). Minority overrepresentation existed across the country and in many instances appeared to be more pronounced in states where minority presence was small.[6] For example, states with larger minority populations (e.g., Alabama, Texas, Washington, D.C.) reported lower index scores, whereas states with smaller minority populations (e.g., Arizona, Iowa, Minnesota) indicated higher index scores.

Minority youth were disproportionately involved at each point in the system, but the stage with the greatest overrepresentation appeared to vary by the state. African American youth were overrepresented in the system more than were Hispanic youth. Recall that the information (index values) representing the identification stage did not generally involve the use of controls

---

6. I would like to thank a reviewer for pointing out the relationship between smaller minority populations and the reporting of larger index scores that indicate greater minority overrepresentation in the juvenile justice system. Because information from the identification stage is descriptive in nature and controls for legal factors are absent, it is difficult to provide firm conclusions regarding the relationship. Drawing on traditional versions of conflict theory, it could be that groups lacking numbers (and economic and political resources) increase their likelihood of arrest and increased social control (e.g., Chambliss & Seidman, 1971; Frazier, Bishop, & Henretta, 1992).

for the factors that might explain minority overrepresentation (i.e., those related to explaining differences in offending and legal considerations). Next, the discussion focuses on state efforts to understand the causes of minority youth overrepresentation in arrests and the juvenile justice system.

The Assessment Stage

In theory, the assessment phase of the DMC initiative should have been based on the results from the identification stage and the minority composition of jurisdictions (Hamparian & Leiber, 1997a; U.S. Department of Justice, 1990). The assessment should have focused on all decision points and multiple jurisdictions and separated out among minority groups. Similar to the results from the identification stage, the review of the state studies revealed gaps in theory versus implementation. Appendix D provides a summary of the assessments conducted by states to address why minority overrepresentation existed.[7]

Because there is no standard procedure for conducting the assessment, individual states varied in their research strategies. Some states did not examine decision making across stages and instead focused on one to two stages (e.g., Mississippi, South Carolina). Some states also focused only on Whites and African Americans (e.g., Georgia) or collapsed all minorities into one group called minority (e.g., Delaware) or non-White (e.g., Florida). Bivariate analysis in the form of cross-tabulations (i.e., race by decision making stage) was also used in a number of studies that sometimes controlled for the seriousness of the offense (e.g., Alabama, North Dakota) to comply with the assessment phase of the DMC requirement. In many ways, the methodological and empirical limitations of these state assessment studies paralleled those that plague research on race and juvenile justice decision making in general (Bishop & Frazier, 1988; Leiber, 1995; Leiber & Stairs, 1999; Pope & Feyerherm, 1992; Pope et al., in press). On a positive note, a majority of the studies used multivariate analyses and qualitative techniques (i.e., surveys, interviews, observations, focus groups) to examine the causes of DMC (e.g., Arizona, Connecticut, Hawaii).

Despite the variability in the analytic strategies, most studies ($n = 32$) found evidence of race differences in juvenile justice outcomes that are not totally accounted for by differential involvement in crime. In 12 states, minority over-

---

7. It is important to note that although the discussion of the results from the assessment stage are generalized to a state, research used jurisdictions within states as the unit of analysis to comply with this phase of the DMC requirement (see Appendix D).

representation was determined to be the result of solely legal factors (i.e., severity of the crime).

Most states that conducted more rigorous assessments by using multivariate techniques showed evidence of direct and indirect race effects on decision making (cf. Hawaii, Massachusetts, Wisconsin). Research in Florida and Maryland, for example, indicated overrepresentation of minority youth throughout the system (Bishop & Frazier, 1990; Iyengar, Wynn, & Perry, 1995). Likewise, minority overrepresentation was found in 10 of the 15 decision points examined in Arizona (Bortner, Burgess, Schneider, & Hall, 1993), whereas in Pennsylvania race effects were evident at all stages but adjudication (Kempf-Leonard, 1992). In Iowa, race effects varied by jurisdiction, stage in the proceedings, and racial group (Leiber, 1992a; 1992b; see also Leiber, in press; Leiber & Jamieson, 1995). In one jurisdiction, Native American youth, for example, were more likely to be released and diverted at intake than were Whites and African Americans. In the same jurisdiction, both Native Americans and African Americans were released at petition once relevant legal and extralegal factors were controlled.

In Ohio, race had a direct effect on detention decisions, and detention status, in turn, affected decisions to commit juveniles to correctional facilities (Dunn, Cernkovich, Perry, & Wicks, 1993). A similar indirect race effect through detention was found in Washington (Bridges, Conley, Beretta, & Engen, 1993), and in Michigan, race operated through the status of the family household (Bynum, Wordes, & Corley, 1993).

Although studied less frequently than any other stage in the system, police decision making was also found to contribute to minority overrepresentation (Bynum et al., 1993; cf. Harris, Huenjke, Rodriguez-Labarca, & O'Connell, 1998). In Connecticut, for example, racial disparity was found at several police decision-making points (length of time held at the police station, use of secure holding, and placement in detention) (Hartstone & Richitelli, 1995). Similar findings were found in Washington, where Bridges and colleagues spent approximately 65 hours conducting participant observation with police officers in three counties with the largest populations of African Americans and Hispanics (Bridges et al., 1993).

In Iowa, the use of semistructured interviews with juvenile justice personnel showed that race bias was often indirectly operating through the respondents' perceptions of minority youth, in particular, African American youth, that were fostered by stereotyping and strong convictions about middle-class values and standards (Leiber, 1993). Beliefs about crime, the family, respect for authority, and the correctional ideology of the court had implications for case processing and outcomes that resulted in the differential treatment of

African Americans compared with Whites. African Americans were believed to be more criminal, reside with a single parent who could not effectively supervise and socialize their children, and lack respect for law and authority. Lack of respect was judged on eye contact, dress, and demeanor. The court's adherence to retribution or the maintenance of order or the protection of society or a legalistic approach had an impact on these beliefs about minorities at some stages and in some jurisdictions to influence decision making and the exertion of social control (Leiber, 1993).

In some states, race and gender interacted to influence decision making even after controlling for legal factors. For example, in Missouri, African American females were more likely to be detained in urban localities, whereas in rural settings, White females were more likely to receive informal supervision than any males or African American females with similar characteristics (Kempf-Leonard, Decker, & Bing, 1990).

Besides the finding of overwhelming evidence to support the presence of race effects in juvenile justice decision making, the locality of the court appeared to be a strong explanatory factor in understanding DMC. Although not addressed in great detail by most studies, a few of the assessments controlled for possible macroeffects or community characteristics on the case processing and outcomes of minorities and Whites. In Ohio, race was not found initially to be predictive of confinement disposition (Dunn et al., 1993). When community characteristics were controlled for in the analysis, however, minority youth were more likely to be given a harsher disposition than White youth. In Washington, county characteristics most associated with disproportionality were the concentration and growth of minorities in the counties, the degree of urbanization, and levels of violent crime and chronic juvenile offending. These contexts affected decision making directly and indirectly (Bridges et al., 1993). In Missouri, community characteristics on decision making were inconsistent. In urban courts, African Americans were more likely than Whites to be detained; in rural courts, race affected both detention and disposition decisions (Kempf-Leonard et al., 1990).

States also used surveys, interviews of decision makers, and focus groups as part of the assessment phase. Some states employed these techniques in conjunction with multivariate analyses (e.g., Hawaii) and/or bivariate analyses (e.g., Illinois). A wide range of responses were offered as to the causes of minority youth overrepresentation. A few states reported responses that emphasized discriminatory policies and procedures, racial stereotyping, and cultural and language barriers as explanations for DMC (e.g., Arizona, California, Oklahoma). The most common explanations of DMC focused on minority criminality and the factors associated with delinquency, such as poverty and the family (e.g., Alabama, Delaware, Nebraska, Texas, Utah).

Other responses also included the need for development of risk assessment tools, use of alternatives to secure corrections, and implementation of cultural sensitivity programs. In New York, for example, explanations for minority overrepresentation emphasized responses to behavioral problems occurring early in the youth's life, opportunities for and the use of probation and diversion, greater ethnic diversity in the workforce, and cultural sensitivity training (Harig, Amared, & Montfort, 1995). In South Carolina, social class rather than race was viewed as the cause of DMC. Responses focused on parental status, family income, and educational status as factors influencing decisions to supervise youth or place youth in restricted environments (Chishom, Teel, & Bashman, 1992).

Of the state assessments that incorporated surveys of youth, some of the respondents provided little or no indication of bias on the part of the juvenile court toward minorities (e.g., Hawaii, Virginia). In other localities, youth indicated police bias in terms of the likelihood of referral to juvenile court (e.g., Connecticut, Iowa, Massachusetts, Mississippi).

DISCUSSION AND CONCLUSION

The incorporation of DMC into the reauthorization of the Juvenile Justice and Delinquency Prevention Act of 1974 has resulted in a number of contributions to addressing the issue of race and involvement with the juvenile justice system. OJJDP, collaborating agencies, and invested persons should be acknowledged and commended for sensitizing states to the issues of minority overrepresentation in the system and racial bias, disseminating information, and providing technical assistance and funding for the development and implementation of initiatives to study and reduce DMC. The results from state efforts to comply with the identification and assessment stages of the DMC requirement, for example, provide information concerning the extent of minority youth overrepresentation in the system across the country, within individual states, and in localities within states. The findings also shed further light on the pervasiveness of racial discrimination within the juvenile justice system and reaffirm the belief that "race still matters" (West, 1993).

In addition, states such as Oregon, Pennsylvania, and Washington and local jurisdictions are funding and implementing strategies to reduce racial bias, use alternatives to secure detention, and prevent crime. These efforts have implications for affecting DMC (Hsia & Hamparian, 1998; Pope & Leiber, in press; U.S. Department of Justice, 2000; Welsh et al., 1996). Although there is no direct evidence linking DMC responses to national trends, the proportion of African Americans at most stages of the juvenile justice system was smaller in 1996/1997 compared with 1990/1991 (Snyder & Sickmund, 1999, p. 192).

Each of these contributions, in many ways, can be attributed to the DMC requirement and justify the continuing need for its reauthorization. Despite these contributions, the review of state attempts to comply with the identification and the assessment stages of the DMC requirement also shows that in many respects, the effort is fraught with problems.

Many states have not provided data for all categories of outcomes (e.g., detention, transfer to adult court) or distinguished and presented index information on these outcomes for multiple minority youth populations or for multiple counties (not evident in tables). Although a number of states have conducted exemplary assessment studies (e.g., Connecticut, Hawaii, Iowa, Missouri, Pennsylvania, Texas, Washington), the problems associated with the identification stage are also evident with states found to be in compliance with the assessment stage. Some states, for example, did not include in the analysis many of the relevant factors that influence juvenile justice decision making, failed to use multivariate analysis or multiple stages, or did not employ both quantitative and qualitative techniques. Findings of nonrace effects or race effects were often based on bivariate comparisons that sometimes involved controlling for crime severity.

Despite the variability in the quality of state efforts to address both the identification and assessment stages of the DMC requirement, few states have been found to be in noncompliance or had their formula grants funding withheld. The question that remains is as follows: What challenges has OJJDP faced in holding states more accountable? In many respects, the answers to these two questions are similar to those discussed by Ira Schwartz (1989), the former administrator of OJJDP, in his book, *(In)Justice for Juveniles: Rethinking the Best Interests of the Child,* which describes the implementation of the Juvenile Justice and Delinquency Prevention Act from 1974 to the mid-1980s. A decade or so later, the ability of states to fully comply with the DMC requirement of the act is also influenced by politics and the complexity of the issue, which includes practical limitations.

The political nature of DMC is not surprising. The topic of race and, in particular, race bias generates much controversy, especially when many people still think of discrimination only in terms of overt, blatant acts such as the Rodney King and Malice Green incidents. Although these occurrences are unfortunate, such blatant forms of discrimination are viewed by many as rare occurrences and declining in significance at both the institutional and the individual level (e.g., Wilson, 1980). Following the changes to the Juvenile Justice and Delinquency Prevention Act in 1992 that designated DMC as a core requirement, OJJDP and contract service providers were faced with educating people about the more common forms of subtle, indirect bias. They also had the daunting task of convincing states that DMC can be explained by both differential involvement in crime and racial bias.

Most of the data as part of the identification and assessment stages were collected during a period of increasing juvenile crime and the war on drugs. Consequently, states often operated on the belief that minorities were overrepresented in the system because they commit more crime and/or more serious crime. Many states were reluctant to spend time and resources on a topic where the answer to the DMC issue was already assumed or known.

Concomitantly, states, juvenile justice specialists, and juvenile courts did not want to be perceived as acting in ways or using procedures that result in disadvantage for minorities. For example, in some states, when race effects were found to remain once controls were employed, emphasis was placed on the greater strength of the legal criteria to predict decision making compared with race (e.g., Delaware). In other words, the presence of the statistically significant race finding(s) was downplayed.[8] States and other invested parties also exerted constant pressure on Congress to not include DMC in the reauthorization of the Juvenile Justice and Delinquency Prevention Act or, at a minimum, to "water down" the DMC requirement (e.g., Coalition for Juvenile Justice, 1999).

In response to these political factors, OJJDP has adopted a judicious approach to implementation of DMC, one which appears to follow the "spirit"

---

8. In Delaware, for example, assessment studies by Miller (1994) and Harris et al. (1998) highlight efforts that have methodological issues and arrive at conclusions that are questionable. The research results need to be viewed from what the studies did and did not do. Miller focused primarily on the back end of the system with dispositional sentencing involving felonies. She used multivariate analysis in the form of stepwise regression and some controls and found race to be a statistically significant predictor but it was the weakest of the predictors. Legal factors were the strongest factors. On the basis of these findings, Miller (1994) concluded that institutional race bias is not present. Although this conclusion may or may not be true, Miller downplays the finding of the race effect and the role that indirect subtle racial bias has in decision making. The research by Harris et al. (1998) also reached a similar conclusion that institutional racial bias is not present, because the findings of the study showed that minorities are not more likely to be charged with serious offenses or multiple charges than are Whites. This study and findings have been classified under the label "point of contact" to justify the possible release of a brochure informing citizens, especially minority citizens, how to conduct themselves when engaging with police officers. The dispersion of the brochure is a good idea. The study and findings by Harris et al., however, have been miscast because the research focuses on once arrest takes place and says nothing about factors leading up to the contact or what takes place when the contact occurs.

of the mandate and attempts to make inroads "to get something done" rather than accomplishing "nothing at all." While the strategy may be a reasonable and wise response to the political and economic realities of the implementation of legislation, it has come at the cost of providing specific instruction, consistency in the determination of compliance, and an accurate picture of DMC and its causes.

The dearth of specific instruction is evident by what states must specifically do to be in compliance, by vague criteria used to determine compliance, and by a lack of knowledge about DMC and research in general by some within the overseeing bodies. OJJDP wanted to provide states with freedom because of the belief that the resources and data needed to ascertain the extent of DMC, determine the cause(s), and address the problem could vary by jurisdiction (U.S. Department of Justice, 1990, p. 5). States were told that there is no "cookbook" formula to address the problem of DMC and the "overriding advice to planners is to provide the best information possible under existing state and local conditions and then to document carefully the sources and limitations of that information" (U.S. Department of Justice, 1990, p. 5).

Accordingly, individual states had to come up with innovative approaches to meet the DMC mandate. Although not an official position of OJJDP, an additional justification for keeping the implementation of the DMC mandate vague and loose is the diffusion of state resistance. By allowing states to come up with their own strategies to address DMC, OJJDP gave the appearance that the federal government was not telling states and localities within states what to do. That is, states and local jurisdictions, to some degree, could feel ownership of the issue.

States were encouraged to contact statistical analysis centers, management information agencies, and local universities for guidance in conducting an assessment study (U.S. Department of Justice, 1990, p. B-6). Further guidance was also available to states through the information provided on the methodologies and experiences of the five pilot states (Coalition for Juvenile Justice, 1993, p. 12; Devine et al., 1998; Rhoden, 1994), technical assistance manuals (U.S. Department of Justice, 1990; 2000), regional workshops, individual state training and technical assistance, and reports and updates. The lack of specific directions and the complexity of the research needed to assess the causes of DMC, however, often resulted in confusion for the states.

States often did not understand how to do an assessment study and/or were not in position to conduct the kind of research needed to identify the causes of DMC. Maintaining compliance with the other three mandates required the simple counting of the number of juveniles in adult jails, the number of status offenders confined, and the number of juveniles in sight or sound of adult incarcerated offenders. Compliance with the DMC identification phase involved a similar process that also included the calculation of proportion indexes. The assessment stage, however, is much more complex than the first three mandates and the identification phase of the DMC requirement (Church, 1994).

The lack of specific instruction also had implications for the reviewing bodies, the State and Tribal Assistance Division (formerly the State Relations and Assistance Division), at the federal level and the State Advisory Groups (SAG) at the state level. The State and Tribal Assistance Division is within OJJDP and administers the State Formula Grants Program and monitors each state's compliance with the four core requirements. Pursuant to Section 223(a)(3) of the Juvenile Justice and Delinquency Prevention Act, the governor in each state that receives formula grants funds must establish an advisory group consisting of a wide range of individuals representing local government, law enforcement, the justice court, a public agency representative concerned with delinquency prevention and treatment, and so forth. The SAG consults with the state on juvenile justice issues, including the four requirements, and approves the use of monies for initiatives and programs dealing with juvenile delinquency and DMC.

Some of the personnel from the State and Tribal Assistance Division and the SAG are not completely knowledgeable on DMC issues, the Juvenile Justice and Delinquency Prevention Act, and/or research in general. This state of affairs, along with the lack of specific criteria to determine state compliance with the assessment stage of the requirement, explains the variability in the kinds and quality of studies conducted.

The SAGs had been provided with even less direction. In response to questions about how rigorous state assessment studies had to be to meet compliance, the *Disproportionate Minority Confinement Technical Assistance Manual* (U.S. Department of Justice, 1990) stated, "The assessment of the reasons for disproportionate minority confinement must be specific and rigorous enough to satisfy the State Advisory Group that it has considered all reasonable explanations for the problem" (p. B-7). The lack of specific criteria and knowledge on the part of the SAG often resulted in a reliance on its own common sense and the judgment of the agency, group, or person conducting the assessment study to determine the merits of the research for meeting the DMC requirement.

Gaps between stated intentions and the actual implementation of policy are a common occurrence and so too is an evolution process or a learning curve that involves the increasing recognition of challenges, barriers, and successes over time. OJJDP, individual states, and consultants have gone through this process in the implementation of the DMC requirement. For example, OJJDP has begun to provide more specific instruction to members of the SAG, juvenile justice specialists, and personnel from the State Relations and Tribal Assistance Division. This specific instruction has come in many forms.

First, training has been provided at both the OJJDP national conference and the regional training conferences on how to address DMC (e.g., Office of Juvenile Justice and Delinquency Prevention, 2000). Personnel from the State Relations and Tribal Assistance Division have also been the recipients of a training session on the requirement and strategies to address the issue. Second, the Disproportionate Minority Confinement Technical Assistance Manual (2000) was revised for the specific purpose of providing the SAG, juvenile specialists, and others (e.g., research agencies) with more direction that included examples of model efforts and was written with the intention of being user-friendly. Third, an updated compliance determination checklist has also been developed for the state representatives and the states that consists of a series of questions with yes and no response categories (U.S. Department of Justice, 2000). More states are now provided DMC compliance determination letters that contain specific steps to take to further enhance the states' efforts to reduce DMC. Fourth, a number of states are receiving intensive technical assistance from OJJDP to provide greater guidance and overcome the shortcomings of previous efforts to comply with the DMC requirement. The intensive technical assistance also involves not only working with the SAG and other state representatives but people and agencies at the local community level. Finally, an in-depth study is underway that examines where states are in terms of compliance with the DMC requirement and includes the identification of promising strategies and interventions toward the reduction of DMC, barriers toward the implementation of these efforts, and technical assistance needs.

Notwithstanding efforts to provide more concrete instruction and information on barriers facing states and promising approaches used by states to reduce DMC on the part of OJJDP, practical considerations have hampered and may continue to hamper the full implementation of the DMC requirement. Some states have chosen not to deal with the complexity of conducting an assessment study that meets social science standards or, in some cases, even the minimum criteria set forth by OJJDP (e.g., differentiating among minority groups). States are often faced with the lack of critical data, such as relevant legal and extralegal factors and the various case outcomes within the juvenile justice system that are in an easily accessible format. Some states opt not to expend the resources (e.g., money, personnel, etc.) needed to manually collect data from juvenile court files and instead use incomplete data. In other instances, the data cannot be collected because no record is kept. Other practical considerations are limited staff, and in many instances, available staff perform a variety of roles with different responsibilities (e.g., formula grants, Title V Grants, Juvenile Accountability Incentive Block Grants). In addition, higher than normal staff turnover rates have proved to be most disruptive in terms of continuity. For example, many new personnel may not be aware of prior efforts to reduce DMC or, for that matter, understand the DMC initiative.

In summary, the politics of race, crime, and racial bias, coupled with state resistance and practical considerations, led OJJDP to adopt a tentative approach to DMC. This judicious strategy resulted in a number of significant contributions to understanding the issue of race and involvement in the juvenile justice system that includes sensitizing states to the issue and, in some instances, (e.g., Connecticut, Pennsylvania, Washington) a reduction in DMC and the adoption of innovative initiatives to address the issue (e.g., Harstone & Richetelli, 2001; Hsia & Hamparian, 1998; McHale, 2001; Oregon Youth Authority, 1999; Sayan, McHale, & Bridges, 2000). At the same time, however, the tentative approach also led to a lack of specific guidance and criteria to evaluate state compliance that resulted in inconsistent implementation of the DMC requirement. OJJDP has begun to address these deficiencies, and these efforts may result in a greater number of states becoming more committed to DMC and information to better inform strategies to reduce the disproportionate representation of minority youth in our juvenile justice system.

APPENDIX A

Identification Stage and Minority Youth Representation in the Juvenile Justice System

Index value[a]

	Minority Youth (%)	Arrests	Secure Detention	Secure Corrections	Adult Jail	Adult Lockups	Transfer to Criminal Court	Probation
Alabama	50.4	1.2	1.3	1.3	0.8	0.0	1.4	1.1
Alaska	28.0	1.4	2.0	2.4	NA	NA	1.4	NA
Arizona	40.3	1.1	1.4	1.6	NA	NA	1.8	NA
Arkansas	22.0[b]	1.6	1.3	2.7	2.2	NA	2.3	NA
California	53.4	1.1	1.2	1.3	NA	NA	NA	NA
Colorado	22.0	1.1	2.3	2.1	1.4	NA	NA	NA
Connecticut	15.3	3.0	4.8	4.5	6.6	2.9	5.2	NA
Delaware	23.6	1.4	2.3	2.7	NA	NA	NA	NA
District of Columbia	85.0	1.1	1.1	1.1	NA	NA	1.0	NA
Florida	45.0	1.7	2.3	2.8	1.9	NA	2.5	1.8
Georgia	35.5	2.1	1.6	1.9	1.8	NA	2.3	NA
Idaho	9.1	2.0	1.5	1.7	1.5	NA	NA	NA
Illinois	NA	0.5	2.1	2.0	0.3	1.2	0.2	NA
Indiana	11.9	NA	4.1	3.2	2.7	3.3	NA	NA
Iowa	4.8	2.7	7.9	6.6	NA	NA	NA	NA
Kansas	11.5	2.6	4.5	3.9	3.0	1.3	NA	NA
Kentucky	9.5	NA	5.5	NA	1.8	NA	NA	NA
Louisiana	38.8	1.5	1.5	2.3	1.4	NA	NA	NA
Maryland[c]	30.0	2.2	2.8	3.4	NA	NA	3.3	NA
Massachusetts	17.2	3.0	3.8	3.3	4.7	2.4	5.0	NA
Minnesota	4.5	1.8	6.7	5.2	2.8	NA	NA	NA
Mississippi	NA	1.3	1.4	1.8	1.2	NA	1.8	NA
Missouri[d]	13.6	1.8	3.4	NA	NA	NA	NA	NA

Montana	16.2	1.1	1.7	1.8	NA	NA	4.3	NA
Nebraska	8.4	1.9	3.6	0.0	NA	NA	0.0	2.1
New Jersey	29.0	2.1	3.3	3.0	NA	NA	3.0	NA
New Mexico	60.0	NA	1.2	1.2	NA	NA	NA	NA
New York	39.0	1.9	2.9	2.4	NA	NA	NA	NA
North Carolina	30.4	1.6	1.7	2.0	NA	NA	NA	NA
North Dakota	7.9	2.3	3.7	4.3	NA	NA	1.3	NA
Ohio	14.3	2.1	NA	3.0	NA	NA	NA	NA
Oklahoma	15.6	1.1	3.3	4.8	1.7	1.2	NA	NA
Oregon	9.1	1.4	2.1	2.1	NA	NA	NA	NA
Pennsylvania	14.3	2.1	5.5	6.1	NA	NA	5.2	NA
Rhode Island	12.4	1.6	2.6	NA	NA	NA	5.3	NA
South Carolina	39.0	1.4	1.7	1.6	1.4	NA	1.9	NA
South Dakota	13.4	NA	3.1	2.2	2.7	NA	NA	2.3
Tennessee	20.0	2.0	3.7	3.0	NA	NA	4.1	1.5
Texas	50.0	NA	1.3	1.6	2.0	1.3	1.3	NA
Utah	11.1	1.0	3.3	4.8	1.7	1.2	0.0	NA
Virginia	27.0	2.2	1.8	2.1	NA	NA	NA	NA
Washington	17.6	NA	2.5	3.7	1.0	NA	NA	NA
West Virginia	5.0	1.8	2.6	2.0	NA	NA	0.0	3.4e
Wisconsin	11.0	1.7	4.9	5.5	1.7	6.8	NA	NA

SOURCE: Updated Hamparian and Leiber (1997a; 1997b).

NOTE: NA = not available.

a. Figure represents index calculated by dividing the percentage of minority juveniles at each decision point by the percentage of minority juveniles in the state's total juvenile population at risk.

b. The data are based on an African American youth population of 22%.

c. The African American youth population is 30%. It appears that most of the minority youth population is African American.

d. Most of the minority population is reported as African American.

e. Out-of-state placements.

APPENDIX B

African American Youth Representation in the Juvenile Justice System

Index Value[a]

	Minority Youth (%)	Arrests	Secure Detention	Secure Corrections	Adult Jail	Lockups	Transfer to Criminal Court	Probation
Alabama	50.4	1.2	1.3	1.3	0.8	0.0	1.4	1.1
Alaska[b]	14.7	NA	1.6	NA	NA	NA	NA	NA
Arizona[c]	4.0	2.5	4.0	4.5	4.1	NA	NA	5.7
Arkansas	22.0	1.6	1.3	2.7	2.2	NA	2.3	NA
California	8.7	2.2	3.0	3.0	NA	NA	NA	NA
Colorado	5.0	3.1	4.4	3.8	1.9	NA	NA	NA
Connecticut	9.6	3.0	4.8	4.7	NA	NA	2.1	NA
Delaware	22.2	NA	2.3	2.7	NA	NA	NA	NA
District of Columbia	85.0	1.1	1.1	1.1	NA	NA	1.0	1.0
Florida	33.0	1.1	1.7	2.1	NA	NA	NA	NA
Georgia	33.5	NA	NA	NA	NA	NA	NA	NA
Illinois	NA	0.6	3.1	2.5	0.5	1.3	0.3	NA
Indiana	9.9	NA	4.1	3.2	2.7	3.3	NA	NA
Iowa	2.3	NA	NA	NA	NA	NA	NA	NA
Kansas	6.8	2.6	4.5	3.9	3.0	1.3	NA	NA
Louisiana[d]	38.8	1.4	1.6	2.2	NA	NA	1.6	NA
Maryland	30.0	2.2	2.8	3.4	NA	NA	3.3	NA
Massachusetts	6.0	4.7	5.9	5.0	3.3	2.9	5.0	3.8
Minnesota	2.9	4.3	10.7	7.1	2.7	NA	9.4	2.5
Mississippi	NA	NA	NA	NA	NA	NA	NA	NA
Missouri	13.6	2.2	3.3	NA	NA	NA	NA	NA
Nebraska	4.2	2.1	NA	0.0	NA	NA	0.0	NA
New Jersey	17.0	2.4	3.8	4.4	1.9	0.0	NA	NA

New Mexico	2.0	NA	1.5	3.5	NA	NA	NA
New York	19.5	2.1	3.2	3.2	NA	NA	NA
North Carolina	28.6	1.6	1.7	2.0	NA	NA	NA
North Dakota	<1.0	NA	NA	NA	NA	NA	NA
Ohio	NA	1.3	NA	3.3	NA	NA	NA
Oklahoma	6.9	NA	NA	NA	NA	NA	NA
Oregon	2.2	2.8	4.2	3.9	NA	NA	NA
Pennsylvania	11.2	NA	NA	NA	NA	NA	NA
Rhode Island	5.7	2.2	NA	5.6	NA	10.2	NA
S. Carolina	36.6	1.4	1.7	1.4	1.4	1.9	NA
Tennessee	20.0	.0	3.7	3.0	NA	4.1	1.5
Texas	12.4	1.6	2.6	2.9	0.0	1.4	NA
Utah	0.7	NA	NA	NA	NA	NA	NA
Virginia[e]	27.0	2.2	1.8	2.1	NA	NA	NA
Washington	3.8	3.9	4.0	6.6	0.0	1.8	NA
West Virginia	4.0	NA	NA	NA	NA	NA	NA
Wisconsin	7.2	2.2	6.6	6.5	1.2	NA	NA

SOURCE: Updated Hamparian and Leiber (1997a; 1997b).
NOTE: NA = not available.
a. Figure represents index calculated by dividing the percentage of minority juveniles at each decision point by the percentage of minority juveniles in the state's total juvenile population at risk.
b. Includes African Americans, Hispanics, Asians, or other in origin.
c. Maricopa County only.
d. Most of the minority population is reported as African American.
e. Washoe County only.

APPENDIX C
Hispanic Youth Representation in the Juvenile Justice System
Index Value[a]

	Minority Youth (%)	Arrests	Detention	Secure Corrections	Secure Jail	Adult Lockups	Transfer to Adult Court	Criminal Probation
Arizona[b]	24.0	1.0	1.5	1.8	NA	NA	1.0	NA
California	34.4	1.3	0.9	1.2	NA	NA	NA	NA
Colorado	17.0	NA	1.9	1.7	1.4	NA	NA	NA
Connecticut	5.7	3.0	4.8	4.0	NA	3.3	10.5	NA
Florida	10.0	1.0	0.7	0.6	NA	NA	NA	NA
Georgia[c]	2.0	NA	NA	NA	NA	NA	NA	NA
Idaho	6.4	NA	NA	NA	NA	NA	NA	NA
Illinois	NA	0.2	0.1	0.9	0.1	0.0	NA	NA
Kansas	3.8	NA	NA	NA	NA	NA	NA	NA
Maine	NA	NA	NA	1.0	NA	NA	NA	NA
Massachusetts	7.6	NA	2.1	2.6	5.3	2.8	1.8	2.7
Nebraska	2.7	1.1	NA	NA	NA	NA	NA	1.3
New Jersey	12.0	1.1	1.5	1.2	2.8	0.0	NA	NA
New Mexico	45.0	NA	1.2	1.3	NA	NA	NA	NA
New York	15.4	1.3	1.6	1.4	NA	NA	NA	NA
Ohio	NA	1.6	NA	2.0	NA	NA	NA	NA
Oklahoma	2.2	NA	NA	NA	NA	NA	NA	NA
Oregon	5.2	0.8	1.3	0.9	NA	NA	NA	NA
Pennsylvania	3.1	NA	NA	NA	NA	NA	NA	NA
Rhode Island	6.7	NA	NA	NA	NA	NA	NA	NA
Texas	37.2	1.2	1.0	1.2	3.0	NA	1.3	NA
Utah	4.9	NA	NA	NA	NA	NA	NA	NA
Washington	2.2	NA	1.1	2.5	1.0	NA	1.1	NA

| Wisconsin | 2.8 | 0.0 | 0.0 | 3.1 | 0.0 | NA | NA | NA | NA |

SOURCE: Updated Hampanan and Leiber (1997a; 1997b).

NOTE: NA = not available.

a. Figure represents index calculated by dividing the percentage of minority juveniles at each decision point by the percentage of minority juveniles in the state's total juvenile population at risk.

b. Maricopa County only.

c. Hispanic and Asian.

Appendix D
Summary of State Assessment Studies

State	Study Sites	Racial/Ethnic Groups Involved	Decision-Making Points Investigated	Analytical Procedures Used	Research Results	Race Effect(s)[a]
Alabama	Statewide, six counties	White/Caucasian, African American	Arrest, detention, court appearance, adjudication, probation, committed to Department of Youth Services, secure facility, or adult jail	Bivariate, surveys with judges	African Americans overrepresented at all points but jail; extent of overrepresenation varied by point of locality	No; overrepresentation due to legal factors
Alaska[b]	Statewide	White/Caucasian, Alaskan Native, African American, Asian, other	Referral, pre-adjudication, detention, intake, court proceedings, supervision	Bivariate	Race differences at all decision points; Alaskan Natives underrepresented in informal probation	No; overrepresentation due to legal factors
Arizona	Pima and Maricopa counties	White/Caucasian, African American, Native American, Hispanic, minority	Detention, adjustment, petition, judicial dismissal, commitment	Regression, interviews with range of individuals, public forums	Race differences at 10 of 15 decision points; extent of differences varied by group, point, and locality	Yes

	Location	Racial groups	Decision points	Methods	Findings	DMC
Arkansas[b]	Statewide, Jefferson, Sebastion, Washington	White/Caucasian, African American, other	Arrest, detention, commitment, waiver	Descriptive, Bivariate	Race differences at all points statewide, minority counties overrepresentation at diversion, extent of differences varied by group and locality	No; overrepresentation due to legal factors
California	Statewide, Los Angeles, San Francisco, Sacramento counties	White/Caucasian, African American, Hispanic/Latino, Asian	Detention, disposition, commitment to California Youth Authority, length of stay	Bivariate, multivariate, analytic models, some controls	Race differences at detention and sentencing; extent of differences varied by group and locality, but greatest for African Americans	Yes
Colorado	City and county of Denver, El Paso County, City of Lakewood, Mesa County	White/Caucasian, African American, Hispanic, other	Arrest, detention	Comparison of juvenile detention screening, and assessment guide to actual detention and placement; cluster profiles; focus groups; surveys of police; descriptive	Race differences varied by group and locality; gender findings noted	Yes

Appendix D (continued)

State	Study Sites	Racial/Ethnic Groups Involved	Decision-Making Points Investigated	Analytical Procedures Used	Research Results	Race Effect(s)[a]
Connecticut	Statewide, 26 police departments, 5 state police barracks, 14 Juvenile Matters Offices	White/Caucasian, African America Hispanic, Asian	Police decisions, petition, detention, official versus unofficial, service needs, probation recommendation disposition, length	Regression, interviews with delinquent offenders, public forums	Differences in African American and Hispanic juveniles at placement in secure confinement; of commitment extent of race differences varied by group and locality, but greatest for African Americans	Yes
Delaware	1. New Castle County	White/Black, Hispanic	Adjudication multivariate analysis, some controls	Descriptive	Minority over-representation due to crime	No; overrepresentation due to legal factors
	2. Statewide, 14 police jurisdictions	White/Black	Number of charges for felonies at arrest	Descriptive	Minority over-representation due to crime	No; evidence of harsher police charging patterns
Florida	1. Statewide, districts, Hillsborough County	White/Caucasian, African American, Hispanic	Referral, detention, prosecution, dispositions,	Descriptive; events associated with decisions	Nonwhite differences at all stages; extent of differences	Yes

State	Sample	Race	Decision Points	Method	Findings	DMC
	2. Statewide	White/Caucasian, non-White	Petition, detention, commitment, transfer to adult court	Analysis, bivariate, regression phone survey with juvenile justice personnel	varied by point and locality; overrepresentation greatest for African Americans Nonwhite differences at all points	Yes
Georgia	1. Sixteen police department and eight juvenile courts in eight counties	White/Caucasian, African American	Arrest, intake, adjudication, court disposition, commitment, placement	Interviews, regression model, path model	Perceptions of race differences at arrest, disposition and commitment; crime severity, demeanor, socioeconomic status, and presence of attorney influences decisions: race has indirect effects through these factors	Yes
	2. Sixteen counties (4 urban, rural)	White/Caucasian, African American	Adjudication, disposition	Archival analysis, scenario with judges and POs, bivariate	African Americans overrepresented at both points; youth treated more	No; overrepresentation due to legal factors

Appendix D (continued)

State	Study Sites	Racial/Ethnic Groups Involved	Decision-Making Points Investigated	Analytical Procedures Used	Research Results	Race Effect(s)[a]
				analysis, regression	severely in rural locality	
	3. Statewide	White/Caucasian, African American	Intake, detention, petition, adjudication, disposition, commitments	Regression	African Americans more likely to receive commitments	African Americans Yes
Hawaii	Statewide, family court, First Circuit, city and county of Honolulu	White/Caucasian, Samoan/African American, Filipino	Delinquent status, delinquent adjusted, petition, adjudication	Regression, focus groups	Minority over-representation at counsel and release and probation; extent of overrepresentation varied by group	No; overrepresentation due to legal factors
Idaho	Six counties	White/Caucasian, Native American, Asian	Arrest, diversion, detention, adult court, adjudication, disposition, commitment	Descriptive, regression, interviews	Minority over-representation, data problems	Unknown
Illinois[b]	26 counties; aggregate data, case-level data	White/Caucasian, African American, Hispanic	Police custody, detention, adult jail lockups, waivers,	Descriptive, bivariate, semistructured interviews with	Minority over-representation at most points and for most localities;	Yes

			corrections	youth		
Indiana[b]	Statewide, 11 counties	White/Caucasian, African American, other	Arrest, pretrial detention, petition, adjudication, sentencing, posttrial treatment	Descriptive, bivariate	African Americans overrepresented greater than Hispanics; Minority over-representation in length of detention, likelihood of petition, and placement of sentencing	No; overrepresentation due to legal factors
Iowa	Four counties	White/Caucasian, African American, Asian, Hispanic, Native American	Intake, petition, adjudication, initial appearance, disposition	Regression, interviews w/ delinquents; youth and decision maker public forums	Racial/ethnic disparity at intake, petition, and disposition	Yes
Maryland	Statewide, breaking counties into six areas	White/Caucasian, African American	Intake/referral, formalization, probation, detention, residential, secure confinement, waiver	Regression	African Americans overrepresented at all points; extent of overrepresentation varied by point and locality; gender findings noted	Yes
Massachusetts	1. Statewide, four counties	White/Caucasian, African American,	Arrest, adjudication,	Regression, surveys with	African Americans overrepresented	No; overrepresentation

Appendix D (continued)

State	Study Sites	Racial/Ethnic Groups Involved	Decision-Making Points Investigated	Analytical Procedures Used	Research Results	Race Effect(s)[a]
		Hispanic, Asian	detention, commitment	personnel, interviews with youth	greater than other minorities and present at all points and localities; other minority overrepresentation differ by locality; minorities overrepresented	due to legal factors
	2. Statewide	White/Caucasian, Hispanic, Asian	Arrest	Census block	Minorities overrepresented due to legal factors	No; overrepresented
Michigan	Police departments and juvenile courts in seven counties	White/Caucasian, African American, Native American, Hispanic	Law enforcement decisions, detention, intake, disposition at formal hearing	Regression; probit scenario and protocol analysis; interview with officers and juveniles in detention; observation	Race differences at all points; African American indirect effects with family; extent of overrepresentation varied by locality; gender findings noted	Yes
Minnesota	16 counties	White/Caucasian, African American,	Arrest, detention, out-of-home	Bivariate, regression,	Race differences at pretrial	Yes

	Sample	Races	Decision points	Method	Findings	DMC
		Native American	placement, waiver	survey of public hearings	detention and out of home; race differences varied by group and locality; presence of counsel important; data problems	
Mississippi	1990 Mississippi youth court data files focusing on county and urban courts	White/Caucasian, African American, non-White	Pretrial detention, final disposition, delinquency	Bivariate; some controls; vignettes; self-report of youth; surveys of police, prosecutors, adjudges	Race differences at pretrial detention and final dispositions	Yes
Missouri	Eight circuits focus on court files	White/Caucasian, African American	Intake, informal supervision, detention, petition, adjudication, disposition out of home, recidivism	Regression	African American overrepresentation at detention, petition, and out-of-home placements; race differences varied by locality; gender findings noted	Yes
Nebraska	1. Two counties	White/Caucasian, African American, Hispanic, Native American, Asian	Detention, petition, arraignment, adjudication,	Regression, survey, interviews	Race differences at detention and final disposition; race	Yes

Appendix D (continued)

State	Study Sites	Racial/Ethnic Groups Involved	Decision-Making Points Investigated	Analytical Procedures Used	Research Results	Race Effect(s)[a]
			disposition		differences varied by locality; gender findings noted; data problems	
	2. Four counties	White/Caucasian, African American, Hispanic, Native American, other	Predetention, petition, secure confinement	Descriptive, regression, interviews, survey	Race differences at each stage; extent of race differences differed by group, point, and locality	Yes
New Jersey[c]	Unknown	White/Caucasian, African American, Hispanic	Committed	Bivariate, some controls	Race differences to commit indirect effects with family makeup	Yes
New Mexico[b]	Statewide, unknown number of counties	White/Caucasian, Native American, Hispanic	Detention, secure corrections	Unknown	Race difference at both decision points; extent of race differences varied by point, groups, and locality	Yes
New York	1. New York City	White/Caucasian, African American, Hispanic	Probation referral, petition, arraignment interview with	Regression with hierarchical strategy, arraignment, and	Race differences at probation referral,	Yes

State	Jurisdiction	Race groups	Decision points	Method	Findings	DMC
	2. Erie and Monroe counties		focus groups	Structural interviews with juvenile personnel and practitioners, focus groups, work shops	sentencing; few differences between African Americans and Hispanics; data problems Perceived police response is different to	No, overrepresentation due to legal factors African Americans; gender discrepancies noted
North Carolina	10 counties	White/Caucasian, African American, Native American	Intake, commitment	Regression, focus groups	Race differences at intake and commitment; race differences varied by group and locality	Yes
North Dakota	Statewide; four reservations	White/Caucasian, African American, Native American, other	Arrest, referral, detention, adjudication, disposition	Descriptive, bivariate	Race differences at all points; extent of differences varied by group and locality; overrepresenation greatest for Native Americans; gender findings noted	Yes
Ohio	Statewide.	White/Caucasian,	Official referral,	Descriptive	Race differences	Yes

Appendix D (continued)

State	Study Sites	Racial/Ethnic Groups Involved	Decision-Making Points Investigated	Analytical Procedures Used	Research Results	Race Effect(s)[a]
	17 counties	African American, minority	detention, adjudication	probabilities, regression, interviews with youth, decision-making simulation	at detention; race/determinants indirect effects with secure confinement; extent of race differences varied by locality	
Oklahoma	Statewide	White/Caucasian, African American, Native American, Hispanic, Asian	Arrest, detention, placement, confinement	Descriptive, bivariate, survey of system personnel	Race differences at point but adjudication; differences greatest for African Americans; differences varied by group and locality	Yes
Oregon	Three counties	White/Caucasian, African American	Unknown	Some controls	Race differences varied by point and locality; race differences at secure confinement especially strong	Yes
Pennsylvania	14 counties	White/Caucasian,	Intake, petition,	Descriptive,	Race differences	Yes

State	Locality	Racial groups	Decision points	Methods	Findings	DMC exists?
		African American, Hispanic	detention, adjudication, disposition	bivariate, regression, interviews with decision makers	at every point but adjudication; race differences varied by group; case processing varied by locality	No; overrepresentation due to legal factors
Rhode Island	Statewide	White/Caucasian, African American, Hispanic, Native American, Asian	Amount of serious crime committed, lack of funds for attorney, background of youths	Individual and group interviews with juvenile justice personnel and community representatives	Minority over-representation	
South Carolina	Chester, Florence, and Richland counties	White/Caucasian, African American	Secure confinement	Descriptive, regression, interviews with focus groups	Race differences at secure confinement	Yes
South Dakota	Statewide, three largest counties	White/Caucasian,	Diversion, minority disposition	Regression adjudication,	Race differences at points; race interaction effects; race difference by locality; gender findings noted; data problems	Yes
Tennessee[b]	Three rural counties and six metropolitan statistical areas	White/Caucasian, African American, minority	Confinement, probation, waiver, diversion	Descriptive, bivariate	Race differences at most points; extent of race differences varied by point and locality	Unknown

Appendix D (continued)

State	Study Sites	Racial/Ethnic Groups Involved	Decision-Making Points Investigated	Analytical Procedures Used	Research Results	Race Effect(s)[a]
Texas	Three localities	White/Caucasian, African American, Hispanic, Asian	Detention at intake, referral to prosecutor, prosecutor's decision, disposition	Logistic regression, survey of practitioners, case scenario evaluation, regression, ANOVA	African American and Hispanic differences at detention and prosecutor's decision; interaction effect with prior referral and latter decision point; extent of differences varied by point and locality; gender findings noted; criminal history strongest determinant of case scenario evaluations	Yes
Virginia[c]	Six court service units	White/Caucasian, African American, Asian, minority	Diversion/petition, detention/release, adjudication/disposition, commitment	Series of studies, bivariate, regression path analysis, youth survey, focus	Race differences at diversion/petition and length of detention; race indirectly related	Yes

				group	to intake through source of complaint; race differences by locality	Yes
Washington	Statewide, six counties	White/Caucasian, African American, North American, Hispanic, Asian	Arrest, referral, detention, diversion, prosecution, adjudication, confinement	Regression, observation, interviews with officials and youth	Race differences varied by point and locality; race indirect effects with prior referral and detention on adjudication and confinement; levels of minority concentration, degree of urbanization, on levels of violent crime key explanatory factors	
West Virginia	33 counties	White/Caucasian, African American, other	Referral, arrest, detention, commitment, placement out of state	Bivariate, some controls	Race differences at detention, commitment, and out-of-state placement; race differences varied by locality; data problems	Yes

Appendix D (continued)

State	Study Sites	Racial/Ethnic Groups Involved	Decision-Making Points Investigated	Analytical Procedures Used	Research Results	Race Effect(s)[a]
Wisconsin	Brown, Fond du Lac, Milwaukee, Rock, and Waukehsa counties	White/Caucasian, African American, Native American, Hispanic, minority	Intake, petition, consent decree, waiver, adjudication, secure confinement	Descriptive, bivariate, multiple classification analysis	Race differences at some points; extent of race differences at case processing varied by group and locality	No; overrepresentation due to legal factors

SOURCE: Updated Hamparian and Leiber (1997a).

a. Race effect is defined as the presence of a statistically significant race relationship with a case outcome that remains once controls for legal factors have been considered. The race effect is considered a "yes" if the effect is present at any decision point and the outcome could be lenient and/or severe.

b. Report could be identification or assessment.

c. Information taken from state plan update or summary report.

REFERENCES

Bilchik, S. (1999). Minorities in the juvenile justice system. *National Report Series Juvenile Justice Bulletin.* Washington, DC: Office of Juvenile Justice and Delinquency Prevention.

Bishop, D., & Frazier, C. (1988). The influence of race in juvenile justice processing. *Journal of Research in Crime and Delinquency, 22,* 309–328.

Bishop, D., & Frazier, C. (1990). A study of race and juvenile processing in Florida (A report submitted to the Florida Supreme Court Racial and Ethnic Bias Study Commission). Gainesville: University of Florida.

Bortner, P., Burgess, C., Schneider, A., & Hall, A. (1993). *Equitable treatment of minority youth.* Phoenix, AZ: Governor's Office for Children.

Bridges, G., Conley, D., Beretta, G., & Engen, R. (1993). Racial disproportionality in the juvenile justice system (Report to the Commission on African American Affairs and Management Services Division/Department of Social and Health Service). Olympia: State of Washington.

Bynum, T., Wordes, M., & Corley, C. (1993). Disproportionate representation in juvenile justice in Michigan (Technical report prepared for the Michigan Committee on Juvenile Justice). East Lansing: Michigan State University.

Chambliss, W., & Seidman, R. (1971). *Law, order and power.* Reading, MA: Addison-Wesley.

Chishom, A., Jr., Teel, S., & Bashman, W. (1992). *An analysis of apparent disparities in the secure confinement of minority juveniles in South Carolina.* Columbia: University of South Carolina.

Church, V. 1994. Juveniles a generation at risk: Meeting disproportionate minority confinement mandates. *Corrections Today,* vol 56, Iss. 7 70–72.

Coalition for Juvenile Justice. (1987). *An act of empowerment.* Washington, DC: Author.

Coalition for Juvenile Justice. (1989). *A delicate balance.* Washington, DC: Author.

Coalition for Juvenile Justice. (1993). *Pursuing the promise: Equal justice for all juveniles.* Washington, DC: Author.

Coalition for Juvenile Justice. (1999). *Preliminary report on 5.254.* Washington, DC: Author.

Devine, P., Coolbaugh, K., & Jenkins, S. (1998). Disproportionate minority confinement: Lessons learned from five states. *Juvenile Justice Bulletin.* Washington, DC: Office of Juvenile Justice and Delinquency Prevention.

Dunn, C., Cernkovich, S., Perry, R., & Wicks. J. (1993). *Race & juvenile justice in Ohio: The overrepresentation & disproportionate confinement of African American & Hispanic youth.* Columbus, OH: Governor's Office of Criminal Justice.

Elliott, D., & Ageton, S. (1980). Reconciling race and class differences in self-reported and official estimates of delinquency. *American Sociological Review, 45,* 95–110.

Farrington, D., Locher, R., Stouthamer-Loeber, M., Van Kammen, W., & Schmidt, L. (1996). Self-reported delinquency and a combined delinquency seriousness scale based on boys, mothers, and teachers: Concurrent and predictive validity for African Americans and Caucasians. *Criminology, 34,* 493–518.

Federal Register. (1991). *Notice of FY 1991 competitive discretionary grant programs and availability of the Office of Juvenile Justice Delinquency Prevention Program an-*

nouncement application kit. Washington, DC: Office of Juvenile Justice and Delinquency Prevention.

Feyerherm, W. (1995). The DMC initiative: The convergence of policy and research themes. In K. Kempf-Leonard, C. E. Pope, & W. Feyerherm (Eds.), *Minorities in juvenile justice* (p. 115). Thousand Oaks, CA: Sage.

Feyerherm, W. (1996). *Disproportionate minority confinement: Lessons learned for the pilot state experiences.* Portland, OR: Portland State University.

Frazier, C., Bishop, D., & Henretta, I. (1992). The social context of race differentials in juvenile justice dispositions. *Sociological Quarterly, 33,* 447–458.

Hamparian, D., & Leiber, M. J. (1997a). Disproportionate confinement of minority youth in secure facilities, 1996 National Report, Prepared for the Office of Juvenile Justice and Delinquency Prevention State Relations and Assistance Division. Washington, DC.

Hamparian, D., & Leiber, M. J. (1997b). *States' progress in reducing disproportionate minority confinement (DMC), 1996, status of the states' report.* Unpublished manuscript. Cedar Falls, IA: University of Northern Iowa.

Harig, T., Amared, S., & Montfort, M. (1995). Disproportionate minority confinement: Preliminary analysis of findings in Erie and Monroe counties. (Prepared for the Juvenile Justice Project). Albany, NY: State Commission of Correction.

Harris, R., Huenke, C., Rodriguez-Labarca, J., & O'Connell, J. (1998). *Disproportionate representation of minority juveniles at arrest: An examination of 1994 changing patterns by race.* Dover: Delaware Statistical Analysis Center.

Hartstone, E., & Richetelli, D. (1995). An assessment of minority overrepresentation in Connecticut's juvenile justice system. (Prepared for the State of Connecticut, Office of Policy and Management Policy Development and Planning Division). Hartford, CT: Spectrum Associates.

Hartstone, E., & Richetelli, D. (2001). A reassessment of minority overrepresentation in Connecticut's juvenile justice system. (Prepared for the State of Connecticut, Office of Policy and Management Policy Development and Planning Division). Hartford, CT: Spectrum Associates.

Hawkins, D., Laub, J., Lauritsen, J., & Cothern, L. (2000, June). Race, ethnicity, and serious and violent juvenile offending. *Juvenile Justice Bulletin.* Washington, DC: U.S. Department of Justice, Office of Juvenile Justice and Delinquency Prevention.

Hindelang, M. (1978). Race and involvement in common law personal crimes. *American Sociological Review, 43,* 93–109.

Hindelang, M., Hirschi, T., & Weis, J. (1981). *Measuring delinquency.* Beverly Hills, CA: Sage.

Hsia, H. (1999, November). OJJDP formula grants program. *Juvenile Justice Bulletin.* Washington, DC: Office of Juvenile Justice and Delinquency Prevention.

Hsia, H., & Hamparian, D. (1998, September). Disproportionate minority confinement: 1997 update. *Juvenile Justice Bulletin.* Washington, DC: Office of Juvenile Justice and Delinquency Prevention.

Huizinga, D., & Elliot, D. (1987). Juvenile offenders: Prevalence, offender incidence, and arrest rates by race. *Crime & Delinquency, 33,* 206–223.

Iyengar, L., Wynn, F., & Perry, D. (1995). *The disproportionate representation of African-American youth at various decision points in the state of Maryland.* Summary Report Prepared for the Maryland Department of Juvenile Justice, Baltimore.

Juvenile Justice and Delinquency Prevention Act of 1974, Pub. L. No. 93–415, §223(a)(23).

Kempf-Leonard, K. (1992). The role of race in juvenile justice processing in Pennsylvania (Prepared for the Center for Juvenile Justice Training and Research). Shippensburg, PA: Shippensburg University.

Kempf-Leonard, K., Decker, S. H., & Bing, R. L. (1990). *An analysis of apparent disparities in the handling of Black youth within Missouri's juvenile justice system.* St. Louis: University of Missouri, Department of Administration of Justice.

Kempf-Leonard, K., Pope, C. E., & Feyerherm, W. (Eds.). 1995. *Minorities in juvenile justice.* Thousand Oaks, CA: Sage.

Krisberg, B., DeComo, R., & Herrera, N. C. (1992). *National juvenile custody trends 1978–1989.* Washington, DC: U.S. Department of Justice, Office of Juvenile Justice and Delinquency Prevention.

Krisberg, B., Schwartz, l., Fishman, G., Eisikovits, Z., Guttman, E., & Joe, K. (1987). The incarceration of minority youth. *Crime & Delinquency, 33,* 173–204.

Leiber, M. J. (1992a). Juvenile justice decision making in Iowa: An analysis of the influences of race on case processing in Scott County. Technical report. Des Moines: Iowa Office of Criminal and Juvenile Justice Planning.

Leiber, M. J. (1992b). Juvenile justice decision making in Iowa: An analysis of the influences of race on case processing in three counties. Technical report. Des Moines: Iowa Office of Criminal and Juvenile Justice Planning.

Leiber, M. J. (1993). The disproportionate overrepresentation of minority youth in secure facilities: A survey of decision makers and delinquents. Paper presented for the State Juvenile Advisory Group of Iowa and the Office of Criminal and Juvenile Justice Planning, Des Moines, Iowa, and the Office of Juvenile Justice and Delinquency Prevention.

Leiber, M. J. (1994). A comparison of juvenile court outcomes for Native Americans, African Americans, and Whites. *Justice Quarterly, 11,* 257–279.

Leiber, M. J. (1995). Toward clarification of the concept of "minority" status and decision-making in juvenile court proceedings. *Journal of Crime & Justice, 18,* 79–108.

Leiber, M. J. (in press). *The contexts of juvenile justice decision making: When race matters* (SUNY Series in Deviance and Social Control). New York: State University of New York Press.

Leiber, M. J., & Jamieson, K. (1995). Race and decision-making within juvenile justice: The importance of context. *Journal of Quantitative Criminology, 11,* 363–388.

Leiber, M. J., & Stairs, J. (1999). Race, contexts, and the use of intake diversion. *Journal of Research in Crime and Delinquency, 36,* 56–86.

Mann, C. R. (1994). A minority view of juvenile "justice." *Washington and Lee Law Review, 51,* 465–478.

McGarrel, E. (1993). Trends in racial disproportionality in juvenile court processing: 1985–1989. *Crime & Delinquency, 39,* 29–48.

McHale, R. (2001). *Minority youth in the juvenile justice system (DMC).* Olympia, WA: Governor's Juvenile Justice Advisor Committee.

Miller, M. (1994). Analysis of the dispositional guidelines for juveniles. Wilmington: Delaware Criminal Justice Council.

Office of Juvenile Justice and Delinquency Prevention. (1998). *Distribution of formula grants by state—FY 1998.* Washington, DC: Author.

Office of Juvenile Justice and Delinquency Prevention. (2000). *Regional training conference: Planning for Tomorrow.* Washington, DC: U.S. Department of Justice, Office of Justice Programs.

Oregon Youth Authority. (1999). *Addressing disparity in treatment of youth and its effect on disproportionate minority confinement.* Salem: Oregon Department of Justice.

Poe-Yamagata, E., & Jones, M. A. (2000). *And justice for some. Building blocks for youth.* Washington, DC: Youth Law Center.

Pope, C., & Feyerherm. W. (I 990a). Minority status and juvenile justice processing: An assessment of the research literature (Part I). *Criminal Justice Abstracts, 22,* 327–385.

Pope, C., & Feyerherm, W. (1990b). Minority status and juvenile justice processing: An assessment of the research literature (Part II). *Criminal Justice Abstracts, 22,* 527–542.

Pope, C., & Feyerherm, W. (1992). *Minorities and the juvenile justice system: Full report.* Washington, DC: Office of Juvenile Justice and Delinquency Prevention.

Pope, C., & Feyerherm, W. (1993). *Minorities and the juvenile justice system: Research summary.* Washington, DC: Office of Juvenile Justice and Delinquency Prevention.

Pope, C., & Leiber, M. J. (in press). *Disproportionate minority confinement (DMC): The federal initiative.* In D. Hawkins & K. Kempf-Leonard (Eds.), *Race, development, and juvenile justice.*

John T. and Catherine MacArthur Foundation, MacArthur Foundation Research Network on Adolescent Development and Juvenile Justice.

Pope, C., Lovell., R., & Hsia, H. (in press). *Synthesis of disproportionate minority confinement (DMC) literature (1989–1999).* Washington, DC: U.S. Department of Justice, Office of Juvenile Justice & Delinquency Prevention.

Rhoden, E. (1994). Disproportionate minority representation: First steps to a solution. *Juvenile Justice, 2,* 9–14.

Roscoe, M., & Morton, R. (1994, April). *Disproportionate minority confinement.* (Fact sheet number 11). Washington, DC: Office of Juvenile Justice and Delinquency Prevention.

Sayan, R., McHale, R., & Bridges, G. (2000, December 12). Washington's systemic and legislative approach to reducing DMC. Presentation at OJJDP's Conference Workshop for Reducing DMC.

Schwartz, I. (1989). *Injustice for juveniles: Rethinking the best interest of the child.* Lexington, MA: Lexington Books

Sickmund, M., Snyder, H., & Poe-Yamagata, E. (1997). *Juvenile offenders and victims: 1997 update on violence.* Washington, DC: Office of Juvenile Justice and Delinquency Prevention.

Snyder, H., & Sickmund, M. (1995). *Juvenile offenders and victims: A national report.* Washington, DC: Office of Juvenile Justice and Delinquency Prevention.

Snyder, H., & Sickmund, M. (1999). *Juvenile offenders and victims: 1999 national report.* Washington, DC: Office of Juvenile Justice Prevention.

Tauke, T. (1987, September 11). *Comments in a hearing of the House Subcommittee on Human Resources.*

Tonry, M. (1995). *Malign neglect: Race, crime anal punishment in America.* New York: Oxford University Press.

U.S. Department of Justice. (1990). *Disproportionate minority confinement technical assistance manual.* Washington, DC: Office of Juvenile Justice and Delinquency Prevention.

U. S. Department of Justice. (2000). *Disproportionate minority confinement technical assistance manual.* Washington, DC: Office of Juvenile Justice and Delinquency Prevention.

Welsh. W. N., Harris, P. W., & Jenkins, P. H. (1996). Reducing overrepresentation of minorities in juvenile justice: Development of community-based programs in Pennsylvania. *Crime & Delinquency, 42,* 76–98.

West, C. (1993). *Race matters.* New York: Vintage.

Wilson, W. (1980). *The declining significance of race: Blacks and changing American institutions.* Chicago: University of Chicago Press.

CHAPTER TEN[*]

THE POLITICS OF RACE AND JUVENILE JUSTICE: THE "DUE PROCESS REVOLUTION" AND THE CONSERVATIVE REACTION[**]

Barry C. Feld

INTRODUCTION

Through the prism of race, this article analyzes the social structural and political context of juvenile justice law reforms over the past half-century. My thesis can be summarized succinctly: Race had two distinct, contradictory and powerful influences on juvenile justice policies during the second half of the 20th century. During the 1950s and 1960s, social structural changes that began several decades earlier motivated the Supreme Court to reassess criminal and juvenile justice practices critically in response to broader concerns about racial discrimination and civil rights. The migration of blacks from the rural South to the industrial North and West in the decades before and after World War II

---

[*] The following article first appeared in *Justice Quarterly, 20* (4), pp. 765–800. Copyright 2003 © by Barry C. Feld. Reprinted with Permission of the Academy of Criminal Justice Sciences.

[**] Three anonymous reviewers provided helpful comments and suggestions to improve this article. Donna Bishop provided extraordinary critical and editorial guidance. A previous version of this article was presented at the annual meeting of the American Society of Criminology, Atlanta, November 2001.

increased the urbanization of blacks and placed issues of racial equality and civil rights on the national political agenda. During the 1950s and 1960s, the Warren Court's civil rights and due-process decisions imposed national legal and equality norms on southern states that still adhered to a segregated, Jim Crow legal regime (Mendelberg, 2001; Powe, 2000). The Court's decisions on school desegregation, criminal procedures, and juvenile justice all reflected a fundamental shift in constitutional jurisprudence to protect individual rights and the rights of racial minorities.

The second phase of juvenile justice legal changes emerged in response to the Court's Gault decision and culminated in "get tough" law reforms that now fall disproportionately on minority offenders. Although protecting minorities' liberty interests provided the impetus for the Warren Court's focus on juveniles' procedural rights, the Court's decisions facilitated and legitimated the increased severity of delinquency sanctions. Moreover, the Court's "Due Process Revolution" coincided with a synergy of campus disorders, escalating baby-boom crime rates, and urban racial rebellions in the mid-1960s. National Republican politicians characterized these events as a crisis of "law and order," appealed to white southern voters' racial antipathy and resistance to school integration, and engineered a conservative backlash to foster a political realignment around issues of race and public policy (Edsall & Edsall, 1992). From the 1970s to the 1990s, conservative Republican politicians pursued a "southern strategy," used crime as a code word for race for electoral advantage, and advocated harsher policies that have affected juvenile justice throughout the nation. Media coverage increasingly put a black face on youth crime that was exploited for political advantage. The increased punitiveness in juvenile justice, which began in the 1970s, continued into the 1990s as a surge in homicides among black youths provided further political incentive to toughen responses to youth crime.

This article synthesizes and analyzes research on history, law, sociology, criminology, current events, race relations, and media studies. The analysis treats changes in juvenile justice law and policy as the dependent variable: the procedural reforms of the 1960s and the harsher substantive sentencing revisions of the 1980s and 1990s. The article treats changes in social, structural, economic, racial, and demographic factors; coverage by the mass media; public attitudes; and political and legal actions as independent variables. Focusing on changes in the juvenile justice laws, it asks and answers important questions. In the first part, it addresses two questions: Why did the Warren Court's constitutional "Due Process Revolution" in juvenile justice happen when it did and as it did, and what were the social, legal, and political consequences? In the second part, it asks and answers the questions: Why did the conservative political backlash that successfully advocated more retributive policies to crack down on youth crime occur when it did and as it did? In both instances, I argue that race and the changing politics of race and crime significantly explain these legal shifts.

THE WARREN COURT'S "DUE PROCESS REVOLUTION" IN JUVENILE JUSTICE

In this section, I argue that in the decades prior to and after World War II, the migration of Blacks from the rural South to the urban North increased minority concentrations in urban ghettos; made race a national, rather than a regional, issue; and provided the political and legal impetus for the civil rights movement (Lemann, 1992). The civil rights movement challenged existing patterns of race relations, especially in the South, and expanded the state's role in protecting racial minorities (Orni & Winant, 1994). During the 1960s, the Warren Court's civil rights, criminal procedure, and juvenile due-process decisions reacted to these structural and racial demographic changes and provided greater safeguards for minorities. Unfortunately, increases in rates of youth crime and urban race riots coincided with the Democratic Party's support for civil rights reforms and the Warren Court's due-process decisions, and conservatives attributed the social unrest to liberal moral laxity and campaigned for "law and order."

Race and the Great Migration

The outbreak of World War I increased the demand for industrial production, curtailed European immigration, and created a need for laborers to work in northern factories (Gottlieb, 1991; Lieberson, 1980; Trotter, 1991). Between 1910 and 1920, more than half a million blacks responded by migrating to non-Southern states, followed by more than three quarters of a million in the 1920s (Massey & Denton, 1993). Between World War I and World War II, the devastation of cotton crops and the mechanization of cotton picking decreased the South's demand for black sharecroppers and increased the out-migration of blacks from the South (Lemann, 1992; Trotter, 1991). Another 400,000 blacks moved to northern cities as a result of worsening economic conditions during the Great Depression.

Depression, Southern racial hostility, Jim Crow laws, Ku Klux Klan violence and lynching, poor segregated schools, and job discrimination drove out even more blacks (Lemann, 1992). During World War II, defense contractors integrated their workforces, and more than 1.5 million blacks left their rural southern homes to work in northern industrial factories. In the 1950s and 1960s, another 1.5 million blacks left the South, and the proportion of blacks which were living in the South decreased from three quarters to about half (Lemann, 1992; Massey & Denton, 1993).

During the Great Migration, blacks almost always moved to cities. In 1910, less than one quarter of blacks lived in cities; by 1940, half did; and by 1960, more than three quarters did. To appreciate the magnitude of the change, in 1870, 80% of blacks lived in the rural South; by 1970, 80% resided in urban locales, half in the North and West (Massey & Denton, 1993). When blacks moved to cities, white hostility forced them to live almost exclusively in urban ghettos. Northern whites reacted to the flood of rural southern migrants with threats and violence and reinforced racial discrimination in housing, education, and employment (Hacker, 1995). White-imposed residential segregation created and enforced the black ghettos that now exist in almost every major city.

Coinciding with the southern exodus, whites began to move from cities to suburbs, isolating blacks in blighted inner-city ghettos. In the period after 1945, federal housing, tax, and mortgage policies subsidized the construction of single-family homes in almost exclusively white suburbs (Katz, 1989). The federal government simultaneously cut mortgage subsidies for the construction of rental units and reduced the availability of mortgage and home-improvement loans in sections of cities that were threatened by the "Negro invasion" (Gottlieb, 1991). The federal interstate highway program facilitated suburban expansion, and easy credit enabled more suburban commuters to purchase automobiles (Gilens, 1999). Even as federal highway policy subsidized the dispersal of whites to the suburbs, the location of interstate roadways disrupted many black communities and created physical barriers to contain their expansion (Katz, 1989). Industrial and employment opportunities began to move from the urban centers to the suburbs as well.

Despite general post-World War II prosperity, the plight of blacks urgently demanded social and legal reforms. The 1950s and 1960s witnessed a basic shift in the understanding of race and racial identities and the emergence of a more assertive civil rights movement that initially challenged segregation in the South and subsequently emerged as a social movement against racism throughout the nation (Omi & Winant, 1994). In 1948, the platform of the Democratic Party convention included a strong civil rights plank, reflecting both northern blacks' growing political influence and white liberals' opposition to segregation. In reaction, then-Democrat governor Strom Thurmond ran as a segregationist "Dixiecrat" in the 1948 presidential election, carried four southern states, and demonstrated the power of race as a basis for political realignment (Edsall & Edsall, 1992). Although Presidents Harry S. Truman and Dwight D. Eisenhower took important steps toward racial equality, such as integrating the military, Congress resisted antidiscrimination and civil rights laws, open housing laws, federal aid to education, and national health insurance. Conservative southern democrats in Congress occupied key committee chairmanships and blocked legislative initiatives for racial equality, social justice, and urban programs. During the Cold War and McCarthy era, conservative congressmen put advocates for civil rights and racial reform on the defensive.

Despite southern recalcitrance, the absence of racial equality and justice posed a national dilemma. The legacy of Hitler's racist crimes and international competition between capitalism and communism for the allegiance of decolonizing Third-World countries required a national response to southern racial violence and domestic apartheid (Kennedy, 1997). During the 1950s and 1960s, the Warren Court's decisions on desegregation, civil rights, and criminal procedures aimed to dismantle the southern caste system of white supremacy that had been established by law and custom and to impose national legal equality norms on the region (Powe, 2000).

Constitutional Protection of "Discrete and Insular" Minorities

The great black migration increased the visibility and awareness of the "American dilemma" and moved matters of race to the center of the nation's and the Warren Court's concerns about civil rights, crime policy, and social justice (Lemann, 1992; Myrdal, 1972). Population shifts made blacks an important electoral force in several swing states, which, in turn, altered the balance of political power and the constituencies of the respective political parties and affected the characteristics of justices whom Presidents Eisenhower, John F. Kennedy, and Lyndon B. Johnson appointed to the Supreme Court (Powe, 2000).

During its 1937–38 term, the Supreme Court reviewed the constitutionality of New Deal laws and distinguished between the scope of judicial review of economic legislation, to which it gave the legislative branch broad authority, and its scrutiny of laws that affected "personal" rights. In the famous Footnote Four of *United States v. Carolene Products* (1938), the Court announced that it would review more closely legislation that affected rights that were enumerated in the Constitution, extend the scope of judicial review to the electoral process to assure political fairness, and "strictly scrutinize" laws that affected racial and "discrete and insular" minorities whose rights could suffer continually from majoritarian legal domination in the political process (Cover, 1982; Powe, 2000). The Court's emerging individual rights agenda recognized that minorities perpetually lost in the political process because of their vulnerability to scapegoating and race-baiting by the white majority (Cover, 1982).

In the South until the 1960s, law, custom, and extra-legal violence combined to create a caste system of white supremacy (Gilens, 1999; Hacker, 1995). Southern whites excluded blacks from the political process; legally dominated them through duly enacted Jim Crow laws; and, for good measure, resorted to violence and terrorism (Cover, 1982). Southern terrorism flourished because law enforcement was almost exclusively local, political, and nonprofessional (Klarman, 2000). Whites resorted to violence when blacks sought to change prevailing racial mores and threatened the lines between superior and subordinate, between whites and blacks. Private terror, formal legal discrimination, and political exclusion combined to disenfranchise and subordinate southern blacks.

In the 1950s and 1960s, racial injustice and urban problems presented volatile issues that Congress failed to address because southern domination prevented the adoption of remedial legislation. It fell to the Court to fill the void in public policy, to pursue racial equality, and to protect individual rights and civil liberties by dismantling the entrenched social and legal order of "separate but equal" (*Plessy v. Feguson*, 1896; Powe, 2000). Although the NAACP Legal Defense Fund attacked "separate but equal" laws in a variety of forums, the crucial battle in the struggle for racial justice and the dismantling of southern apartheid occurred in the effort to desegregate schools. In *Brown v. Board of Education* (1954), the Warren Court struck down the "separate but equal" doctrine. Although *Brown* ordered states to desegregate with "all deliberate speed," southern leaders challenged the "lawfulness" of the Court's decision and urged "massive resistance" to federal judicial usurpation of "states' rights" (Powe, 2000). Southern opposition to court-ordered desegregation in the 1950s, the Barry Goldwater Republican campaign of 1964, and the George Wallace and Richard Nixon campaigns of 1968 demonstrated the power of racial appeals and "rightwing populism" as political organizing principles (Edsall & Edsall, 1992).

Pressure generated by the civil rights movement and the nationally televised violent southern repression of black protests eventually led to passage of the Civil Rights Act of 1964, which banned discrimination in schools and public accommodations, and the Voting Rights Act of 1965, which prohibited procedures designed to impede blacks' exercise of the franchise. Passage of the Civil Rights and Voting Rights Acts ended the legal foundations of the "southern way of life" and established a national legal norm of equality about race to which Congress and the Court obliged the South to conform (Mendelberg, 2001).

Criminal Procedure and the "Due Process Revolution"

As early as the 1920s and 1930s, the Supreme Court sporadically used the Fourteenth Amendment's Due Process Clause to review states' criminal justice administration and to protect blacks from southern injustice in cases like *Moore v. Dempsey* (1923), *Powell v. Alabama* (1932), and *Brown v. Mississippi* (1936), cases that involved mob-dominated trials, the appointment of defense counsel in capital cases on the day of the trial, and confessions extracted by torture (Kennedy, 1997). Southern appellate courts regarded the formalities of any criminal trial, however procedurally inadequate, as preferable to lynch-mobs' summary execution, whereas the Supreme Court believed that a criminal trial actually should determine whether a defendant was guilty or innocent (Kennedy, 1997; Klarman, 2000). Although oversight of state criminal procedures required the Court to depart from a century of legal tradition and principles of federalism, the Court's limited role in superintending southern criminal justice marked the beginning of its efforts to impose national legal norms of equality on regional deviation from elementary procedural expectations (Klarman, 2000).

By the 1960s, the issue of race was linked with distrust of governmental benevolence, concern about criminal justice decision making, rising rates of youth crime, urban disorders, the crisis of law and order, and the Supreme Court's due-process jurisprudence. The Court's criminal-procedure decisions responded to the structural and racial demographic changes described earlier and attempted to protect minority citizens from abuses of state power. The Court's criminal-procedure decisions followed closely on its civil rights opinions because those who were accused of crimes in the states consisted disproportionately of the poor, minorities, and the young. Several themes integrate the Court's due-process jurisprudence: a greater emphasis on individual liberty and equality, a distrust of state power, and a desire to impose the rule of law on administrative and police discretion (Graham, 1970; Powe, 2000). The Court's decisions redefined the relationship between individuals and the state; endorsed an adversarial, rather than a paternalistic, model to resolve disputes; and reflected the crucial link among race, civil rights, and criminal justice policies.

In re Gault and the "Due Process Revolution" in Juvenile Justice

During the 1960s, several forces eroded support for the "rehabilitative ideal" on which Progressives founded the original juvenile court and led the Court to give delinquents procedural safeguards. Left-wing critics described rehabilitative programs as coercive and discriminatory instruments of social control through which the state oppressed the poor and minorities (American Friends Service Committee, 1971). Liberals criticized the exercise of discretion by clinical personnel because these personnel treated similarly situated offenders differently and often invidiously (Allen, 1981; Mauer, 1999). Conservatives argued that rehabilitation "coddled criminals" and advocated "law and order" in response to rising crime rates and urban riots (Cullen & Gilbert,1982). By the 1970s, criticism of the rehabilitative model from the Left, Right, and Center shifted the focus of sentencing from the offender to the offense; placed greater emphasis on consistency, uniformity, and proportionality; and resurrected long-discredited modes of public and political penal discourse about retribution and punishment (Allen, 1981; Garland, 2001).

No systematic reexamination of juvenile courts occurred until the 1960s. The Supreme Court fired its first salvo in *Kent v. United States* (1966), in which it observed that "the child receives the worst of both worlds: he gets neither the protections accorded to adults nor the solicitous care and regenerative treatment postulated for children." *Kent* required some procedural due process in waiver proceedings in which a judge decided whether to transfer a youth from juvenile to criminal court for prosecution as an adult.

The following year, in *In re Gault* (1967), the Court concluded that many aspects of juvenile justice administration violated the Constitution and required a substantial overhaul. *Gault* identified two crucial disjunctions between the rhetoric and reality of juvenile justice: the theory versus the practice of "rehabilitation" and the differences between the procedural safeguards afforded adult criminal defendants and those available to delinquents.[1] Rather than accept uncritically the Progressives' rehabilitative rhetoric, *Gault* examined the punitive realities of juvenile justice. It candidly appraised the realities of recidivism, the failures of rehabilitation, the stigma of a label of delinquency, the breaches of confidentiality, the conditions of confinement, and the arbitrariness of the hearing process. *Gault* mandated some procedural due-

---

1. *Gault* involved the delinquency adjudication and institutional confinement of a youth who allegedly made a lewd telephone call of the "irritatingly offensive, adolescent, sex variety" to a neighbor woman. The police took 13-year-old Gault into custody, detained him overnight without notice to his parents, and required him to appear at a hearing the following day. A probation officer filed a petition that alleged simply that Gault was delinquent. The juvenile court judge heard no witnesses or sworn testimony, kept no record of the proceedings, and actively interrogated Gault about his involvement. After adjudicating him delinquent, the judge committed him to the state training school for the duration of his minority—up to six years—even though an adult who was convicted of a similar offense could have received only a $50 fine or two months' imprisonment.

process safeguards for delinquents who were charged with crimes and faced confinement: advance notice of charges, a fair and impartial hearing, the right to counsel, the right to confront and cross-examine witnesses, and the privilege against self-incrimination. Once *Gault* granted delinquents the privilege against self-incrimination, proponents of juvenile courts no longer could characterize proceedings either as "noncriminal" or as "nonadversarial." The Fifth Amendment privilege, more than any other provision of the Bill of Rights, provides the foundation of an adversary process and a primary mechanism to maintain equality between the state and the individual (Feld, 1999). *Gault* reflected the Warren Court's belief that constitutional rights and adversarial procedures would restrict state power and assure the regularity of law enforcement and justice administration.

In re Gault perceived a clear need for some procedures to protect delinquents and minority offenders. Throughout its opinion, the Court cited the contemporaneous findings of the President's Commission on Law Enforcement and the Administration of Justice (1967). A survey conducted for the commission reported that in 74% of the 207 larger juvenile courts that served populations of 100,000 or more, nonwhite juveniles constituted up to 40% of those against whom courts filed delinquency petitions. Five percent of the largest urban courts reported that nonwhites constituted up to 60% of the petitioned delinquents. Virtually all the juveniles who appeared in juvenile courts were not represented by counsel. Only 3% of the courts reported that lawyers accompanied delinquents in 40% or more of the cases, and only 10% reported that counsel appeared in even 20% or more of delinquency cases (President's Commission, 1967). Other analyses from the mid-20th century also provided evidence of racial biases in the handling of juveniles. A study of juvenile court dispositions in 1964 reported that black juveniles were referred for formal processing and committed to the state youth authority more often than were white juveniles with similar offenses and prior records (Arnold, 1971). An earlier study compared the characteristics of black and white delinquents who were committed to a state institution. It found that black youths were younger, had fewer prior court appearances or institutional commitments, committed fewer and less serious offenses, and received fewer probationary sentences than did the confined white delinquents and attributed the differences in patterns of commitments for blacks to the lack of other placement options (Axelrad, 1952).

In subsequent due-process decisions, the Court further amplified the criminal nature of delinquency proceedings. In *In re Winship* (1970), the Court held that the state must prove delinquency by the criminal standard of "beyond a reasonable doubt," rather than by lower civil standards of proof. The Court required the highest standard of proof to protect juveniles from unwarranted convictions, to guard against abuses of governmental power, and to ensure public confidence in the administration of justice. In *Breed v. Jones* (1975), the Court held that "double jeopardy" precluded the criminal reprosecution of a youth as an adult after adjudication as a delinquent in a juvenile court for the same offense. The Court posited a functional equivalence and identity of defendants' interests in delinquency and criminal trials.

In *McKeiver v. Pennsylvania* (1971), the Court declined to extend all the procedural safeguards of adult criminal prosecutions to juveniles. *McKeiver* held that the Constitution does not grant the right to a jury trial in delinquency proceedings because "due process" requires only "accurate fact finding," which a judge could provide as well as a jury. Unlike *Gault,* which emphasized both accurate fact finding and protection against governmental oppression, *McKeiver* denied that delinquents required protection from the state, invoked the mythology of the paternalistic juvenile court judge, and rejected the concern that closed juvenile court hearings actually could prejudice the accuracy of fact finding.

Gault and its progeny precipitated a procedural revolution that unintentionally, but inevitably, transformed the juvenile court from its original Progressive conception of a social welfare agency into a legal one. Progressive reformers intervened on the basis of a child's "real needs"—social circumstances, environment, and the need for rehabilitation—and regarded proof of a specific offense as secondary (Zimring, 2002). Despite *McKeiver*'s denial of a jury trial, *Gault* and *Winship* imported the adversarial model, defense attorneys, the privilege against self-incrimination, the criminal standard of proof, and the primacy of legal guilt as a prerequisite to state intervention. By emphasizing some degree of criminal procedural regularity, the Court altered juvenile courts' focus from "real needs" to "criminal deeds" and shifted the focus of delinquency proceedings from a social welfare inquiry into a quasi-criminal prosecution. Formalizing the connections between criminal behavior and sanctions highlighted the criminal-law foundation of juvenile courts that Progressives had tried to obscure. Providing juveniles with some criminal procedural safeguards also legitimated the imposition of more punitive sentences. Once states grant a semblance of procedural justice, however inadequate, juvenile courts more readily depart from a purely "rehabilitative" model. Although the Court provided procedural rights to protect minorities' liberty interests, affording those rights permitted sanctions to escalate. Those increasingly punitive penalties would fall disproportionately heavily on minority offenders.

Responses to the "Due Process Revolution": Rights, Race Riots, and Conservative Reaction

Despite the complex structural, racial, and demographic changes during the 1960s, critics of the Warren Court simplistically attributed the turmoil on college campuses, rising crime rates, and urban racial disorders to the Court's decisions on criminal procedures and civil rights (Mauer, 1999). During the late 1960s, liberals and conservatives interpreted the causes of social unrest differently. Liberals attributed crime and poverty to social structural conditions and racial and economic inequality, whereas conservatives subscribed to more individualistic explanations and blamed people who made bad choices for crime or poverty and argued that social welfare programs only encouraged irresponsibility (Beckett, 1997; Beckett & Sasson, 2000).

During the second half of the 1960s, the civil rights movement shifted its focus from ending apartheid and legally sanctioned inequality to even more difficult issues of structural, economic, and social inequality nationwide. By the late 1960s, federal judges began to prescribe remedies to reduce racial inequality with far-reaching impacts on local schools, housing, and jobs. Under pressure of federal mandates, the Aid to Families with Dependent Children's welfare rolls expanded, the proportion of black recipients increased, and politicians and the public linked poverty and dependence on welfare with race (Gilens, 1999). The Court's decisions in the 1960s brought to the fore a host of other contentious social and moral issues—sexual privacy, contraception, and school prayer—that further fueled a conservative backlash (Edsall & Edsall, 1992; Powe, 2000). Because of President Johnson's leadership and the Warren Court's decisions, the public associated Democrats with the new liberal and "rights" agenda and the interests of blacks (Edsall & Edsall, 1992). The Court's decisions eroded political support for expanding civil rights by pitting the interests of blacks and working-class ethnic whites and traditionalists and liberals against each other. By the end of the decade, the unfortunate confluence among the Court's decisions, rising crime and urban riots had important implications for race relations, domestic politics, and crime policy.

Criminologists have long recognized that urbanization per se contributes to higher rates of crime. A variety of structural factors: the anomie, stresses, and strains of urban life; the erosion of family and informal social controls; population density, anonymity, and heterogeneity; income inequality; and family disruption contribute to higher rates of urban crime. In addition to the post World War II racial migration and urbanization, the baby boom generation, born after World War II, created a demographic bulge, and rates of crime and delinquency began to escalate in the 1960s as the cohort entered adolescence. During the 1960s, urban riots rocked American cities as blacks reacted violently to decades of segregation, deprivation, and alienation. Harlem experienced the largest race riot since World War II in 1964, and Watts exploded in riot in 1965. In 1966, 38 riots erupted; 164 more riots occurred during the first nine months of 1967 (Lemann, 1992). The National Advisory Commission on Civil Disorders (1965), popularly called the Kerner Commission, attributed the riots to racial discrimination in employment, education, social services, and housing. Established in the aftermath of the riots, the Commission (1968, p. 1) warned that the United States "was moving toward two societies, one black, one white—separate and unequal."[2] The Commission noted the media's role in exacerbating racial divisions.[3]

Despite the Kerner Commission's sympathetic findings about the structural "root causes" of urban crime and racial disorder, the riots changed many whites' perceptions of the legitimacy of blacks' grievances; enabled many whites to attribute crime and dependence on welfare to individual choices, rather than to structural forces; and provided the context of more conservative political appeals that were based on race in public policies (Mendelberg, 2001). In addition, divisions within the civil rights movement between nonviolent, church-led moderate leaders and radical "black power" advocates produced a fragmentation of efforts and added a more ominous rhetoric to blacks' claims for equality (Omi & Winant, 1994).

Between 1964 and 1968, urban riots, black-power rhetoric, violence and confrontations, soaring rates of black illegitimacy and welfare expenditures, rising rates of youth crime, and student protests against the Vietnam War combined to threaten middle-class traditions and strengthen conservative opposition. Many whites associated these social ills with blacks, which they believed had failed to take advantage of the equal opportunity that the civil rights and voting laws afforded (Gilens, 1999; Hacker, 1995).

---

2. Recognizing the historical prevalence and persistence of segregation, discrimination, and poverty, the commission cautioned that the continuation of current policies would "make permanent the division of our country into two societies; one, largely Negro and poor, located in the central cities; the other predominantly white and affluent, located in the suburbs" (National Advisory Commission, 1968, p. 22).

3. "By failing to portray the Negro as a matter of routine and in the context of the total society, the news media have...contributed to the Black-White schism in this country" (National Advisory Commission, 1968, p. 383).

Conservative Backlash and the Inversion of Juvenile Jurisprudence

By the early 1970s, urban riots, escalating crime rates, dissatisfaction with the treatment model in penology, and the emerging "politics of crime" prompted calls for a return to classical principles of criminal law. Between 1960 and 1970, the number of serious and violent crimes more than doubled and produced a markedly more conservative public opinion about crime and punishment (Garland, 2001). By the 1970s, liberal as well as conservative critics of the "rehabilitative ideal" and indeterminate sentences began to swing the penal-policy pendulum toward proportionality, determinate sentences, and "just deserts" (von Hirsch, 1976). The just-deserts critique produced strange philosophical and political bedfellows: liberals who were concerned about discretion and discrimination, civil libertarians who were concerned about individual liberty and autonomy, and conservatives who denounced treatment as being "soft on crime" and who advocated "law and order" and a reduced role of the state in welfare (Garland, 2001; Mauer, 1999). Because liberals criticized rehabilitation and indeterminacy as arbitrary and discriminatory, they lacked a coherent alternative policy on crime when conservatives proposed to crack down on criminals.

The sources of these changes in penal policies lay in broader ideological and structural changes and the politics of crime and race (Feld, 1999; Garland, 2001). In this section, I argue that the economic and structural transformation of cities during the 1970s and 1980s led to the emergence of a racially isolated and impoverished underclass. Macrostructural, economic, and racial demographic changes that occurred in cities during the 1970s and 1980s and the escalation of homicide rates among black youths in the late 1980s facilitated the politics of crime and produced the more punitive juvenile justice policies of the early 1990s. One factor that contributed to "get tough" politics was the epidemic of crack cocaine and the gun violence and youth homicides that accompanied the deindustrialization of the urban core and the emergence of the black underclass (Blumstein, 1995; Feld, 1999; Massey & Denton, 1993). The second factor was media coverage that disproportionately put a black face on young criminals and reinforced the white public's fear and racial animus. The immediate source of the crackdown was conservative politicians who used *crime* as a code word to make racial appeals for electoral advantage with pledges to get tough (Mendelberg, 2001). Misgivings about the ability of juvenile courts either to rehabilitate violent offenders or to protect public safety bolstered policies to prosecute a larger number of youths as adults. Culminating in the late 1980s and early 1990s, almost every state enacted laws either to simplify the transfer of youths to criminal courts or to require juvenile court judges to impose determinate or mandatory minimum sentences on those who remained within a more punitive juvenile system (Feld, 1998; Torbett et al., 1996). Both strategies de-emphasize rehabilitation and the needs of offenders, stress personal and justice-system accountability and punishment, and base dispositions on the seriousness of the offense and prior record. These changes inverted juvenile justice jurisprudence and sentencing policies—from rehabilitation to retribution, from an emphasis on the offender to the seriousness of the offense, from a concern with "amenability to treatment" and a child's "best interests" to public safety and punishment—and shifted discretion from the judicial to the legislative or executive branches.

Transformation of the Economy and Cities and the Rise of the Urban Underclass

Between the prosperous post-World War II years and the early 1970s, employment in the steel, automobile, construction, and manufacturing industries provided semiskilled high school graduates with good-paying jobs. These opportunities proved especially beneficial for black men who moved to the northern cities and provided the foundation for stable, two-parent, black working-class communities (Hacker, 1995). In the 1970s, the transition from an industrial to an information and service economy began to reduce job prospects in the manufacturing sectors. Because of the timing of the Great Migration, blacks' experiences differed from those of earlier European immigrants and placed them at a significant economic and structural disadvantage during the postindustrial transition (Katz, 1989; Lieberson, 1980; Massey & Denton, 1993). Between 1969 and 1984, employment in manufacturing decreased from 26% to 19% of the workforce, while employment in the service sectors increased from 13% to 28% (Katz, 1989). In 1973, for the first time since the post-World War II period of sustained growth began, inflation-adjusted real hourly wages stagnated and then declined—by 2.8% in 1974 and 0.7% in 1975 (Edsall & Edsall, 1992). Black and white working-class Americans previously had experienced their strongest gains in the automobile and steel industries. In the globalized economy of the 1970s and 1980s, overseas competition had profound racial consequences as low-skill, entry-level jobs disappeared or migrated to other nations. White blue-collar workers, already under stress as their wages, benefits, and middle-class status eroded, strongly resented affirmative action programs to extend jobs and seniority to blacks.

Economic prospects in postindustrial cities increasingly depended on skills and education. The transition to an information and service economy produced a widening gap in earnings between high school and college graduates as those with a better education prospered and those with fewer skills foundered (Katz, 1989). In fewer than 20 years, the gap between high school and college graduates' earnings widened because the former earned less and the latter earned more. As recently as 1975, college graduates earned only about 25% more than did high school graduates (Wilson, 1996). Two decades later, the average difference in earnings was almost 100%, as college graduates' earning capacity increased and high school graduates' real earnings declined about 25% (Jencks, 1992; National Research Council, 1993). However, only 13.1% of blacks aged 25–34 had college degrees, compared with 24.5% of whites, and the proportion of blacks aged 18–24 who were enrolled in college declined during this period while that of whites increased (Edsall & Edsall, 1992).

Recall that during the post–World War II era, governmental highway, housing, and mortgage policies contributed to the growth of predominantly white suburbs surrounding increasingly poor and minority urban cores. As blacks migrated to cities, whites simultaneously began to move from cities to suburbs. Urban renewal and highway construction disrupted, destroyed, and quarantined many urban black communities. The isolation of blacks in ghettoes did not "just happen" and did not reflect exclusively the housing preferences of racial minorities. Rather, public policies and private institutional arrangements created and sustain racial segregation, amplify and exacerbate the harmful consequences of concentrated poverty, and adversely affect the economic and social welfare of black Americans (Massey & Denton, 1993; Sampson & Lauritsen, 1997). Seventy percent of poor whites live in non-poverty areas, compared with only 16% of poor blacks. Conversely, fewer than 7% of poor whites live in areas of concentrated poverty, compared with 38% of poor blacks (Mauer, 1999). Blacks are far more likely than are whites to be poor and, if they are poor, to live in areas of concentrated poverty. Whites' perceptions of blacks sustain housing, education, and welfare policies that contribute to criminogenic urban slums. In turn, the adaptive behaviors of poor blacks reinforce whites' view of minorities as dangerous and undeserving people to be kept at a distance (Katz, 1989; Massey & Denton, 1993). The migration of whites to suburbs, the growth of service jobs in suburbs, the bifurcation of the economy on the basis of education, and the concentration of poverty among blacks in cities altered the political balance. Between 1970 and 1986, the suburban population, overwhelmingly white and voting in higher proportions, grew from 40% to 45% of the nation's total to constitute nearly an electoral majority. Because the majority of black voters are heavily concentrated in urban areas, they have relatively little influence over politicians who represent predominantly white districts (Hacker, 1995). The emergence of the suburban population as a virtual electoral majority has enabled white voters to satisfy their public service needs for schools, parks, police, and roads through local and county tax expenditures, has weakened their ties to increasingly black cities, and has reduced whites' self-interest in investing in state or federal programs that primarily benefit blacks and the poor.

The Black Underclass. The macrostructural economic changes that are associated with the postindustrial transition had a cumulative, deleterious impact on urban minority residents (Wilson, 1987; 1996). Job losses occurred primarily in those higher-paying, lower-skilled manufacturing industries to which urban minorities previously had greater access, and job growth occurred in the suburbs and in sectors of the economy that required levels of education that were higher than many urban minority workers possessed (Wilson, 1987). As a result of the economic, spatial, and racial reorganization of cities, the past two decades witnessed the emergence of a black underclass, living in concentrated poverty and in racial, social, and cultural isolation (Jencks & Peterson, 1991; Katz, 1993; Wilson, 1987). Structural changes reduced black men's employment prospects and the pool of marriageable men. Incarceration policies, which disproportionately affect minority men, restrict subsequent employment opportunities and place unskilled black men at a further economic disadvantage (Mauer, 1999). As marriage to unemployed or unemployable black men became less attractive, unwed childbearing and female-headed households increased among poor black women (Wilson, 1987; 1996). Following passage of the civil rights legislation, many middle-class blacks took advantage of economic opportunities to leave the ghettoes. Their mobility deprived minority communities of a base of human capital for social stability and amplified the effects of concentrated poverty among the "truly disadvantaged" who were left behind (Wilson, 1987).

Crack Cocaine and Black Youth Homicide

In the mid-1980s, crack cocaine markets exploded in the inner cities, young drug dealers armed themselves, and the rates of homicide among black youths escalated sharply (Blumstein, 1995; Cook & Laub, 1998; Zimring, 1998). The increase in homicide provided the immediate political impetus to "get tough" on youth crime in general. Because of real racial differences in rates of violent offending, "getting tough" effectively meant targeting young black men. The mass media depict and the public perceives delinquents primarily as poor, urban young black men. Politicians manipulated and exploited these racially tinged perceptions with demagogic pledges to crack down on youth crime, which the public understands as a code word for young black men (Beckett & Sasson, 2000; Mendelberg, 2001).

The Federal Bureau of Investigation reported that rates of serious crime overall, juvenile crime, and violent juvenile crime have followed roughly similar patterns—increasing from the mid-1960s until 1980, declining during the mid-1980s, rebounding to another peak in the early 1990s, and then declining dramatically (Feld, 1999; Snyder & Sickmund, 1999; Zimring, 1998). Between 1965 and 1980, the rates of overall juvenile violent crime and homicide doubled, followed by a second, sharp upsurge between 1986 and 1994 (Cook & Laub, 1998; Reiss & Roth, 1993). These shifts provided the backdrop for public and political concerns about youth crime and the subsequent legal changes (Feld, 1999; Torbet et al., 1996).

Although conservatives had long criticized juvenile courts for excessive lenity (Zimring, 2000), states changed their juvenile waiver and delinquency-sentencing laws in the late 1980s and early 1990s in response to two specific changes in patterns of youth crime and violence—race and guns. Lethal violence and victimization are highly concentrated in the interstices of social disadvantage, and since the mid-1960s, the police have arrested black juveniles for violent offenses—murder, rape, robbery, and aggravated assault—at rates about five times greater than those of white youths and for homicide, at a rate about seven times greater than that of white youths (Feld, 1999; Zimring, 1998). Beginning in 1986, rates of youth homicide escalated sharply, and the arrest rates of black and white juveniles diverged abruptly (Cook & Laub, 1998). Between 1986 and 1993, arrests of white juveniles for homicide increased about 40%, while those of black youths jumped by 278% (Snyder & Sickmund, 1999). The use of guns by juveniles accounted for most of the escalation in youth homicide. Although the number of homicide deaths that juveniles caused by means other than firearms remained relatively stable between 1984 and 1994, the number of deaths they caused by firearms quadrupled (412%) (Feld, 1999; Zimring, 1996; Zimring & Hawkins, 1997). Over the decade, arrests of adolescents for homicide nearly tripled, and the use of firearms by juveniles accounted for almost the entire increase (Feld, 1999; Zimring, 1996). Because of the disproportionate involvement of black youths in violence and homicide, almost all the "excess homicides" occurred within the urban black male population (Cook & Laub, 1998). Analysts have attributed the dramatic increases in black youth homicides to the violent crack-cocaine industry that emerged in large cities during the mid- to late 1980s (Blumstein, 1995; Cook & Laub, 1998).

Media coverage of the intersections of race, guns, and homicide fanned a public "panic" that supported political efforts to repress youth crime. Gang

violence, drive-by shootings, and the disproportionate involvement of minorities in homicides inflamed the public's fear. Conservative politicians, un-
encumbered by racial scruples, promoted and exploited the public's fears for
electoral advantage, decried a coming generation of "superpredators" suffer-
ing from "moral poverty," and demonized young people to muster support for
harsher sentencing and transfer policies that disproportionately affected minority offenders (Miller, 1996; Zimring, 1998).

The Black Face of Youth Crime in the Media

As a result of social changes since World War II, most black and white
Americans live more residentially segregated lives now than they did a century
ago (Kinder & Mendelberg, 1995; Massey & Demon, 1993). Although some
whites know about the black underclass from personal contact with urban
poverty, from being victims of crime, or from family members' or friends' reports of their experiences, most of whites' knowledge about blacks comes from
news reports about welfare, crime, or unemployment. Media reports tend to
reinforce racial prejudice and stereotypes (Dorfman & Schiraldi, 2001; Edsall
& Edsall, 1991).

People are "cognitive misers." Stereotypes enable them quickly to simplify
and organize complex social experiences and to place people into meaningful
categories by focusing on information that confirms the stereotype and ignoring or interpreting information that contradicts it. Whites' stereotypes of
blacks function as a perceptual screen that admits supporting evidence and
blocks contradictory data (Entman & Rojecki, 2000). The term *offender* itself
elicits a predictable, negative stereotype—a young, lower-class, physically un-
attractive black man who was involved in a violent crime (Roberts, 1992).
News professionals who socially construct "news" unconsciously may cater to
their white viewers' or readers' stereotypes and use images, pictures, and stories with a racial content that their viewers more readily will recognize and
that will tap into their emotional responses to a story (Gilens, 1999).

Crime is socially constructed, and "frames" represent alternative ways to
understand crime and have different policy implications (Beckett & Sasson,
2000). The policy choice to get tough on youth crime reflects the ascendance
of certain ways of interpreting and framing crime in the political and media
cultures and a decision to emphasize punishment and imprisonment policies
over more humane alternatives (Mauer, 1999). In recent decades, the nature
and content of media coverage have reinforced conservative interpretations of
crime, put a black face on it, and intensified popular support for punitiveness.
Although news coverage may reflect public concerns, it more often influences

them by priming popular perceptions by the weight of coverage attached to an issue (Valentino, 1999). Public attitudes typically reflect the claims and narratives that dominate political rhetoric and media portrayals about crime, rather than react to real changes in crime rates and dictate political responses (Beckett, 1997; Roberts, 1992).

News media coverage has systematically distorted reality by disproportionately overreporting violent crime and by overemphasizing the role of minority perpetrators in committing violent crimes and thereby has affected public perceptions (Dorfman & Schiraldi, 2001). The overemphasis on violence and race primes racial stereotypes and prejudice and amplifies, rather than challenges, politicians' claims about the need for harsher policies toward criminals.

Media coverage: Crime is violent. Most people know about the world around them from local television news (Entman, 1990; Oliver, 1999; Roberts, 1992). The social construction of "news" is a complex process that reflects journalistic values and routine practices, the entertainment value of the content, and the sociopolitical context of its creation. To increase audience shares and advertising revenues, local news programs favor an action-news format that focuses on frightening and sensational violence because these stories are concrete, visual, and emotionally powerful. In standard coverage of news about crime, an anchor announces a violent crime, an on-the-scene reporter follows with a firsthand account of the offense from victims or bystanders, and then the focus shifts to the offender's identity and police efforts to apprehend the perpetrator. The standard script of local crime news typically contains two elements (Gilliam & Iyengar 2000; Gilliam, Iyengar, Simon, & Wright, 1996). The first element is that crime—murder, rape, robbery, or gang behavior— is violent. The second element features the "usual suspects"—minority perpetrators. Combining images of violence and race exerts a pervasive and cumulative effect on public opinion. Viewers who are exposed to violent and racial imagery tend to support more punitive policies (Gilliam et al., 1996; Peffley, Shields, & Williams, 1996).

The media's depictions of crime do not accurately reflect real rates of crime, the proportion of crime that is violent, or the proportion of crime that is committed by minorities. Instead media coverage systematically distorts and misrepresents reality (Dorfman & Schiraldi, 2001). Local and network television news and news magazines devote more coverage to violent crime than they do to any other subject and disproportionately overreport the rarest types of crime, such as murder and rape—"if it bleeds, it leads" (Entman & Rojecki, 2000). During the 1990s, violent crime decreased 20% while news coverage increased 83%, and homicides declined by one third while network news coverage increased 473% (Dorfman & Schiraldi, 2001). Murder accounts for less than 1% of all crime, but constitutes more than one quarter of all crime coverage (Beckett & Sasson, 2000; Gilliam & Iyengar, 2000; Gilliam et al., 1996). The nearly exclusive focus on the most unusual, violent crimes creates the misleading impression that such crimes are common and prevalent. Moreover, the media typically depict violent crimes involving strangers, even though acquaintances or intimates commit most violent crimes and such coverage tends to reinforce a perception of criminals as outsiders and predators.

Coverage of news about crime tends to be episodic, rather than contextual—that is, to focus on individual stories, rather than on the broader social context—and rarely analyzes neighborhood conditions or individual or community risk factors that contribute to crime (Entman & Rojecki, 2000). The lack of reporting about context leaves a misleading impression that violence is exclusively attributable to individual offenders' bad choices, rather than to structural factors, and thereby reinforces conservatives' interpretations of crime. News coverage exacerbates the gap between reality, as reflected in crime statistics and trends, and the public's perceptions of reality. It fails to provide the information that the public needs to make reasoned judgments or to evaluate politicians' claims about crime and justice policies (Dorfman & Schiraldi, 2001; Roberts, 1992). The media's coverage of the administration of criminal justice typically emphasizes failures of the system—defendants who are freed on "legal technicalities" by lenient judges—and then advocates for more severe punishment as the remedy (Miller, 1996; Roberts, 1992).

Several factors skew the news coverage of local crimes. One is the availability of news stories to journalists who operate under time and logistical constraints. Another is the suitability, interest, and importance of stories for the intended audience (Gilens, 1999). Large media markets span several political jurisdictions and focus on the general coverage of sports, weather, crime, disasters, and human-interest features, rather than on the politics or policies of a particular municipality (Entman & Rojecki, 2000; Gilens, 1999). Crime fascinates the public, and for-profit media seek to gain an increased market share by presenting crime stories that have greater entertainment value than do longer analytical news features. Reporters who are working under the pressure of deadlines select subjects that are close at hand. Because most news producers and most blacks are located in urban areas, their geographic proximity leads to minorities' overrepresentation in crime stories (Gilens, 1999; Valentino, 1999). The media can produce crime stories efficiently by using official sources, which also lend an aura of credibility. Local police departments are open 24 hours a day for late-breaking news (Mauer, 1999). The tendency of news organizations to use law enforcement agencies as official sources of information affects the depiction, coverage, and content of reporting of crime news. The police may focus on violent crimes when they have higher clearance rates to portray themselves more favorably. Similarly, politicians generate crime news stories to shape public attitudes and promote policies on crime that they believe will provide them with political benefits (Beckett & Sasson, 2000; Tonry, 1995). Because journalists and editors consume the news they produce, the "reality" that they depict affects their own perceptions, the editorial decisions that they make, and the stories that they subsequently present.

Media coverage: Criminals are black. The bias toward overreporting violent crime reinforces the connection between race and crime. Although blacks commit violent crimes at higher rates than do whites, the coverage of crime news depicts blacks' commission of these crimes even more disproportionately than their actual rates (Gilliam et al., 1996; Hurwitz & Peffley, 1997). Over half the crime stories on local television news explicitly refer to the race or ethnicity of the offenders, 59% of the stories of violent crimes implicate minority offenders, and blacks constitute the largest identified group of minority offenders (Gilliam & Iyengar, 2000; Gilliam et al., 1996). Media reports portray black defendants who are arrested for violent crimes negatively and depict them anonymously, handcuffed or spread-eagled in police custody, and poorly dressed more often than they do white offenders (Beckett & Sasson, 2000; Entman, 1992; 1994; Peffley et al., 1996). Depictions of unidentified, "nameless" black suspects reinforce white viewers' racial stereotypes and create a heightened perception of blacks as threatening, menacing, and requiring physical restraint (Entman, 1992; Peffley, Hurwitz, & Sniderman, 1997). Conversely, crime news stories more often depict victims as female, white, and affluent, although white affluent women experience less victimization than do other demographic groups, especially blacks. The "newsworthiness" of crime stories increases with white victims, decreases with black victims, and is the strongest when crime is interracial, even though most crimes are intra-racial (Dorfman & Schiraldi, 2001).

The skewed emphasis on violence, the disproportionate overrepresentation of blacks as perpetrators, and the under-representation of blacks as victims systematically mislead the public and skew their understanding of crime and justice. Moreover, such coverage promotes pejorative stereotypes, reinforces whites' perceptions of blacks as dangerous, and bolsters conservatives' interpretations of crime and advocacy of punishment (Gilliam & Iyengar, 2000; Mendelberg, 2001).

Politics of Race and Crime

The adoption of harsh laws to punish youth crime in the early 1990s culminated in the politicization of criminal and juvenile justice policies that began several decades earlier. Social problems, such as crime, emerge in a process of social construction among conflicting and competing interpretations with different policy prescriptions. Claims makers, such as politicians, compete for public acceptance of the interpretations or frames they prefer and the policies they prescribe. The media play a crucial role in shaping popular culture and creating the mindset within which politicians frame issues involving race and crime for public consumption (Entman & Rojecki, 2001). Over the past three decades, conservative politicians have successfully influenced public perceptions about the threat of crime; attributed the causes of crime to individual choices, rather than to social structural forces; assigned responsibility for unacceptably high crime rates to lenient justice-system policies; and promoted campaigns to crack down on crime as part of a broader electoral strategy.

Following *Brown v. Board of Education* (1954), civil rights activists responded to southern "massive resistance" with direct action and civil disobedience to desegregate public facilities. When activists used disruptive strategies, such as sit-ins, southern politicians and law enforcement officials characterized the protesters as criminals and mobs, fomented by "outside agitators" and communists, and sometimes repressed them violently. Subsequently, conservative politicians equated political dissent and crime, identified the civil rights movement's use of civil disobedience as a cause of crime, and urged its swift and severe suppression (Beckett, 1997). Thus, race and crime became linked early in conservative political discourse.

Divisions within the Democratic Party between racial and social policy liberals and conservatives and northerners and southerners first emerged in 1948. By the 1960s, the civil rights movement heightened the visibility of black oppression in the South and forced the national Democratic Party to choose between its white southern and black northern constituencies. Although most Americans agreed in theory with the norms of racial equality, many disagreed with the specific means that the courts and regulatory agencies developed to remedy inequality and harbored racial resentments (Mendelberg, 2001). Many of the remedies instituted by the Warren Court to end discrimination and racial segregation and to grant legal and procedural rights to unpopular groups, such as criminal defendants, became associated in the public mind with the liberal agenda of the Democratic Party. The burden of integrating schools, housing, and employment fell more heavily on blue-collar and lower-middle-class white ethnic neighborhoods in the North and across the South. The expanding "rights revolution" and the associated social and cultural changes disturbed and angered many members of the white ethnic working- and lower-middle classes, who bore the brunt of change—civil rights for minorities, employment and reproductive rights for women, protection for criminal defendants, and affirmative action and racial preferences in hiring (Edsall & Edsall, 1992).

During the turbulent 1960s, the sharp rise in youth crime and urban racial disorders evoked fears of "crime in the streets" and provoked cries for "law and order." Republican politicians ascribed the escalating crime, campus disorders, urban riots, and social upheavals to the Warren Court and liberal Democratic policies. Crime and welfare policies became central issues in partisan politics and acquired a racial coloration as conservatives cast blacks and their Democratic allies as the villains (Gilens, 1999; Mendelberg, 2001). The polarization between the two major political parties on issues of race became explicit during the 1964 presidential contest between Lyndon Johnson, whose leadership led to the passage of the 1964 Civil Rights Act, and Barry Goldwater, a staunch conservative and opponent of the law (Edsall & Edsall, 1992). Democratic support for civil rights for blacks alienated white southern voters, and that election presaged a racial political realignment as voters began to identify clear differences between the two parties on a host of race-related issues. Although the initial civil rights agenda focused on providing fundamental citizenship rights for blacks, such as the right to vote and equal access to public accommodations, the post-1964 agenda addressed broader goals of implementing rights and ensuring equality of outcomes for blacks, often through the use of racial preferences.

Conservatives strongly opposed governmental actions to redistribute public and private goods jobs, education, housing, and the like—to achieve greater racial equality. During the mid-1960s, the long-standing distinctions between the deserving and undeserving poor and the stereotypic belief that blacks were lazy became intertwined when poor blacks came to the media's and public's attention (Gilens, 1999). Negative media coverage of crime and welfare reinforced public perceptions and political depictions of blacks as criminals and undeserving (Edsall & Edsall, 1992; Gilens, 1999). The civil rights movement changed perceptions of the Democratic and Republican parties, and conservative politicians used crime control, affirmative action, and welfare as racially tinged "wedge issues" with which to distinguish themselves from Democrats in order to woo southern white and ethnic voters (Beckett, 1997; Edsall & Edsall, 1992).

In 1968, Alabama Governor George Wallace redefined the white backlash as right-wing populism against moral, racial, and cultural liberalism. Similarly, Richard Nixon's 1968 presidential campaign attributed urban riots and rising crime rates to liberal "permissiveness" and criticized the Warren Court for "coddling criminals" and "handcuffing the forces of law and order." Nixon's strategy effectively straddled the conflict between public support for the abstract principle of racial equality and growing public opposition to government-prescribed remedies for inequality. Nixon articulated the views of many white Americans who believed that it was wrong to deny blacks basic citizenship rights, but who also opposed court and government-imposed residential, employment, and educational integration (Mendelberg, 2001).

Republican political strategists found a responsive audience among white southerners, suburbanites, socially conservative ethnic Catholics, and blue-collar workers to foster a political realignment around racial issues. Pursuing Phillips's (1969; see also Orni & Winant 1994) "southern strategy," Republicans courted these new constituencies with racially charged code words, such as *law and order* that indirectly evoked racial themes without explicitly challenging egalitarian ideals. The Republican's southern strategy ruptured the Democrats' New Deal economic coalition of the "have-nots" and produced a party realignment along issues of race, rather than of socioeconomic class. Political reforms that were introduced in the Democratic Party after the 1968 convention proved more advantageous to the articulate and well-educated veterans of the civil rights, women's, and antiwar movements than to the traditional blue-collar and ethnic ward politicians in the competition for delegates. As more progressive forces dominated the national Democratic Party, Republicans depicted them as liberal elitists who were bent on imposing an alien racial and cultural agenda. Divisive issues, such as school busing to achieve integration in northern cities and tax and welfare policies, brought home starkly the implications of the liberal agenda to lower-middle- and working-class urban ethnic residents and suburban voters (Edsall & Edsall, 1992). Because of the perceived association between race, on the one hand, and violence, crime, and illegitimacy, on the other, liberals failed convincingly to address increasingly conservative public attitudes that were spurred by rising rates of crime and welfare. The inability of liberals effectively to debate issues associated with race enabled conservative Republicans to propose simplistic, politically popular policies on a host of contentious issues and to push the debate in a more conservative direction (Mendelberg, 2001). Only in the early 1990s under President Bill Clinton, for example, could national Democrats respond to Republican's exploitation of the crime issue by embracing an equally tough rhetoric and fostering a bipartisan policy consensus for law and order (Garland, 2001; Beckett & Sasson, 2000).

Code Words to Appeal to Anti-Black Sentiments

It is "politically incorrect" to express overtly racist sentiments, and research on "modern racism" has attempted to identify closely related, indirect indicators of racial hostility, such as anti-black emotional affect, resistance to blacks' political demands, and the denial that discrimination or racism persists (Entman & Rojecki, 2000). Modern racism "is composed of a general and diffuse 'anti-black affect' combined with disaffection over the continuing claims of blacks on white resources and sympathies, rancor rooted in an attachment to traditional American, individualist values and in a conviction that racism has disappeared" (Entman, 1990, p. 333). These views emerge in media coverage and political discourse about welfare and crime.

Crime and welfare now serve as coded issues that enable politicians implicitly to invoke race—some white Americans' negative views about blacks—without explicitly playing the "race card" (Gilens, 1996; Mendelberg, 2001). Code words are phrases that indirectly conjure racial themes, but do not directly challenge egalitarian ideals, that politicians can use to appeal implicitly to racial resentment without providing clear evidence of racism or an intent to discriminate (Dvorak, 2000; Omi & Winant, 1994). By the 1970s, conservative politicians recognized that terms like *law and order* and *individual rights* evoked racial understandings, and, by the 1980s, words like *welfare, fairness,* and *groups* had acquired racial meanings as a backlash against liberal policies (Dvorak, 2000; Edsall & Edsall, 1991).

For the past 35 years, "sound-bite" politics, symbols, and rhetoric have shaped penal policies as politicians have feared being labeled "soft on crime" and have avoided thoughtful discussions of complex issues of crime policy (Beckett, 1997). In this unreflective and punitive environment, politicians have exploited racially tinged words and perceptions for political advantage with promises to get tough and crack down on youth crime, which the public understands as a code word for young black men (Beckett, 1997). The use of code phrases enables politicians to convey a well-known but implicit meaning—such as an appeal to whites' racial hostilities—but to deny any racist interpretation (Kinder & Mendelberg, 1995; Miller, 1996). Race provides a focus for political conflicts over values, culture, and the allocation of resources and implicates a host of policy issues—social welfare, neighborhood schools, the distribution of the tax burden, crime, drugs and violence, family structure, and political allegiances (Omi & Winant, 1994).

In the past 35 years, conservative politicians and the mass media have pushed crime to the top of the political agenda by focusing on sensational and violent crimes to promote more punitive policies for political purposes. Since the late 1960s, Republican politicians in national elections have recognized the value of using anticrime rhetoric to appeal to white voters (Tonry, 1994, 1995). Moreover, politicians generate crime news stories to shape public attitudes and promote crime policies that they believe will provide them with a political advantage.[4] The focus in George Bush's 1988 presidential campaign on Willie Horton, a convicted black murderer who was released on furlough and burglarized and stabbed a white middle-class man and raped a woman, tapped voters' anger over criminal defendants' and prisoners' rights through the threatening archetype of the black male rapist of a white woman (Anderson, 1995; Mendelberg, 2001). Although the Bush campaign claimed that the Horton advertisement was about Michael Dukakis's "soft on crime" attitudes, not about race, many analysts concluded that the appeal mobilized whites' racial prejudices, rather than their concerns about crime policies (Anderson, 1995; Mendelberg, 1997, 2001). By the early 1990s, the words *youth crime* had acquired a coded meaning, and juveniles had become a symbolic "Willie Horton" (Beckett, 1997; Beckett & Sasson, 2000).

Punitiveness an Juvenile-Transfer and Sentencing Policies

The politicization of crime policies and the public and political connections between race and youth crime provided a powerful incentive to transform juvenile justice jurisprudence (Zimring, 1998). Questions about the effectiveness and legitimacy of the "rehabilitative ideal" that emerged in the 1960s increasingly eroded the traditional interventionist rationale of the juvenile justice system and evoked a sense of failure among both practitioners and the public (Garland, 2001; Zimring, 2000).[5] Political opportunism and

---

4. After Republican politicians declared a "war on drugs" in the1980s, they provided a steady stream of interviews, and media coverage of drug stories increased sharply. These news stories focused on crack, rather than powder, cocaine; emphasized that crack was a drug of the black inner city; increasingly depicted cocaine users as poor and nonwhite; participated in the creation of a "moral panic"; reinforced get-tough rhetoric; and abetted conservatives' advocacy of punitive laws (Beckett & Sasson, 2000; Tonry, 1995). Analyses of network coverage of the war on drugs between 1981 and 1988 reported that as the focus of law enforcement shifted from powder to crack cocaine, "the media frame shifted dramatically from white, suburban drug users in need of therapy to riveting images of violent black drug offenders in the inner city who were beyond the point of rehabilitation" (Hurwitz & Peffley, 1997, p. 395). Such complicity by the media reinforced get-tough political rhetoric and abetted conservatives' advocacy of punitive laws, such as the Federal Sentencing Guidelines' crack-versus-powder cocaine sentencing differential that produced a dramatically disproportionate impact on the rates of conviction and incarceration of blacks (Kennedy, 1997; Miller, 1996; Tonry, 1995).

5. Zimring (2000, 2002) argued that two rationales supported the creation of the original juvenile court: diversion and intervention. The diversionary rationale rested on the idea that a separate juvenile court for adolescents would avoid the life destructive consequences of criminal punishments simply by doing less harm. The interventionist rationale and the "rehabilitative ideal" asserted that treatment would affirmatively improve young

the accumulating perception that "nothing works" fostered a greater legislative emphasis on punishment. The overarching jurisprudential themes of these legal changes include a shift from rehabilitation to retribution, from sentences based on the needs of the individual offender to those based on the seriousness of the offense, and from "amenability to treatment" to public safety and accountability and a transfer of discretion from judges to prosecutors (Feld, 1998; 1999).

Waiver policies. Within the past two decades, particularly in reaction to the increase in homicides among black youths in the late 1980s and early 1990s, virtually every state revised its transfer laws to facilitate the prosecution of more juveniles in criminal court (Feld, 1995; 1998; Torbet et al., 1996). Juvenile justice policies became especially punitive toward youths who were charged with violent and drug crimes, the offense categories to which black youths contribute disproportionately. Statutory changes use offense criteria in waiver laws as dispositional guidelines to structure and limit judicial discretion, to guide prosecutorial charging decisions, or automatically to exclude certain offenses from the jurisdiction of the juvenile court (Feld, 1998; McCord, Widom, & Crowell, 2001; Torbet et al., 1996). The changes in waiver laws reflect a fundamental cultural and legal reconceptualization of youths from innocent and dependent children to responsible and autonomous adultlike offenders. Politicians' sound bites: "adult crime, adult time" or "old enough to do the crime, old enough to do the time" exemplify the reformulation of adolescence and represent policies on crime that provide no formal recognition of youthfulness as a mitigating factor in sentencing (Feld, 1997). Controlling for the seriousness of the offense, juvenile court judges are more likely to transfer minority youths than white youths to criminal court, and the disparities are the greatest for youths who are charged with violent and drug offenses (Poe-Yamagata & Jones, 1999). Once states try youths as adults, criminal court judges sentence them as if they are adults, impose the same sentences, send them to the same prisons, and even execute them for the crimes they committed as children (Feld 1998; *Stanford v. Kentucky,* 1989).

---

offenders' life chances. Research in the 1960s and 1970s questioned the effectiveness of treatment interventions for adults or juveniles "what works" and led to the decline of support for the "rehabilitative ideal" (Allen, 1981; Martinson, 1974). More recent research has indicated that some treatment programs may improve the correctional outcomes for young offenders (Lipsey & Wilson, 1998). However, it is exactly because evaluation research has identified the components of effective treatment programs that some other explanation is required for the substantial legislative abandonment of the treatment or interventionist rationale of juvenile justice. I argue that it is the politics of race, not the inefficacy of treatment, which explains changes in the "culture of control" and the abandonment of the commitment to rehabilitation (Garland, 2001).

Sentencing policies. The jurisprudential shifts from offender to offense and from treatment to punishment that inspired changes in waiver policies affect the sentences that judges impose on delinquent offenders as well (Feld, 1988). Progressive reformers envisioned a *parens patriae* welfare system that minimized procedural safeguards and maximized discretion to focus on youths' "real needs." The impetus to get tough impels judges to punish delinquents more severely, and these harsher sanctions—pretrial detention and postadjudication incarceration—disproportionately affect minority youths (Feld, 1999; Poe-Yamagata & Jones, 1999).

Several indicators reveal that juvenile court judges increasingly punish youths for their past offenses, rather than treat them for their future welfare. Legislative preambles and court opinions explicitly endorse punishment as an appropriate component of juvenile sanctions. States' juvenile codes increasingly use the rhetoric of system accountability, individual responsibility, punishment, and public safety, rather than a child's welfare or "best interests" (Feld, 1988; 1998). States' sentencing laws increasingly provide for determinate or mandatory minimum sentences on the basis of the seriousness of the offense (Feld, 1998; Torbet et al., 1996). Half the states use some type of offense-based criteria to guide sentencing discretion (Sheffer, 1995; Torbet et al., 1996). Some use sentencing guidelines to impose presumptive, determinate sentences that are based on age, offense, and prior record (Feld, 1998; Sheffer, 1995). Others impose mandatory sentences that prescribe minimum terms of confinement or level of security placement on the basis of age and offense (Sheffer, 1995; Torbet et al., 1996). States' departments of corrections have administratively adopted security classification and release guidelines that use offense criteria to specify proportional or mandatory minimum terms of confinement (Feld, 1998). All these sentencing provisions—determinate and mandatory minimum laws and correctional and parole-release guidelines—share the common feature of offense-based dispositions that explicitly link the length of time that delinquents serve to the seriousness of the crimes they committed, rather than to their "real needs" (McCord et al., 2001). They use offense criteria to rationalize and achieve proportionality in sentencing decisions, to increase the penal bite of sanctions, and to allow legislators to demonstrate symbolically how "tough" they are.

Empirical evaluations of juvenile court judges' sentencing practices have reported two consistent findings. First, the principles of the criminal law—present offense and prior record—explain most of the variance in juvenile court sentences. Because every state defines juvenile courts' delinquency jurisdiction on the basis of the commission of a criminal act, juvenile court judges' sentencing practices focus primarily on the present offense and prior record when the judges sentence delinquents. Every methodologically rigorous study of juvenile court sentencing practices has reported that judges focus primarily on the seriousness of the present offense and prior record (Bishop & Frazier, 1996; Feld, 1999). Because juvenile court judges heavily consider legal variables when they process youths, real differences in rates of criminal behavior by black youths account for part of the racial disparities in the administration of justice. Various measures of delinquency—official data on arrests and convictions, self-report surveys, and surveys of crime victims—have indicated that black youths have higher rates of serious offending than do white youths (McCord et al., 2001). Some of these differences in rates of offending reflect black youths' greater exposure to risk factors that are associated with crime and violence—segregation, isolation in concentrated poverty, inadequate schools, poor health care, and the like (McCord et al., 2001).

After researchers have controlled for legal variables, which account for differences in rates of offending by race, the individualized justice of juvenile courts has consistently produced racial disparities in processing and sentencing minority offenders (Kempf-Leonard, Pope, & Feyerherm, 1995; Miller, 1996; Pope & Feyerherm, 1992). *Parens Patriae* ideology legitimates individualization and exposes "disadvantaged" youths to more extensive controls. In a society that is marked by great inequality, those who are most "in need" are also those who are most "at risk" for juvenile court intervention. The structural context of the administration of juvenile justice also places minority youths at a dispositional disadvantage. Urban courts are more procedurally formal and sentence all delinquents more severely (Feld, 1991); they have greater access to detention facilities, and detained youths receive more severe sentences than do those who remain at liberty. Because proportionally more minority youths live in urban environs, the geographic and structural context of the administration of juvenile justice may interact with race to produce the overrepresentation of minority youths in detention facilities and correctional institutions (Feld, 1999; Snyder & Sickmund, 1999).

The juvenile justice process entails successive decisions—intake, petition, detention, adjudication or waiver, and disposition—and even small racial disparities produce larger cumulative differences. In 1997, black youths made up about 15% of the population aged 10–17, 26% of juvenile arrests, 30% of delinquency referrals, one third of petitioned delinquency cases, and 40% of inmates in public long-term institutions (McCord et al., 2001). Minority youths are overrepresented at each successive step of the decision-making process, with the greatest disparities occurring in the initial stages (Sampson & Lauritsen, 1997; Snyder & Sickmund, 1999). McCord et al.'s (2001, p. 257) analysis of the effects of discretionary decision-making reported that "at almost every stage in the juvenile justice process the racial disparity is clear, but not extreme. However, because the system operates cumulatively, the risk is compounded and the end result is that black juveniles are three times as likely as white juveniles to end up in residential placement."

In 1988, Congress amended the Juvenile Justice and Delinquency Prevention Act and required states that received federal funds to ensure equality of treatment on the basis of race and to examine the disproportionate confinement of minorities in detention facilities and institutions (42 U.S.C. § 5633(a)(16) (1994)). A number of states responded to the mandate of the act, evaluated juvenile justice administration, and reported racial disparities in their systems. After controlling for legal variables, 41 of 42 states found that minority youths were overrepresented in secure detention facilities, and all 13 states that analyzed postadjudication placements found that minorities were disproportionately confined (Pope, 1994). When judges sentence juveniles, minority youths receive disproportionately more out-of-home placements and serve longer periods in custody than do white youths who are committed for similar offenses (Poe-Yamagata & Jones, 1999).

The recent "get-tough" amendments to juvenile sentencing statutes have had a substantial and disproportionate impact on minority youths in confinement. An examination of the proportional changes in the racial composition of institutional populations for the 1985–95 period, which corresponds with the era of punitive changes in sentencing laws, revealed that the overall number of youths who were in custody on any given day increased almost 40%, from 49,322 to 68,983 (Feld, 1999). Despite the overall increase in daily custody populations, the percentage of white juveniles who were confined in public facilities declined 7%, while the percentage of black juveniles who were confined increased almost 63%. The overall increases and proportional changes reflect the sharp growth in minority youths in confinement. Because of these changes in the numerical composition of confined delinquents, the proportion of white juveniles in custody declined from 44% to 32% of all confined youths, while the proportion of black juveniles increased from 37% to 43% and that of Hispanic juveniles increased from 13% to 21% (Feld, 1999).

CONCLUSION

The issue of race had two distinct and contradictory influences on juvenile justice theory and practice during the second half of the 20th century. Initially, the Warren Court's "Due Process Revolution" and *Gault* attempted to enhance civil rights, protect minority citizens, and limit the coercive powers of the state. But *Gault*'s provision of procedural rights at trial legitimated punishment and fostered a procedural and substantive convergence with criminal courts. The second phase of the reform of juvenile justice reflects the confluence of macrostructural, economic, and racial demographic changes that occurred in U.S. cities between the 1960s and the 1980s: the emergence of a black underclass living in concentrated poverty and the rise in gun violence and youth homicides. Mass media portrayals and political rhetoric have firmly established in the public mind the connection between race and youth crime (Mendelberg, 2001). Politicians exploit these racial perceptions for political advantage.

Just as Progressive reformers did a century ago, we face the same "conservative" versus "liberal" policy choices between controlling and punishing errant individuals and initiating social structural changes to reduce the developmental risks that some young people face. Concentrated poverty, racial isolation, and the ensuing youth crime and violence are the cumulative consequences of public policies that produce patterned inequality. Unfortunately, our public policy debates about poverty and inequality, the allocation of social resources and benefits, and welfare and crime have become intertwined with questions of race. Poor blacks that live in concentrated poverty are effectively segregated from the social, economic, and political mainstream and engage in behaviors of which the dominant culture disapproves. The mass media convey biased and misleading images that incite white viewers' fear and indignation and activate stereotypes and prejudices. Conservative politicians exploit voters' sensitivities to matters of race with coded messages that are designed to sustain a right-wing coalition and to promote racial animus. As a result, Americans engage in a subterranean discourse on race without confronting its reality. As long as the white public and politicians identify long-term poverty and its associated problems—unemployment, drug abuse, criminality, and illegitimacy—as a black condition that is separate from the mainstream of American society, policy makers can evade a sense of governmental responsibility or public obligation. The political, media, and public association of the image of the criminal with that of the urban black male has fostered punitive policies, rather than expanded employment or educational opportunities to prevent crime. For adult offenders, harsher policies, such as those associated with the "war on drugs," have quadrupled rates of confinement with a disproportionate and debilitating impact on blacks (Mauer, 1999; Tonry, 1995). For youths, harsher policies have transformed the juvenile court into a punitive agency for the social control of "other people's children" (Feld, 1999; Grubb & Lazerson, 1982). Rather than address issues of public policy and political economy that contribute both to racial and social inequality and to the skewed distribution of crime, politicians use coded rhetoric to evoke racial resentments, to ascribe primary responsibility for crime and poverty to errant individuals, and to evade our collective obligation to all our children.

REFERENCES

Allen, F. A. (1981). *The decline of the rehabilitative ideal: Penal policy and social purpose.* New Haven, CT: Yale University Press.

American Friends Service Committee. (1971). *Struggle for justice.* New York: Hill & Wang.

Anderson, D. C. (1995). *Crime and the politics of hysteria: How the Willie Horton story changed American justice.* New York: Random House.

Arnold, W. R. (1971). Race and ethnicity relative to other factors in juvenile court dispositions. *American Journal of Sociology, 77,* 211–227.

Axelrad, S. (1952). Negro and white male institutionalized delinquents. *American Journal of Sociology, 57,* 569–574.

Beckett, K. (1997). *Making crime pay: Law and order in contemporary American politics.* New York: Oxford University Press.

Beckett, K., & Sasson, T. (2000). *The politics of injustice: Crime and punishment in America.* Thousand Oaks, CA: Pine Forge Press.

Bishop, D. M., & Frazier, C. S. (1996). Race effects in juvenile justice decision-making: Findings of a statewide analysis. *Journal of Criminal Law and Criminology, 86,* 392–413.

Blumstein, A. (1995). Youth violence, guns, and the illicit-drug industry. *Journal of Criminal Law and Criminology, 86,* 10–36.

Cook, P. J., & Laub, J. H. (1998). The role of youth in violent crime and victimization. *Crime and Justice: A Review of Research, 24,* 27–64.

Cover, R. M. (1982). The origins of judicial activism in the protection of minorities. *Yale Law Journal, 91,* 1287–1316.

Cullen, F. T., & Gilbert, K. E. (1982). *Reaffirming rehabilitation.* Cincinnati, OH: Anderson.

Dorfman, L., & Schiraldi, V. (2001). *Off balance: Youth, race and crime in the news.* Washington, DC: Youth Law Center, Building Blocks for Youth.

Dvorak, R. (2000). Cracking the code: "De-coding" color-blind slurs during the congressional crack cocaine debates. *Michigan Journal of Race & Law, 5,* 611–663.

Edsall, T. B., & Edsall, M. D. (1991). Race. *Atlantic Monthly, 267,* 53–86.

Edsall, T. B., & Edsall, M. D. (1992). *Chain reaction: The impact of race, rights and taxes on American politics.* New York: W. W. Norton.

Entman, R. M. (1990). Modern racism and the images of blacks in local television news. *Critical Studies in Mass Communication, 7,* 332–345.

Entman, R. M. (1992). Blacks in the news: Television, modern racism and cultural change. *Journalism Quarterly, 69,* 341–361.

Entman, R. M. (1994). Representation and reality in the portrayal of blacks on network television news. *Journalism Quarterly, 71,* 509–520.

Entman, R. M., & Rojecki, A. (2000). *The black image in the white mind: Media and Race in America.* Chicago: University of Chicago Press.

Feld, B. C. (1988). Juvenile court meets the principle of offense: Punishment, treatment, and the difference it makes. *Boston University Law Review, 68,* 821–915.

Feld, B. C. (1991). Justice by geography: Urban, suburban, and rural variations in juvenile justice administration. *Journal of Criminal Law and Criminology, 82,* 156–210.

Feld, B. C. (199b). Violent youth and public policy: A case study of juvenile justice law reform. *Minnesota Law Review, 79,* 965–1128.

Feld, B. C. (1997). Abolish the juvenile court: Youthfulness, criminal responsibility, and sentencing policy. *Journal of Criminal Law and Criminology, 88,* 68–136.

Feld, B. C. (1998). Juvenile and criminal justice systems' responses to youth violence. *Crime & Justice: An Annual Review, 24,* 189–261.

Feld, B. C. (1999). Bad kids: Race and the transformation of the juvenile court. New York: Oxford University Press.

Garland, D. (2001). The culture of control: Crime and social order in contemporary society. Chicago: University of Chicago Press.

Gilens, M. (1996). Race coding: White opposition to welfare. *American Political Science Review, 90,* 593–604.

Gilens, M. (1999). Why Americans hate welfare: Race, media, and the politics of antipoverty policy. Chicago: University of Chicago Press.

Gilliam, F. D., Jr., & Iyengar, S. (2000). Prime suspects: The influence of local television news on the viewing public. *American Journal of Political Science, 44,* 560–573.

Gilliam, F. D., Jr., Iyengar, S., Simon, A., & Wright, O. (1996). Crime in black and white: The violent, scary world of local news. *Harvard International Journal of Press Politics, 1* (3), 6–23.

Gottlieb, P. (1991). Rethinking the Great Migration: A perspective from Pittsburgh. In J. W. Trotter, Jr. (Ed.), *The Great Migration in historical perspective: New dimensions of race, class and gender* (pp. 68–82). Bloomington: Indiana University Press.

Graham, F. P. (1970). *The Due Process Revolution: The Warren Court's impact on criminal law.* New York: Hayden Books.

Grubb, W. N., & Lazerson, M. (1982). *Broken promises: How Americans fail their children.* New York: Basic Books.

Hacker, A. (1995). *Two nations: Black and white, separate, hostile and unequal.* New York: Macmillan.

Hurwitz, J., & Peflley, M. (1997). Public perceptions of race and crime: The role of racial stereotypes. *American Journal of Political Science, 41,* 375–401.

Jencks, C. (1992). *Rethinking social policy: Race, poverty, and the underclass.* New York: HarperCollins.

Jencks, C., and Peterson, P. E. (1991). *The urban underclass.* Washington, DC: Brookings Institution.

Katz, M. B. (1989). *The undeserving poor: From the War on Poverty to the war on welfare.* New York: Pantheon Books.

Katz, M. B. (Ed.). (1993). *The underclass debate: Views from history.* Princeton, NJ: Princeton University Press.

Kempf-Leonard, K., Pope, C., & Feyerherm, W. (Eds.). (1995). *Minorities in juvenile justice.* Thousand Oaks, CA: Sage.

Kennedy, R. (1997). *Race, crime, and the law.* New York: Random House.

Kinder, D. R., & Mendelberg, T. (1995). Cracks in American apartheid: The political impact of prejudice among desegregated whites. *Journal of Politics, 57,* 402–424.

Klarman, M. J. (2000). The racial origins of modern criminal procedure. *Michigan Law Review, 99,* 48–97.

Lemann, N. (1992). *The promised land: The great black migration and how it changed America.* New York: Random House.

Lieberson, S. (1980). *A piece of the pie: Black and white immigrants since 1880.* Berkeley: University of California Press.

Lipsey, M. W., & Wilson, D. B. (1998). Effective intervention for serious juvenile offenders. In R. Loeber & D. P. Farrington, (Eds.), *Serious and violent juvenile offenders: Risk factors and successful interventions* (pp. 313–345). Thousand Oaks, CA: Sage.

Martinson, R. (1974). What works? Questions and answers about prison reform. *The Public Interest, 35,* 22–54.

Massey, D. S., & Denton, N. A. (1993). *American apartheid: Segregation and the making of the underclass.* Cambridge, MA: Harvard University Press.

Mauer, M. (1999). *Race to incarcerate.* New York: New Press.

McCord, J., Widom, C. S., & Crowell, N. A. (2001). *Juvenile crime, juvenile justice.* Washington, DC: National Academy Press.

Mendelberg, T. (1997). Executing Hortons: Racial crime in the 1988 presidential campaign. *Public Opinion Quarterly, 61,* 134–157.

Mendelberg, T. (2001). *The race card: Campaign strategy, implicit messages, and the norm of equality.* Princeton, NJ: Princeton University Press.

Miller, J. G. (1996). *Search and destroy: African-American males in the criminal justice system.* New York: Cambridge University Press.

Myrdal, G. (1972). *An American dilemma* (Vols. 1 & 2). New York: Pantheon Books.

National Advisory Commission on Civil Disorders. (1968). Report. Washington, DC: U.S. Government Printing Office.

National Research Council. (1993). *Losing generations: Adolescents in high-risk settings.* Washington, DC: National Academy Press.

Oliver, M. B. (1999). Caucasian viewers' memory of black and white criminal suspects in the news. *Journal of Communication, 49,* 46–60.

Omi, M., & Winant, H. (1994). *Racial formation in the United States: From the 1960s to the 1980s.* New York: Routledge.

Peffley, M., Hurwitz, J., & Sniderman, P. M. (1997). Racial stereotypes and whites' political views of blacks in the context of welfare and crime. *American Journal of Political Science, 41,* 30–60.

Peffley, M., Shields, T., & Williams, B. (1996). The intersection of race and crime in television news stories: An experimental study. *Political Communications, 13,* 309–327.

Phillips, K. (1969). *The emerging Republican majority.* New Rochelle, NY: Arlington House.

Poe-Yamagata, E., & Jones, M. A. (1999). *And justice for some.* Washington, DC: Building Blocks for Youth.

Pope, C. E. (1994). Racial disparities in the juvenile justice system. *Overcrowded Times, 5,* 1–4.

Pope, C. E., & Feyerherm, W. H. (1992). *Minorities and the juvenile justice system.* Washington, DC: US. Department of Justice, Office of Juvenile Justice and Delinquency Prevention.

Powe, L. A., Jr. (2000). *The Warren Court and American politics.* Cambridge, MA: Harvard University Press.

President's Commission on Law Enforcement and the Administration of Justice. (1967). Task force report: Juvenile delinquency and youth crime. Washington, DC: U.S. Government Printing Office.

Reiss, A. J., Jr., & Roth, J. A. (Eds.). (1993). *Understanding and preventing violence.* Washington, DC: National Academy of Science.

Roberts, J. V. (1992). Public opinion, crime, and criminal justice. *Crime and Justice: A Review of Research, 16,* 99–164.

Sampson, R. J., & Lauritsen, J. E. (1997). Racial and ethnic disparities in crime and criminal justice in the United States. *Crime and Justice: A Review of Research, 23,* 311–374.

Sheffer, J. P. (1995). Serious and habitual juvenile offender statutes: Reconciling punishment and rehabilitation within the juvenile justice system. *Vanderbilt Law Review, 48,* 479–512.

Snyder, H. N., & Sickmund, M. (1999). Juvenile offenders and victims: A national report. Washington, DC: Office of Juvenile Justice and Delinquency Prevention.

Tonry, M. (1994). Racial politics, racial disparities, and the war on drugs. *Crime & Delinquency, 40,* 475–494.

Tonry, M. (1995). *Malign neglect: Race, crime, and punishment in America.* New York: Oxford University Press.

Torbet, P., Gable, R., Hurst, H., IV, Montgomery, I., Szymanski, L., & Thomas, D. (1996). State responses to serious and violent juvenile crime: Research report. Washington, DC: Office of Juvenile Justice and Delinquency Prevention, National Center for Juvenile Justice.

Trotter, J. W., Jr. (1991). Black migration in historical perspective: A review of the literature. In J. W. Trotter, Jr. (Ed.), *The Great Migration in historical perspective: New dimensions of race, class and gender* (pp. 1–21). Bloomington: Indiana University Press.

Valentino, N. A. (1999). Crime news and the priming of racial attitudes during evaluations of the president. *Public Opinion Quarterly, 63,* 293–320.

von Hirsch, A. (1976). *Doing justice.* New York: Hill & Wang.

Wilson, W. J. (1987). *The truly disadvantaged.* Chicago: University of Chicago Press.

Wilson, W. J. (1996). *When work disappears: The world of the new urban poor.* New York: Alfred A. Knopf.

Zimring, F. (1996). Kids, guns, and homicide: Policy notes on an age-specific epidemic. *Law and Contemporary Problems 59,* 25–37.

Zimring, F. (1998). *American youth violence.* New York: Oxford University Press

Zimring, F. (2000). The common thread: Diversion in juvenile justice. *California Law Review, 88,* 2477–2495.

Zimring, F. (2002). The common thread: Diversion in the jurisprudence of juvenile courts. In M. K. Roeenheim, F. E. Zimring, D. S. Tannenhaus, & B. Dorhn (Eds.), *A century of juvenile justice* (pp. 142–157). Chicago: University of Chicago Press.

Zimring, F., & Hawkins, G. (1997). *Crime is not the problem: Lethal violence in America.* New York: Oxford University Press.

Cases Cited

Breed v. Jones, 421 U.S. 519 (1975).
Brown v. Board of Education, 347 U.S. 483 (1954).
Brown v. Mississippi, 297 U.S. 278 (1936).
In re Gault, 387 U.S. 1 (1967).
In re Winship, 397 U.S. 358 (1970).
Kent v. United States, 383 U.S. 541 (1966).
McKeiver v. Pennsylvania, 403 U.S. 528 (1971).
Moore v. Dempsey, 261 U.S. 86 (1923),
Plessy v.Feguson, 163 U.S. 537 (1896).
Powell v. Alabama, 287 U.S. 42 (1932).
Stanford v. Kentucky, 492 U.S. 361 (1989).
United States v. Carolene Products, 304 U.S. 144 (1938).

Chapter Eleven

Reducing Juvenile Delinquency: Lessons Learned

Helen Taylor Greene and Everette B. Penn

Introduction

With repeated media images of street crime, school violence, and gang activity, uncontrolled youth crime and maladaptive behavior appear to be prevalent in the United States. The reality is that most youths never have contact with the juvenile or criminal justice systems. In fact, most youths in the nation, regardless of race, are not involved in delinquent activities, much less serious, violent, or chronic offenses. There are approximately 73 million youths under the age of eighteen of whom an estimated 1.3 million were arrested in 2002 (U.S. Census Bureau, 2002; Federal Bureau of Investigation, 2003). In this context, we have prevented juvenile delinquency through a network of families, schools, churches, and communities working together. National data indicate a steady downward trend in juvenile arrests and victimizations since 1994 (Federal Bureau of Investigation, 2003; Rennison & Rand, 2003). In spite of this more accurate portrayal of youth crime, the plight of some American youths is troubling. According to the same national data that indicate juvenile crime has decreased, there are also a disproportionate number of delinquent and criminal acts committed by minorities, especially African-Americans. Howell notes (2003):

> Minority youth, particularly black youngsters...are bearing the brunt of the punitive juvenile justice reforms that the panic over juvenile violence has wrought.... [T]hey have suffered the largest increases in

arrest rates, court referrals, and rates of detention, incarceration, and transfer to the criminal justice system. (p. 40)

Long before the creation of the first juvenile court in 1899, the United States took a protective posture in regard to curtailing youths from becoming adult criminals. Relying on the concept of *parens patriae,* the state became the "ultimate parent," responsible for correcting and protecting youths. Understanding the need for prevention of delinquency, various religious, social, and civic groups coalesced in their efforts to "save" wayward youths and help them become productive members of society (Feld, 1999; Platt, 1969). Unfortunately, even the benign intentions of these "Child Savers" were marred by racial and economic inequalities. Discrimination against African-Americans in prevention programs and facilities was common (Ward, 2001; Young, 1994). More than likely this was also the case for Asian-American, Latino-American, and Native American youths. In spite of racism, segregation, and deplorable social, economic, and political conditions that strongly correlate to delinquency and crime (Shaw & McKay, 1942), minority groups have made a commitment to the betterment of their youths independent of government intervention. Their beliefs and values about hard work, achievement, and respect for the law have facilitated the development of generations of youths who were neither delinquent nor in the juvenile justice system. The often unspoken "American Dream"—the dream for each generation to do better than the previous one—has also applied to these minority groups and their positive beliefs and values; involvement in crime and delinquency, though often inevitable for some minority groups, was not acceptable to most.

The purpose of this chapter is to examine what we have learned about reducing juvenile delinquency by focusing on prevention strategies that have emerged during the past two decades. Our goal is to identify approaches that are promising for all youths, but we will emphasize minority youths. We begin with an overview of delinquency prevention and intervention, followed by a discussion of what strategies do not work. We then discuss what strategies do work and present several important issues and challenges, including ways of targeting child delinquents, educational initiatives, and ways of preventing female delinquency. The chapter concludes with a discussion of future research needs.

DELINQUENCY PREVENTION AND INTERVENTION

Prevention science and prevention ideology emphasize the importance of eliminating the causes of human disorder, generally (Coie et al., 1993) and, more specifically, juvenile delinquency (Bynum & Thompson, 2002). Coie et al. (1993) offered prevention science as an approach to understanding risk and protective factors for mental health. In the past decade prevention science and risk and protective factors have been used to promote a better understanding of criminal and delinquent behavior (Black, Howard, Kin, & Ricardo, 1998; Keenan, 2001; Loeber & Farrington, 2001; Siegel, 2002). Briefly, risk factors foster delinquency, while protective factors reduce it. Both have internal and external aspects. For example, there can be individual as well as family, school, and community risk and protective factors.

Prevention programs are often classified into primary, secondary, and tertiary efforts. Primary prevention refers to programs and strategies designed to prevent the occurrence of delinquency by modifying conditions in the environment. Bloom (1996) views primary prevention as a three-dimensional optimistic concept—prevention, protection, and promotion of a desired objective. Secondary and tertiary interventions refer to efforts directed at children and adolescents who are involved in delinquency at either early stages or as recidivists. Prevention and intervention strategies can be further classified as either universal (aimed at all youths) or selective (targeting at-risk youths). Howell (2003) notes the importance of another concept, "youth development," that focuses on the over all well-being of youths and assisting them in growing up healthily in every aspect—physically, intellectually, psychologically, emotionally, and socially. A new focus in prevention, developmental prevention, links it to programs for infant, child, and adolescent stages of development; aims at more than one risk factor that affects developmental processes; and involves entire communities (Howell, 2003; Tonry & Farrington, 1995).

In 1996, the United States Congress mandated that the attorney general provide an evaluation of the effectiveness of programs designed to prevent youth violence, risk factors for youth violence in the community, families, and schools, as well as the effectiveness of programs designed to increase protective factors against delinquency (Sherman, Gottfredson, MacKenzie, Eck, Reuter & Bushway, 1997). The authors concluded:

> [T]he effectiveness of Department of Justice (DOJ) funding depends heavily on whether it is directed to the urban neighborhoods where youth violence is highly concentrated. Substantial reductions in national rates of serious crime can only be achieved by prevention in areas of concentrated poverty, where the majority of all homicides in the nation occur, and where homicide rates are 20 times the national average. (p. 1)

A primary recommendation of the report was that the DOJ needed to provide better guidance about what works, fund more rigorous testing, and identify model programs. These issues are particularly relevant for prevention and intervention efforts targeting minority youths since they often are the residents of the urban neighborhoods which Sherman et al. (1997) and Sherman (1998) describe. While the decrease in juvenile arrests and victimizations that has occurred since 1994 is encouraging, explanations for these decreases rarely point to delinquency prevention and intervention programs. This is due, at least in part, to the difficulty in determining program effectiveness that often perpetuates funding programs that do not work.

The Juvenile Justice Cycle

The 1950s is identified as the era when American (white) youths began to rebel against their parents and develop a youth culture (England, 1967). A decade later, and throughout the 1960s and 1970s, during a social revolution that would reshape America, the United States Supreme Court eroded the unchallenged discretion of juvenile courts (see, for example, *Kent v. United States,* 1966; *In re Gault,* 1967; *In re Winship,* 1970; *McKeiver v. Pennsylvania,* 1971; *Breed v. Jones,* 1975). In the late 1960s, there were calls for changes in both criminal and juvenile justice issued by the President's Commission on Law Enforcement and the Administration of Justice.

By the 1970s rehabilitative and prevention-focused programs had given way to a more punitive juvenile justice system that has prevailed for more than twenty years. Over time, juvenile court proceedings began to resemble those in adult criminal courts (Butts & Mears, 2001). During the 1990s a threat of youth violence previously unmatched in America was forecast. Termed as "superpredators" and brought to the forefront of the media by James Alan Fox and John DiIulio., Jr., these youths were identified as juveniles in the inner cities. The solution was more cops, more prisons, "and less 1960's-style nonsense about the 'root causes'" (DiIulio, 1994, p. 7). Juvenile justice rehabilitation practices were seen as relics of an unsuccessful past, as states prepared for the worst, changed laws, and made tremendous fiscal outlays preparing for the superpredators. Although such a creature did not emerge, the damage was done and the course was set. From the late 1990s until the present, spending money on punishment prevailed over spending money on cost-effective prevention.

The cost of get-tough policies is further evidence of what does not work. For example, to house a juvenile for one year in a Regional Youth Detention Center costs $41,245. For a state operated facility the cost rises to $56,940 and up to $166,800 for an intensive residential program (Bailey & Paisley, 2004).

With states and local governments facing financial difficulties, alternatives to costly incarceration must be sought. Thus, shifting juvenile justice policies from costly ineffective ones to cost-effective prevention practices is in the best interests of juveniles, the general public and government agencies. Recent findings by Cohen, Rust, Steen, and Tidd (2004) present the cost of crime as a figure of the costs for the victim and for the criminal justice system. Cohen et al. (2004) make it clear that past estimates were low since their own estimates place the costs of burglary as high as $30,000; of serious assault, $86,000; of rape and sexual assault, $313,000; of armed robbery, $314,000; and of murder, $11,000,000. Further, their findings provide support that the public is willing to pay, through higher taxes, for cost-effective, crime prevention policies and practices. Thus, the public's willingness would overcome the state and federal governments' limited resources and crime prevention would indeed receive more financial support.

The RAND Corporation (Greenwood, Model, Rydell, & Chiesa, 1996) provides research that supports prevention programs as a cost-effective crime prevention method. In a study that compared four crime prevention approaches to California's "Three Strikes and You're Out" law, their findings indicated that youth crime prevention programs, including high school graduation incentives, parent training, and delinquent supervision, were more cost-effective per 1 million dollars spent. High school graduation incentive programs prevented 250 serious crimes; parent training 160; and delinquent supervision 70. In comparison, the Three Strikes law prevented 62 serious crimes per $1 million spent. No longer can the public coffers afford ineffective, wasteful strategies to curtail juvenile crime.

The authors believe the pendulum of juvenile justice treatment is moving toward prevention rather than retribution, punishment, and revenge. The greatest factor creating this change in the United States is the inability of states to maintain the high cost of "get tough" justice. In order for this new approach to juvenile justice in the United States to be successful, there must be a body of literature that demonstrates the effectiveness of juvenile delinquency prevention.

WHAT DOES NOT WORK

In order to understand what works to prevent juvenile delinquency, the antithesis must be understood: What does not work, and why? By knowing what does not work, a body of literature can be identified that focuses on the elements, characteristics, theory, and practices that have not been effective, thus making it easier to define and recognize what does work to prevent juvenile delinquency. Through an analysis of such juvenile justice literature, the reader can know what approaches and strategies do not work in preventing juvenile crime. Recent research points to the ineffectiveness of such programs as curfew laws (McDowall, Loftin & Wiersema, 2000); scared straight programs (Finckenauer & Gavin, 1999); boot camps (MacKenzie, 2000); punishment in adult facilities (Howell, 1996); out-of-home placements (Burns and Goldman, 1999); Drug Abuse Resistance Education (DARE) programs (Durlak, 1997; Lundman, 2001); confinement in large correctional facilities (Coalition for Juvenile Justice, 1999); and zero tolerance policies (Howell, 2003).

To summarize, ineffective programs are those that either use general deterrence or "one size fits all" programming, rather than addressing the specific risk factors found in the individual, family, peer group, school, and neighborhood. Instead of addressing issues related to risk factors, ineffective practices often adhere to a "get tough" philosophy, rooted in punishment. Often, a "we versus they" practice unfolds, which further distances youth from parents, teachers, social institutions, and persons in authority, thereby undermining the social bonding process. Also, programs that work to engage families and communities in finding and choosing alternatives to crime may be discounted because they are slow to show success and can often be difficult to measure (Brownstein, 2000). Public policies are creatures of political cycles, which consist of elections, budgets, and crisis management. Consequently, success must be quick and easily measured. Being able to show an increase in arrests, convictions, and length of sentences fits the bill and makes the "get tough" philosophy an *easier* practice than a *best* practice.

WHAT WORKS

Ever since Martinson (1974) presented a scathing review of correctional programs and concluded that few of them worked, there has been a considerable amount of research directed at determining what works, not only in corrections but in all aspects of criminal justice, including crime prevention. Sherman (1998) acknowledged the difficulty in ascertaining what works. In order to determine what works Sherman et al. (1997) decided to focus on whether there was reasonable certainty that a program had any beneficial effect at all in preventing crime. They classified programs according to what works, what doesn't work, what's promising, and what's unknown. A program found to work was believed to "reduce risk factors for crime in the kinds of social contexts in which they have been evaluated, and for which the findings should be generalizable to similar settings in other places and times" (p. 4). Although Sherman et al. (1997) concluded that there are no community-based crime prevention programs with "proven effectiveness" (p. 26), there are a number of promising delinquency and prevention programs that are believed to work. Promising programs are those for which "the level of certainty from available evidence is too low to support generalizable conclusions, but for which there is some empirical basis for predicting that further research could support such conclusions" (p. 4). Gang violence prevention and volunteer mentoring were found to be promising. This research is particularly relevant because of its emphasis on identifying successful prevention programs in inner-city communities that are often characterized by multiple, external risk factors, including segregation, poverty, and disorganization.

In 1996, the Center for the Study and Prevention of Violence (CSPV), at the University of Colorado at Boulder, launched a national violence prevention initiative to identify violence prevention programs that are effective. The project, called Blueprints for Violence Prevention, has identified prevention and intervention programs that meet a strict scientific standard of program effectiveness. Program effectiveness is based upon an initial review by CSPV and a final review and recommendation from an advisory board comprised of seven experts in the field of violence prevention. Program criteria include formal evaluation, demonstrated significant treatment effects, sustained effects for at least one year, replication in at least one location, and benefits that exceed costs. Eleven Blueprint programs claim to have been effective in reducing adolescent violent crime, aggression, delinquency, and substance abuse. Another twenty-one programs have been identified as promising. The Office of Juvenile Justice and Delinquency Prevention (OJJDP) funds CSPV to sponsor program replication. To date, two programs, multisystemic therapy and mentoring have been replicated the most. Multisystemic therapy (MST), replicated in thirty States, is a multidimensional home-based family therapy program designed for young chronic and violent offenders and their parents. The goal of MST is to help parents deal effectively with their child's behavior problems, including disengagement from deviant peers and poor school performance (Center for the Study and Prevention of Violence, 2004).

Mentoring programs are in operation throughout the United States. They intervene with youths at risk of entering or reentering the juvenile justice system and aim to develop a population of healthy youths through structured relationships with caring adults. Cairns and Cairns (1994) call mentors "lifelines" who provide guidance and protection against risk factors. Mentoring aims to improve academic performance, as well as reduce school dropout rates, youth gang involvement, and delinquency (Samuels, 2003). One of the oldest mentoring programs is Big Brothers Big Sisters. Newer programs focus specifically on aiding maladjusted youth away from delinquency and antisocial behavior (Samuels, 2003). Recently there has been a shift in mentoring funding to faith-based and other community-based organizations (OJJDP, 2003). This may add to the availability of mentors since mentor organizations are often in demand of mentors, especially of minority men.

Contemporary delinquency programs that utilize a multidimensional framework which targets families, schools, peers, and communities are believed to be an effective delinquency prevention strategy. OJJDP recommends developing a community planning process to foster a targeted and coordinated juvenile justice and delinquency prevention and intervention system. One example of a multidimensional framework that has proven to be effective is the Comprehensive Strategy Framework (Howell, 2003). This approach includes various community strategies (Mobilization/Assessment/Planning/Implementation/Evaluation) and aims to strengthen families, promote juvenile delinquency prevention, intervene immediately and effectively when delinquent behavior occurs, and control the small number of violent and habitual offenders. It includes prevention and early intervention, prevention among all youths, early intervention with disruptive children and child delinquents, a system of graduated sanctions, and a parallel continuum of treatment alternatives, immediate interventions, and sanctions (Howell, 2003).

More recently, OJJDP has identified effective interventions for serious and/or violent juveniles and child offenders that include interpersonal skills training, individual counseling, and behavioral programs. Parent-child treatment programs for preschool children, problem-solving skills training, and anger-coping therapy for school-age children are deemed to be the most effective interventions for children and adolescents with conduct problems. Finally, there are several other approaches that have not been fully evaluated but that are promising, including community-oriented policing, teen courts, violence prevention programs, and juvenile or community assessment centers (Howell, 2003).

What Works for Minority Youths

Overall, we do not know enough about what works exclusively for minority youths. Arguably, since minorities, especially African-Americans, comprise a disproportionate number of delinquent youths, some successful programs, such as multisystemic family therapy and mentoring, are probably effective for at least some minority youths. However, without specific disaggregated information, generalizations require a great deal of caution. At the very least we need to know what proportion of the study samples are minority youths in programs that purport to be effective. If an effective delinquency prevention or intervention strategy is based on a study sample that includes at least 50 percent minority youths, it could be viewed as effective for minority youths. Unfortunately, information on the race/ethnicity of participants is not usually readily available in studies of "what works." Another important issue is the exclusion of strategies that specifically target minority youth in the prevention evaluation literature. For example, culturally specific programs, including Afrocentric rites of passage programs for males and females, have been overlooked, with few exceptions (King, Holmes, Henderson, & Latessa, 2001; Woolredge, Hartman, Latessa, & Holmes, 1994). Vega, Gill, and Associates' (1998) explanation of how historical culture conflicts and discrimination manifest differently in minority youths' drug use and how these different manifestations might guide delinquency prevention efforts has received very little empirically based attention (outside drug prevention research).

Understanding culture and cultural differences are critical to developing effective prevention programs (Valentine, De Jong, & Kennedy, 1998). Cultural identity has been the focus of many Afrocentric programs operated by public and independent schools as well as by numerous community organizations. Schiele (1998) notes that human service workers should be familiar with these programs for the benefit of their clients, while Graham (1999) emphasizes the importance of African-centered social work. Afrocentric programs directly and indirectly target delinquency. Many juvenile justice intervention strategies include Afrocentric information for clients in secure confinement and community placements. This information may include pictures of African-Americans, maps of Africa, books, etc. Rites of passage programs, perhaps the most common Afrocentric approach, are more comprehensive and aim to foster positive youth development by preparing youths for the challenges they face. Rites of passage programs are used in both community and therapeutic settings (Warfield-Coppock, 1992). Although we know little about the longitudinal effectiveness of Afrocentric rites of passage programs for preventing delinquency, they have been found to be effective in preventing drug and alcohol use (Belgrave, Townsend, Cherry, & Cunningham, 1997). Culturally relevant programs that stimulate self-esteem and educational interest and that promote future goals may be an effective prevention strategy for other minority groups, such as Native Americans, Hispanics, and Asians (Van Stelle, Allen, & Moberg, 1998; Petoskey, Van Stelle, & De Jong, 1998; Zane, Aoki, Ho, Huang, & Jang, 1998).

One example of an antiviolence intervention that utilizes cultural identity is the program Making attitude Adjustments in order to Lead more Effective lives (MALE). This program, developed by Berry (2000), seeks to address hy-permasculine attitudes and beliefs of incarcerated African-American males. MALE teaches a proactive approach to masculinity in group therapy. The program was found effective in Ohio prisons and has been replicated in several other correctional facilities (Murray, 2003). MALE may be successful with other minority and majority youths since it seeks to promote resilience. Resiliency refers to ones' ability to adapt positively to a negative environment. Proponents of resilience emphasize that some youths overcome stressful environments (Bloom, 1996). Programs that focus on resilience seek not only to identify protective factors but also to equip youth with coping strategies. While resilience has received some attention in prevention research, the role of culturally unique protective factors remains unclear (Miller & MacIntosh, 1999). The lack of information on (1) cultural relevance and (2) resilience prevention and intervention strategies is related to several more specific issues and challenges presented below.

Important Issues and Challenges

There are several topics that must not be neglected when developing effective prevention and intervention strategies for minority youths. We choose to highlight the importance of early detection of child delinquency, educational strategies, and the prevention of female delinquency. Of course, other relevant topics are worthy of consideration, such as involvement in gangs and alcohol and drug use. Since a considerable amount of research on these topics already exists, they will not be discussed in this chapter.

Targeting Child Delinquency

Chronic juvenile offenders and recidivists account for a great deal of delinquency (Siegel, 2002). Often, these offenders begin their delinquent acts at a very early age and do not mature out of them. OJJDP, in the Study Group on Very Young Offenders, concluded, "Early antisocial behavior may be the best predictor of later delinquency" (Wasserman et al., 2003, p. 2). This antisocial behavior includes oppositional rule violations and aggression. To address this growing problem, several states, including Michigan and Minnesota, have developed programs to intervene in the lives of these youths as early as possible (Loeber, Farrington, & Petechuk, 2003). The Michigan Early Offender Program (EOP) "provides specialized, intensive in-home interventions to youth who are age 13 or younger at the time of first adjudication and who have had two or more prior police contacts" (p. 11). Interventions include individual-ized treatment, group therapy, assistance with school preparation, and short-term detention (Burns et al., 2003). The Minnesota Delinquents Under 10 Program uses a Wraparound Network that includes community-based organizations, an integrated service delivery team, a critical support person or mentor, and a corporate sponsor that funds extracurricular activities. Canada has focused on child delinquency since the 1980s and now provides funding for Community Teams for Children Under 12 Committing Offenses and a National Information Center on Very Young Offenders (Burns et al., 2003).

Educational Strategies

Consistently, educational achievement has been correlated with delin-quency prevention (Maguin & Loeber, 1996; Gottfredson, 2001). Since continuing an education provides future economic opportunities, socialization, and a commitment that requires time, education has an effect on youths that extends through the age of twenty-five. Therefore, school dropouts were more delinquent than a comparison group that remained in school (Thornberry, Moore & Christensen, 1985). Moreover, there is a strong association between delinquency and school performance, especially among black male children. Effective academic performance decreases the risk of delinquency (Maguin & Loeber, 1996). Finding strategies that encourage attachment to school and success in it reduces delinquency and improves the quality of life for the student and for future generations. Arguably, the group most in need of such educational intervention strategies are African-Americans, who represent 17 percent of the total school population yet account for 32 percent of suspensions and 30 percent of expulsions (Skiba, Michael, Nardo & Peterson, 2000). Also African-American males are three times more likely to be in remedial or special education classes as compared to their White counterparts. Overall, an African-American male has a 1 in 4 chance of becoming a high school dropout and a 1 in 12 chance of graduating from college (Bailey & Paisley, 2004).

It has been observed that students (especially black boys) become uninterested in school after the fourth grade. Kunjufu (1995) calls this phenomenon the "Fourth Grade Failure Syndrome" and states that its onset originates from years of tender, nurturing, and supportive moments in programs such as Head Start from the first through the third grade. But when children move to the intermediate grades, the learning pedagogy changes to a competitive, individualistic, and much less socially interactive style. Perhaps as the students begin to adhere to the standard of a "middle class measuring rod" (Cohen, 1955), they are unable to make an adjustment to the new learning environment and thus become uninterested in school and increase their likelihood of delinquent behavior. Solutions to the problem of the "Fourth Grade Failure Syndrome" include parental involvement, mentoring, and a supportive learning environment (Kunjufu, 1995; Howell, 2003; Bailey and Paisley, 2004).

Lessons learned early become precursors of expected behavior and allow for the use of social skills, patience, personal responsibility, and the ability to work independently, thus averting the onset of the "Fourth Grade Failure Syndrome." Programs that target antisocial behavior and promote social norms throughout a student's academic tenure are an important part of adaptation and bonding to a school environment. Such programs have been found to show improvements in pro-social behavior and in decreased disruptive behavior in school and at home (Conduct Problems Prevention Research Group, 1999).

Parental involvement throughout the child's education cannot be overlooked. As an education consultant to many inner-city schools and their districts around the United States, Kunjufu (1995) notes that as the age of the child increases, the involvement of parents decreases. He states that he sees 80 percent of parents attending Head Start functions, 30 percent attending elementary school events, and almost no parental involvement in high schools. Keeping parents involved in their children's education involves the training of parents to be active participants. Recent media campaigns have stressed the importance of parents talking with their children and asking questions about school, friends, activities, and goals. Hopefully, such campaigns will be successful in providing children and youths with more care and nurturing, especially when these are needed most. The importance of parental involvement, along with that of the immediate family, has been shown to be a factor in a youth's receiving less harsh and intrusive sanctions when he or she comes into contact with the justice system (Frazier & Bishop, 1995).

Finally, providing a supportive environment for all youths, especially minority youths, has centered on single sex, mono-racial educational programming. Largely based in African-American populations, these programs are often termed "rites of passage programs" in which youths learn that a "good" life is "Godlike" and thus a life grounded in virtue and morality (Harvey & Rauch, 1997). Through meetings after school and on weekends, students receive assistance with schoolwork and learn about contributions made by African-Americans. A prerequisite in many of these programs is active participation of parents. Without the parental involvement the child cannot participate. Rights of passage programs often involve the whole family, mentoring, and school officials. Parents attend meetings to discuss the progress of their children in school as well as in social settings. Parents learn how to support their children's dreams and ideas and improve their self-esteem. Evaluations of these programs consistently demonstrate improved success in school, increased self-esteem and better relations with family and others (Bailey & Paisley, 2004).

Female Delinquency

Increased interest in girls' delinquency has brought attention to the dearth of information about gender-specific prevention and intervention strategies. Although female delinquency has always occurred much less frequently than male delinquency, young females' increased participation in more violent crimes, including aggravated and other assaults, has received much more attention than their historical pattern of arrests for larceny-thefts, running away, and prostitution. According to Chesney-Lind & Shelden (2004), white and Hispanic females are more likely to report consuming alcohol than black females, who report greater involvement in assault and sexual activity. Young females at risk for precocious sexuality and teen pregnancy deserve much more attention in prevention strategies in light of the potential impact both may have on adolescent girls and their offspring. According to the National Campaign to Prevent Teen Pregnancy (NCPTP), children of teen mothers are more likely to be born prematurely, are more likely to repeat a grade (50 percent), are less likely to complete high school, have higher rates of abuse and neglect, and are more likely to live in poverty. Additionally, sons of teen mothers are 13 percent more likely to end up in prison (NCPTP, 2004).

The United States has the highest rates of teen pregnancy/births in the industrialized world. While the teen pregnancy rate has continued to decline since 1990, there is considerable variation according to race/ethnicity. In 2000 the rate for non-Hispanic whites was 54.7 per 1,000 girls aged 15–19; the rate for Hispanics was 137.9 per 1,000; and the rate for blacks was 153.3 per 1,000 (NCPTP, 2004). One-third of both male and female high school students in the United States reported being sexually active in 2001. Black males (52%) and black females (39%) are much more likely to be sexually active than white males (31%) and white females (32%) and than Hispanic males (36%) and Hispanic females (34%) (Child Trends Data Bank, 2004). Although the black teen birth rate was cut in half between 1991 and 2002, a recent study of low-income black urban youths (aged 16–20) revealed that teenage parenting was more realistic than abstaining from sex, getting married, or having a successful future (NCPTP, 2004). Even though teen pregnancy prevention is considered to be a worthwhile strategy, traditional prevention efforts such as health care services and sex education classes are failing these teens (NCPTP, 2004).

Current efforts aimed at reducing teen pregnancy include funding for maternity group homes, abstinence education, family planning, promoting responsible fatherhood, and mentoring children of prisoners. The National Campaign to Prevent Teen Pregnancy, Girls, Inc., and rites of passage programs for girls address both abstinence and sexuality. A recent study of urban teens cautioned that efforts to reduce teen pregnancy may fail if community values and norms are not supportive and do not provide countermessages. Successful prevention strategies must focus on the emotional and physical consequences of sex and early pregnancy (Motivational Educational Entertainment, 2004). More attention must also be devoted to sexual assaults of young girls that might contribute to other delinquent acts.

Gender-specific programs have received considerable attention during the past several years (Acoca, 1999; Bloom, Owen, Deschenes, & Rosenbaum, 2002; Howell, 2003; Morgan & Patton, 2002). These programs have not been fully implemented nationwide, nor is there enough information currently available about their effectiveness. If gender-specific prevention and intervention programs are to be effective, they must target girls between the ages of eight and fifteen and take into consideration their emotional and social development as well as how risk and protective factors contribute to their delinquency (Bloom et al., 2002). Bloom et al. (2002) identified "family issues, sexual, physical, and emotional abuse, and inadequate academic and social skills" as risk factors specific to girls (p. 53). Existing gender-specific programs that focus on these issues, that are cost-effective, and that are easily replicated should also be funded.

FUTURE RESEARCH ISSUES

During the next decade more attention must be devoted to identifying effective delinquency prevention and intervention strategies, as Sherman et al. (1997) recommended several years ago. While we do know a little more about what prevention programs work, such as the Blueprints, we still do not know enough about what works for minority youths. We also do not know enough about either developmental crime prevention or the effectiveness of the comprehensive strategy and of culturally specific programs. We do know that prevention programs continue to be underfunded while ineffective programs that do not work continue to be funded. Increasing funding for prevention and intervention programs that are effective is not a panacea. Funding must also be made available for other strategies, including youth (teen) courts, preparing children for entering school, increasing parents' involvement in their children's education, and enhancing after-school programs. There is also a need to invest in other strategies, such as culturally specific programs, leadership development, and faith-based initiatives, in order to better understand their potential as cost-effective approaches that can be replicated. It is also time to develop a body of prevention knowledge that not only identifies but also specifies how to counter risk factors and strengthen protective factors. Our understanding of how race/ethnicity and gender influence risk and protective factors also needs to improve. Recent delinquency and victimization research by McGee (2003) and McGee & Baker (2002) indicates that African-American males and females differ in their reaction to victimization. McGee & Baker (2002) note, "[T]here is evidence to suggest that prevention programs aimed at strengthening protective factors would be more effective in reducing risk factors by considering variations in coping strategies utilized by adolescents" (p. 309).

As juvenile justice passes 105 years of existence, the hope is that prevention programs will move from select literature to widely used practice. In juvenile justice courts around the country, the real and ever present fact is that minority youths, especially Blacks and Hispanics, often make up the majority of cases, detentions and placements. Future research that focuses specifically on these groups will contribute to the return of juvenile justice to its original purpose of prevention while promoting equal justice for all.

REFERENCES

Acoca, L. (1999). Investing in girls: A 21st-century strategy. *Juvenile Justice, 6,* 3–13.

Bailey, D., & Paisley, P. (2004). Developing and nurturing excellence in African American male adolescents." *Journal of Counseling and Development, 82* (Winter 2004) 10–17.

Belgrave, F. Z., Townsend, T. G., Cherry, V. R., & Cunningham, D. M. (1997). Influence of an Afrocentric worldview and demographic variables on drug knowledge, attitudes, and use among African American youth. *Journal of Community Psychology, 25,* 421–433.

Berry, J. (2000). An outcome evaluation of the Making attitude Adjustments in order to Lead more Effective lives (MALE) intervention program. *Dissertation Abstracts International,* 61, AA19995870.

Black, M. M., Howard, D. E., Kim, N., & Ricardo, I. B. (1998). Interventions to prevent violence among African American Adolescents from low-income communities. *Aggression and Violent Behavior, 3,* 17–33.

Bloom, B., Owen, B., Deschenes, E. P., & Rosenbaum, J. (2002). Moving toward justice for female juvenile offenders in the new millennium. *Journal of Contemporary Criminal Justice, 18,* 37–56.

Bloom, M. (1996). Primary prevention and resilience: Changing paradigms and changing lives. In R. L. Hampton, P. Jenkins, & T. P. Gullotta. (Eds.), *Preventing Violence in America* (pp. 87–114). Thousand Oaks, CA: Sage Publications.

Breed vs. Jones. (1975). 421 U.S. 517

Brownstein H. (2000). *The social reality of violence and violent crime.* Boston: Allyn and Bacon.

Burns, B. & Goldman, S. (Eds.). (1999). *Promising practices in Wraparound for children with serious emotional disturbances and their families: Systems of care.* Washington, D.C.: American Institute for Research, Center for Effective Collaboration and Practice.

Burns, B. J., Howell, J. C., Wig, J. K. Augimeri, L. K., Welsh, B. C., Loeber, R., & Petechuk, D. (2003). *Treatment, services, and intervention programs for child delinquents.* Washington, D.C.: OJJDP. (NCJ 193410)

Butts, J. A. & Mears, D. P. (2001). Reviving juvenile justice in a get-tough era. *Youth & Society, 33,* 169–198.

Bynum, J. E. & Thompson, W. E. (2002). *Juvenile delinquency: A sociological approach.* Boston, MA: Allyn & Bacon.

Cairns, R., & Cairns, B. (1994). *Lifelines and risks: Pathways of youth in our time.* New York: Cambridge University Press.

Center for the Study and Prevention of Violence (2004). Blueprints for violence prevention overview. Retrieved: http://www.Colorado.edu/cspv/blueprints/index.html.

Chesney-Lind, M. & Shelden, R. (2004). *Girls, delinquency, and juvenile justice.* Belmont, CA: Wadsworth.

Child Trends Data Bank (2004). Sexually active teens. Retrieved: http://www.childtrendsdatabank.org/pdf/23_PDF.pdf.

Coalition for Juvenile Justice. (1999). *Ain't no place anybody would want to be: Conditions and confinement for youth.* Washington, D.C.: Author.

Cohen, A. (1955). *Delinquent boys: The culture of the gang.* New York: Free Press.

Cohen, M., Rust, R., Steen, S., & Tidd, S. (2004). Willingness-to-pay for crime control programs. *Criminology 42* (1), 89–109.

Coie, J. D., Watt, N. F., West, St. G., Hawkins, J. D., Asarnow, J. R., Markman, H. J., Ramey, S. L., Shure, M. B., & Long, B. (1993). The science of prevention: A conceptual framework and some directions for a national research program. *American Psychologist, 48,* 1013–1022.

Conduct Problems Prevention Research Group. (1999). Initial impact of the fast track prevention trial for conduct problems: I. The high risk sample. *Journal of Clinical Psychology, 67,* 648–657.

DiIulio, J. J., Jr. (1994). America's ticking crime bomb and how to defuse it. *Wisconsin Interest, Spring/Summer,* 1–8.

Durlak, J. (1997) *Successful programs for children and adolescents.* New York: Plenum.

England, R. W. (1967). A theory of middle class juvenile delinquency. In E. W. Vaz (Ed.), *Middle class juvenile delinquency.* New York: Harper & Row.

Federal Bureau of Investigation (2003). *Crime in the United States, 2002.* Retrieved: http://www.fbi.gov/ucr/cius_02/pdf/4sectionfour.pdf.

Feld, B. (1999). *Bad kids: Race and the transformation of the juvenile court.* New York: Oxford University Press.

Finchenauer, J. O., & Gavin, P. W. (1999). *Scared straight: The panacea phenomenon revisited.* Prospect Heights, IL: Waveland.

Frazier, C. E., & Bishop, D. (1995). Reflections on race effects in juvenile justice." In K. Leonard, C. Pope, & W. Feyerherm (Eds.), *Minorities in juvenile justice* (16–46). Thousand Oaks, CA: Sage Publications.

Gottfredson, D. C. (2001). *Schools and delinquency*. New York: Cambridge University Press.

Graham, M. J. (1999). The African-centered worldview: Toward a paradigm for social work. *Journal of Black Studies 30*, 103–122.

Greenwood, P. W., Model, K. E., Rydell, C. P., & Chiesa, J. (1996). *Diverting children from a life of crime: Measuring costs and benefits*. Santa Monica, CA: RAND.

Harvey, A., & Rauch, J. (1997). A comprehensive Afrocentric rites of passage program for black male adolescents. *Health and Social Work, 22* (1), 30–38.

Howell, J. C. (1996). Juvenile transfers to the criminal justice system: State-of-the-art. *Law and Policy, 18,* 17–60.

Howell, J. C. 2003. *Preventing & reducing juvenile delinquency: A comprehensive framework*. Thousand Oaks, CA: Sage Publications.

In re Gault. (1967). 387 U.S. 1; 87 S. Ct. 1248.

In re Winship. (1970.) 397 U.S. 358.

Keenan, K. (2001). Uncovering preschool precursor problem behaviors. In R. Loeber & D. P. Farrington (Eds.), *Child delinquents: Development, intervention and service needs* (pp. 117–134). Thousand Oaks, CA: Sage Publications.

Kent v. United States. (1966). 383 U.S. 541. 86 S. Ct. 1045, 16 L.Ed.2d 84.

King, W., Holmes, S. T., Henderson, M. L. & Latessa, E. J. (2001). The community corrections partnership: Examining the long-term effects of youth participation in an Afrocentric diversion program. *Crime & Delinquency, 47,* 558–572.

Kunjufu, J. (1995). *Countering the conspiracy to destroy black boys* (Vol. 4). Chicago: African American Images.

Loeber, R. & Farrington, D. P. (Eds.), (2001). *Child delinquents: Development, intervention and service needs* (pp. 117–134). Thousand Oaks, CA: Sage Publications.

Loeber, R., Farrington, D. P. & Petechuk, D. (2003). *Child delinquency: Early intervention and prevention*. Washington, D.C.: U.S. Department of Justice.

Lundman, R. J. (2001). *Prevention and Control of Juvenile Delinquency* (3rd ed.). New York: Oxford University Press.

Maguin, E, & Loeber, R. (1996). Academic performance and delinquency. *Crime and Justice, 20,* 145–264.

Martinson, R. (1974). What works? Questions and answers about prison reform. *The Public Interest, 35,* 22–54.

MacKenzie, D. L. (2000). Evidence-based corrections: Identifying what works. *Crime & Delinquency, 46,* 457–471.

McDowall, D., Loftin, C. & Wiersema, B. (2000). The impact of youth curfew laws on juvenile crime rates. *Crime & Delinquency, 46,* 76–91.

McGee, Z. T. (2003). Community violence and adolescent development: An examination of risk and protective factors among African American youth. *Journal of Contemporary Criminal Justice, 19,* 293–314.

McGee, Z. T. & Baker, S. R (2002). Impact of violence on problem behavior among adolescents: Risk factors among an urban sample. *Journal of Contemporary Criminal Justice, 18,* 74–93.

McKeiver v. Pennsylvania. (1971). 403 U.S. 528

Miller, D. B. & MacIntosh, R. (1999). Promoting resilience in urban African American adolescents: Racial socialization and identity as protective factors. *Social Work Research, 23,* 159–170.

Morgan, M. & Patton, P. (2002). Gender-responsive programming in the justice system: Oregon's guidelines for effective programming for girls. *Federal Probation, 66,* 57–65.

Motivational Educational Entertainment (2004). Retrieved: http://www.meeproductions.com (as cited in National Campaign to Prevent Teen Pregnancy).

Murray, B. (2003). Bringing the anti-violence message to young black males. *Monitor on Psychology, 34.* Retrieved: http://www.apa.org/monitor/julaug03/bringing.html.

National Campaign to Prevent Teen Pregnancy. (2004). Retrieved: http://www.teen-pregnancy.org.

Office of Juvenile Justice and Delinquency Prevention (2003). Mentoring makes a difference. *OJJDP News@ A Glance, 11,* 1–6. Washington, D.C.: U.S. Department of Justice. NCJ 202802.

Petoskey, E. L., Van Stelle, K. R., De Jong, J. A. (1998). Prevention through empowerment in Native American community. In J. Valentine, J. A. De Jong, & N. Kennedy (Eds.), *Substance abuse prevention in multicultural communities* (pp. 147–162). New York: The Haworth Press.

Platt, A. M. (1969). *The child savers: The invention of delinquency.* Chicago: University of Chicago Press.

Rennison, C. M. & Rand, M. R. (2003). *Criminal victimization, 2002.* Washington, D.C.: U.S. Department of Justice.

Samuels, L. (2003). Mentoring programs. In D. McShane & F. Williams (Eds.), *Encyclopedia of juvenile justice.* Thousand Oaks, CA: Sage Publications.

Schiele, J. H. (1998). Cultural alignment, African American male youths, and violent crime. *Journal of Human Behavior, 1,* 165–181.

Shaw, C. R. & McKay, H. D. (1942). *Juvenile delinquency in urban areas.* Chicago: University of Chicago Press.

Sherman, L. W. (1998). *Preventing crime: An overview.* Washington, D.C.: National Institute of Justice. Retrieved: http://www.ncjrs.org/pdffiles/171676.pdf.

Sherman, L. W., Gottfredson, D., MacKenzie, D., Eck, J., Reuter, P., Bushway, S. (1997). *Preventing Crime: What Works, What Doesn't, What's Promising.* Washington, D.C.: U.S. Department of Justice.

Siegel, L. J. (2002). *Juvenile delinquency: The core.* Belmont, CA: Wadsworth.

Skiba, R. J., Michael, R. S., Nardo, A. C., & Peterson, R. (2000). The color of discipline: Sources of racial and gender disproportionality in school punishment. (Policy Research Report No. SRS1) Lincoln: University of Nebraska.

Thornberry, T. P., Moore, M., & Christenson, R. L. (1985). The effect of dropping out of high school on subsequent criminal behavior. *Journal of Research in Crime and Delinquency, 30,* 55–87.

Tonry, M. & Farrington, D. P. (1995). Strategic approaches to crime prevention. In M. Tonry & D. P. Farrington (Eds.), *Building a safer society: Strategic approaches to crime prevention* (pp. 1–20). Chicago: University of Chicago Press.

United States Census Bureau (2002). *Census 2000 redistricting data summary file for states.* Washington, D.C.: Author. Retrieved: http://www.census.gov/population/www/cen2000/phc-t1.html.

Valentine, J., De Jong, J. A. & Kennedy, N. (1998). (Eds.), *Substance abuse prevention in multicultural communities* (pp. 53–60). New York: The Haworth Press.

Van Stelle, K. R., Allen, G. A., & Moberg, D. P. (1998). Alcohol and drug prevention among American Indian families: The family circles program. In J. Valentine, J. A. De Jong, & N. Kennedy (Eds.), *Substance abuse prevention in multicultural communities* (pp. 53–60). New York: The Haworth Press.

Vega, W. A., Gil, A. G., & Associates. (1998). *Drug use and ethnicity in early adolescence.* New York: Plenum Press.

Ward, G. F. (2001). *Color lines of social control: Juvenile justice administration in a racialized social system, 1825–2000.* Unpublished doctoral dissertation, University of Michigan, Ann Arbor.

Warfield-Coppock, N. (1992). The rites of passage movement: A resurgence of African-centered practices for socializing African American youth. *The Journal of Negro Education 16,* 471–482.

Wasserman, G. A., Keenan, K., Tremblay, R. E., Cole, J. D., Herrenkohl, T. I., Loeber, R., & Petechuk, D. (2003). *Risk and protective factors of child delinquency.* Washington, D.C.: U.S. Department of Justice.

Wooldredge, J., Hartman, J., Latessa, E., & Holmes, S. (1994). Effectiveness of culturally specific community treatment for African American juvenile felons. *Crime & Delinquency, 40,* 589–598.

Young, V. D. (1994). Race and gender in the establishment of juvenile institutions: The case of the south. *Prison Journal, 74,* 224–266.

Zane, N., Aoki, B., Ho, T., Huang, L., & Jang, M. (1998). Dosage-related changes in a culturally responsive prevention program for Asian American youth. In J. Valentine, J. A. DeJong, & N. Kennedy (Eds.), *Substance abuse prevention in multicultural communities* (pp. 105–126). New York: The Haworth Press.

Name Index

Subject Index

S

School shootings, 11–13, 25
Segregation, 190, 198, 201, 208, 215, 220, 224, 229
Sentencing discretion, 132, 214
Sentencing policies, 200, 204, 212–214
Sentencing practices, 214–215
Sentencing, 40, 42, 44–45, 56, 61, 63, 114, 128, 132–133, 136, 155, 167, 171, 175, 188, 194, 200, 204, 212–216, 219
Racial disparities, 4, 6, 43–44, 215–216, 220–221
September 11, 2001, 35, 125
Service economy, 200–201
Shadow of Hate in America, 132, 134, 138
Slavery, 58, 61–63, 99, 110, 132, 138
Social control, 17, 20, 22, 25, 43, 53, 63, 68, 149, 152, 183, 194, 217, 219, 241
Social distance, 60, 126, 129, 132–138
Social disorganization, 24, 47, 53, 55, 63, 113
Social learning, 17–18, 20–26, 101, 108
Social learning/differential association, 17–18, 23
Soft on crime, 199, 211–212
Sound bites, 213
Southern racial hostility, 189
Southern strategy, 188, 208, 210
Stanford v. Kentucky, 213, 222
State Advisory Groups, 157
State and Tribal Assistance Division, 157–158

State Assessment Studies, 147, 150, 157, 166
State Formula Grants Program, 157
State relations and Assistance Division, 157–158, 182
State-sanctioned homicide, 131
Stereotypes, 61, 109, 117, 204–205, 207, 217, 219–220
Street Terrorism Enforcement and Prevention Act, 115
Study Group on Very Young Offenders, 232
Subculture lifestyle, 53

T

Targeting Child delinquents, 224
Teen Pregnancy, 235–236, 240
Three strikes and You're Out, 227
Title IV Grants, 90
Tribal Youth Program, 90

U

Uniform Crime Report, 14
United Nations, 135–136, 138–139
Convention on the Rights of the Child, 136–137
United States Census, 3, 7, 28, 44, 63, 240
United States Census Bureau, 7, 28, 44, 63, 240
United States v. Carolene Products, 191, 222
Urban riots, 189, 194, 197–199, 209
U.S. Department of Education, 83
U.S. Department of Health and Human Services, 83
Substance Abuse and Mental Health Services Administration, 26